TESLA

TESLA

MASTER OF LIGHTNING

BY MARGARET CHENEY & ROBERT UTH

TECHNICAL EDITOR, JIM GLENN

BARNES & NOBLE BOOKS
NEW YORK

This book is dedicated to Simonida, whose love of Tesla made it all happen.

ACKNOWLEDGMENTS

The authors would like to acknowledge the following persons who made this work possible:

Leland I. Anderson for his wisdom, knowledge, and life-long commitment to keeping Tesla's name and legacy before the public; Velimir Abramović and Marija Sesić whose intellectual contributions and friendship were invaluable; William Terbo and the late Nicholas Kosanovich, directors of the Tesla Memorial Society; Harry Goldman for his always illuminating *Tesla Coil Builders Association News;* John W. Wagner for his unwavering commitment to the truth; Charlotte Muzar for her support; Zoran Amar, Dennis Whitehead, Joseph Webster, Rusty Kolb, and Vernon Mangold for their knowledge and assistance; the many distinguished academics and engineers who shared their wisdom, perspectives, and time; Phillip L. Holmes for his inspiration; the Tesla Museum, past director Aleksandar Marin ić, and present director Branimir Jovanović, for providing some of the research and photographic materials for this project, showing the friendship between Yugoslavia and America; James and Judy Hardesty for expertise and friendship; Ken and Jim Corum for their scientific efforts in exploring Tesla's high-frequency experiments; Charles Ruch, Westinghouse historian, who contributed valuable insight and materials; the National Museum of American History, Smithsonian Institution, for its cooperation; our publisher, Barnes & Noble Books, especially John J. Kelly for his vision and Lynne Arany for her editorial experience and guiding hand; Clifford D. Conner and Walter M. Havighurst for copyediting and proofreading; Radomir and Mary Perica for their creative assistance; Peter and Trish Wright, for their faith; Michael Noble for his dedication and skill; and to numerous other friends and researchers, who know their contributions well, we extend our deepest gratitude.

Nikola Tesla

PREFACE   vi

CHAPTER   1. AN OLD WORLD CHILDHOOD   3

2. GENIUSES COLLIDE   13

3. WAR OF THE CURRENTS   23

4. HIGH FREQUENCY   35

5. LIONIZED AND IONIZED   47

6. NIAGARA FALLS   55

7. WHO INVENTED RADIO?   65

8. X-RAYS, EARTHQUAKES AND ROBOTS   75

9. COLORADO SPRINGS   85

10. WARDENCLYFFE TOWER   97

11. POWERHOUSE IN A HAT   109

12. HONORS, WELCOME AND OTHERWISE   117

13. WAR BY ELECTRICAL MEANS   125

14. POET AND VISIONARY   133

15. A WEAPON TO END WAR   141

16. ENIGMATIC TO THE END   149

17. THE PAPER TRAIL   157

18. THE COSMIC SIGNATURE   167

REFERENCES   175

BIBLIOGRAPHY   179

INDEX   181

PHOTO CREDITS   184

PREFACE

History closed quietly over memory of Nikola Tesla when he died at the height of the Second World War. Somehow textbooks, encyclopedias, and museum archives managed to lose the proud genius who may have been the greatest inventor of any age, not only giving us the electrical basis of our modern civilization but correctly pointing science to the ionospheric circuit in the heavens. Since my first book about Tesla in 1981, interest in him has grown steadily and so has information about this extraordinary human being.

That the memory of him survives is a tribute to the passions he inspired in a few scientists, engineers, and researchers who refused to let him be forgotten. His memory is also preserved today by a phalanx of lay admirers, not the least of whom are his fellow Yugoslavs at home and in the U.S. and Canada. In recent years the troops have ranged from ardent third-grade students in Michigan, to Ivy League scholars, U.S. senators, California rock stars, retired school-teachers, journalists, filmmakers, poets, and sculptors.

This book provides a rare glimpse into Tesla's genius and the "wonder-world of electricity" he created. The reader will find two hundred and fifty historic photographs and illustrations, and important new research, including previously unpublished letters and papers as well as interviews with leading contemporary authorities. This book, along with Robert Uth's documentary of the same name, *Tesla: Master of Lightning*, and Jim Glenn's *The Complete Patents of Nikola Tesla* (Barnes & Noble Books, 1994) also contribute to our growing knowledge of one of the world's most important inventors.

Tesla is indisputably the father of alternating current power generation and transmission. His AC technology, first introduced on a large scale at Niagara Falls in 1896, remains unchanged and unchallenged to this day. The same holds true for Tesla's "Apparatus for Transmission of Electrical Energy," patented in 1900, which is still the basis for transmitting and receiving all radio and television signals. These two technologies alone merit the recognition and gratitude of every inhabitant on this planet.

Like other great inventors, Tesla was a true Renaissance man. He turned fresh loam across half-a-dozen fields of science. He patented hundreds of inventions, crafted his own tools, built his own machines, practiced and consulted as an electrical engineer, handled his own press relations with dexterity and *élan*, and was even known to write poetry. Not only did this 19th-century polymath perform such heavy roles under one hat, he was also an environmentalist, a health and nutrition advocate, a philosopher, and many would say a visionary genius.

Tesla was a "heroic" inventor—something we need more of today. He looked at invention as a way to improve the lot of mankind, not just a means of enhancing wealth, or meeting the demands of the marketplace. He never married, though he was a convivial socialite. With respect to his work, he was a loner. He once confided to a relative that he did not wish to be swayed by corporate generosity and, in truth, there was little danger. His indifference to corporate and academic alliances, not to mention a certain testiness toward fellow engineers, plus the fact that he had no offspring to carry on his name, lay at the root of the obscurity which befell him.

Well aware of the irony of his position, Tesla wrote sulkily to the *New York World* in 1919, "No amount of praise is too much to bestow upon Edison for his vigorous pioneer work, but . . . had the Edison companies not finally adopted my invention they would have been wiped out of existence, and yet not the slightest acknowledgment of my labors has ever been made by any of them."

Though few inventors have contributed more to the development of the United States as a world power, the prestigious Smithsonian Institution has never substantially acknowledged Tesla's contribution. His alternating current generator, for example, is included in the museum's exhibit on Thomas Edison. The Institution has also been reluctant to credit Tesla's critical role in the invention of radio even though the U.S. Supreme Court affirmed his patent priority over Marconi in 1943. In the Smithsonian's defense, attempts have been made to produce a special Tesla exhibition in cooperation with the Nikola Tesla Museum in Belgrade. However, a decade of fighting in that region has prevented the project from coming into fruition.

As a result of this historical bias, Tesla's major inventions are usually attributed to others. And since reference books are revised only periodically, they too remain generally inadequate on the scope of Tesla's contributions to our modern electronic culture.

Following Tesla's death, another set of peculiar circumstances added to his obscurity. Virtually forgotten in the United States, his remaining possessions were shipped to his native Yugoslavia and placed in the Tesla Museum in Belgrade. With the onset of the Cold War, Western researchers interested in his work encountered the frustrating obstacle of geography and the political barrier of the Iron Curtain. Because of revolutionary ideas he advanced for electronic weapons, many of Tesla's technical papers in the United States disappeared or became cloaked in top-secrecy. In the end, it was Tesla's incredible vision that inspired the U.S. Strategic Defense Initiative or "Star Wars" program.

But Tesla's inventions are not science fiction fantasy. Every time we turn on a light, or a radio, or operate a remote control we continue his legacy. His name should be respected everywhere electricity flows.

MARGARET CHENEY
Hollister, California
June 1999

An Old World Childhood

Tesla's birthplace in Smiljan, Yugoslavia

Nikola Tesla, inventor *extraordinaire*, was born of Serbian parents who lived near the western edge of the Austro-Hungarian Empire. The area, known as Lika, eventually became part of Yugoslavia, and is today located in Croatia near the border of Bosnia. He was born at midnight between July 9 and 10, 1856; his birthday was always observed on the tenth. A lifelong pacifist, he would always claim to be equally proud of his Serbian and Croatian heritage.

He was the second son of Georgina (Djuka) Mandić and the Reverend Milutin Tesla. Georgina was brilliant and inventive but unschooled; his erudite father was an ill-paid parish priest. Their little house stood near the Serbian Orthodox Church in the pretty village of Smiljan, between the Adriatic Sea and a range of mountains called the Velebit.

Part of a close family, Nikola had a brilliant older brother, Dane, and three sisters, Milka, Angelina, and Marica, who doted on the small boy. His happy pastoral childhood was shattered at the age of five when Dane, whom his parents considered the family genius, was killed in a horse-riding accident. The loss of his brother afflicted Nikola with a lifelong sense of obligation to his parents to compensate for their sadness, and of guilt that he, rather than Dane, had survived. He often drove himself to mental exhaustion in an effort to merit his parents' love. "Anything I did that was creditable," he later wrote, "merely caused my parents to feel their loss more keenly. So I grew up with little confidence in myself." Psychologists today might conclude that he suffered from an obsessive-compulsive disorder, manifested in various forms of eccentric behavior.

Young Niko, his parents, and his sisters were all gifted with phenomenal memories, which were assid-

From left: Milutin Tesla, Nikola's father; Milka, Angelina, and Marica, Tesla's sisters

In 1939 Tesla made several trips to the Yugoslav embassy in Washington, D.C. There he was introduced to Pola Fotić, the eight-year-old daughter of Ambassador Kontstantin Fotić. The aging inventor and the young girl struck up a warm friendship based on a mutual love for their childhood cats.

As a result, Tesla wrote *A Story of Youth Told by Age,* and dedicated it to Pola. In it he described his cat named Mačak and his first experience with electricity:

> [As a child] the fountain of my enjoyment [was] our magnificent Mačak. . . . Now I must tell you of a strange and unforgettable experience which bore fruit in my later life. It happened that on the day of my experience we had a cold drier than ever observed before. It was dusk of the evening

Pola Fotić in 1940

> and I felt impelled to stroke Mačak's back. What I saw was a miracle which made me speechless from amazement. Mačak's back was a sheet of light and my hand produced a shower of erupting sparks loud enough to

be heard all over the place. My father was a very learned man, he had an answer for every question. "Well," he finally remarked, "this is nothing but electricity, the same thing you see on the trees in a storm." My mother seemed charmed. "Stop playing with this cat," she said, "he might start a fire." I was thinking abstractedly: Is nature a gigantic cat? If so who strokes its back? It can only be God, I concluded.

> I cannot exaggerate the effect of this marvelous night on my childish imagination. Day after day I asked myself what is electricity and found no answer. Eighty years have gone by since and I still ask the same question, unable to answer it (Tesla 1939).

uously developed by the Rev. Tesla's advanced concepts of child rearing. The first few years of the boy's life, however, were carefree and exceedingly active and adventurous. He romped on their picturesque small farm with the domestic animals, geese, and pigeons, and got into more than the normal variety of boyish scrapes.

His mother's family were among the earliest landowners in the area, and included several inventors. He began to emulate his gifted mother when still a child, observing how she created numerous useful appliances, such as a mechanical eggbeater, to help with her household duties. Others she invented to assist with supervision of the farm work.

His father, in addition to being a distinguished clergyman, was a writer and poet who signed his articles "Man of Justice." Milutin Tesla joked that if all the classics of literature were destroyed, he would be

able to restore them from memory. He had a substantial library in which Nikola, who soon learned to read, immersed himself. Afraid that the boy would ruin his eyes, the father took away the candles used for reading at night. After that Nikola made his own candles from scraps of wax, and stuffed rags under his bedroom door so that the light of guilty learning could not leak out.

Georgina, who had been deprived of education as a girl, memorized the musical Serbian poetry and recited it to her children. Watching his mother constantly working and reciting poetry made Nikola believe that she "would have achieved great things had she not been so remote from modern life and its multifold opportunities."

"Although I must trace to my mother's influence whatever inventiveness I possess," he was to write,

Above: Josif Tesla, brother of Nikola's father

Left: Pajo Mandić, brother of Nikola's mother

the training [my father] gave me must have been helpful. It comprised all sorts of exercises…guessing one another's thoughts, discovering the defects of some form or expression, repeating long sentences, or performing mental calculations. These daily lessons were intended to strengthen memory and reason and especially to develop the critical sense, and were undoubtedly very beneficial (Tesla 1919a).

Nikola's uncles on his mother's side were relatively wealthy, and most were either clergy or military men. They included Nikolai Mandić, His Eminence the Archbishop of Sarajevo and Metropolitan of the Serbian Orthodox Church in Bosnia; Uncle Pajo, a general-staff colonel in the Imperial Austro-Hungarian army; and Uncle Trifun, a well-known hotelier and landowner. The three uncles would later assist their talented young nephew with his education and subsequent passage to America.

Young Nikola had his heart set on becoming an engineer but was "constantly oppressed," he later wrote, by "being intended from my very birth for the clerical profession." His father was inflexible on this point. The army was equally determined that he should perform military service.

Despite the emotional stresses of his childhood the future inventor did enjoy moments of triumph. At the age of six, at a demonstration of the town's new fire engine, he managed to make it work after futile efforts by the captain and crew. The hose of the engine, with one end plunged into a nearby lake, was producing no water whatever, to the mystification of the mayor and village elders. Young Tesla saved the day by plunging into the icy water and straightening the collapsed suction hose.

Tesla's home and primary school in Gospić

This bit of celebrity came just in time to restore him to favor with his father, who had entrusted his son with the job of ringing the church bell on Sundays. On the first Sabbath of his new responsibility, impetuous Nikola rang the bell perfectly, then raced down the stairs from the belfry, only to land on the long skirts of the mayor's wife, ripping them from her body, he later recalled, with a noise "that sounded like a salvo of musketry fired by raw recruits." The clergyman was long mortified by that disaster.

As a youth, Tesla exhibited a peculiar trait that he considered the basis of all his invention. He had an abnormal ability, usually involuntary, to visualize scenes, people, and things so vividly that he was sometimes unsure of what was real and what imaginary. Strong flashes of light often accompanied these images. Tormented, he would move his hand in front of his eyes to determine whether the objects were simply in his mind or outside. He considered the strange ability an

affliction at first, but for an inventor it could be a gift.

Tesla wrote of these phenomena and of his efforts to find an explanation for them, since no psychologist or physiologist was ever able to help him. "The theory I have formulated," he wrote much later,

is that the images were the result of a reflex action from the brain on the retina under great excitation. They certainly were not hallucinations, for in other respects I was normal and composed. To give an idea of my distress, suppose that I had witnessed a funeral or some such nerve-wracking spectacle. Then, inevitably, in the stillness of the night, a vivid picture of the scene would thrust itself before my eyes and persist despite all my efforts to banish it. Sometimes it would even remain fixed in space though I pushed my hand through it (Tesla 1919a).

To no one's surprise Nikola performed brilliant-

Top: The "Real Gymnasium" (secondary school) in Carlstadt, Croatia, where Tesla studied for three years.

Right: Gramme dynamo, 1877 (Courtesy Smithsonian Institution)

Tesla and his contemporaries often spoke of electricity as a fluid, which is still a useful analogy: there is an "amount" of flow (amperage), a "pressure" to move it (voltage), and together they provide a certain measure of power (wattage). At a more exact level of description, however, the electricity we know and use arises from properties of fundamental particles within the atom.

All the atoms that make up ordinary matter occur by nature in an electrically balanced state, with as many positive charges (protons) as negative (electrons). In some materials, especially in metals like copper, this may be a fragile balance. The electrons most distant from the nucleus, almost completely masked from positive charges at the center, are all but free to depart the neighborhood. Any pronounced positive tug will set them drifting in their direction, creating in fact an electrical flow, or "current."

Drifting may seem too tame a term for the kind of powerful and dangerous display encountered when something goes wrong with the wiring. Nonetheless, individual electrons don't move through ordinary wires in purposeful straight lines. A measurable "progress" toward the positive end only amounts to an inch or two per second. However, the effect of charge, its electrical "field," is felt along a wire almost immediately; all the loosely held electrons begin to migrate nearly simultaneously.

A field may be thought of as a forceful influence spread about in space. And electrical fields, as it turns out, have a surprising duality: they are always accompanied by magnetic fields, and vice versa. Every charged particle carries its own field and interacts with every other field.

The double nature of the electromagnetic field manifests physically in a simple geometrical way: magnetic force spreads at right angles to the direction of its electrical component. Were an electrical attraction—a field—to exist across this page from, say, left to right,

A remarkable electric display in Spokane Washington, 1912. (Courtesy National Archives)

its magnetic aspect would be felt coming out of the page. But this only describes a very steady state of affairs, just an unvarying electric field with a constant magnetic force hovering about. Should anything change—for example, should its strength grow and diminish periodically—it would create ripples in the field, as the field's force values working out from the center drop or rise. Such changes are wavelike; in fact, they are electromagnetic waves.

Were the waves to arrive at an even spacing of around a half-millionth of a millimeter between them, we would perceive them as light (orange, in this case). Somewhat longer spacings we detect as infrared, microwave, and radio; shorter ones as ultraviolet, X-rays, and gamma rays. At whatever frequency we register them, we always clock them at the speed of light.

ly in school, first in his village at the age of five; then a year later, moving with his family to the nearby city of Gospić, where he attended public school for four years, followed by three at the Real Gymnasium at Carlstadt in Austria. There, excited by the chance to work with mechanical models, he built several small turbines that he loved to operate. By the age of ten, he was obsessed with the possibilities of vacuums, and was "passionately fond" of mathematics, performing calculations in his head more rapidly than his teacher could write them on the board. He was at first suspected of cheating.

Niagara Falls, from Goat Island, circa *1867. (Courtesy Library of Congress)*

During this period Tesla saw a steel engraving of Niagara Falls. In his mind there appeared a huge waterwheel being turned by the powerful currents. He told his uncle, Josif Tesla, that he would go to America one day and capture energy in this way. Thirty years later he did exactly that. Despite his early creativity Tesla did not begin to think of himself as an inventor until he was an adult.

Tesla graduated from the gymnasium in 1873 at age seventeen. At that time, a cholera epidemic was sweeping the country. His parents urged him not to return but he did so, and at once caught the disease. This illness became a turning point in his life, for he craftily exacted an important concession from his father. The Reverend Milutin Tesla promised his son that if he survived, he would be allowed to attend the renowned Austrian Polytechnic School at Graz to study engineering.

The same ill health apparently exempted the young man from military service, and he was sent by his father into the mountains for a restorative year of roughing it. Roaming in the wild, he encountered lightning storms and avalanches that inspired him to ponder deeply the mysteries of nature. Incredible ideas started taking shape in his brain.

He conceived of building a tube to carry mail under the Atlantic Ocean, but found the mathematics involved in the frictional resistance of pipe to water flow beyond his skills. This problem he would recall later while inventing a unique bladeless turbine. He also envisioned constructing a great elevated ring around the equator. Its scaffolding, once knocked away, would leave the ring free to rotate at the speed of earth, somewhat like the geosynchronous satellites of today. But in the end it was the magic of electricity that measured up to his dreams of world-transforming inventions.

At the Polytechnic School Tesla began his studies in mechanical and electrical engineering. Professor Poeschl, his physics teacher, showed him a new Gramme machine that could be used as both a motor and a generator. Early electric motors operated on direct current electricity, and required a sparking device called a commutator to reverse the direction of the current. In this way, a rotary motion was created in the machine.

After watching it for a time, Tesla suggested it might be possible to do away with the sparking connections. This, his amused professor said, would be like building a perpetual motion machine! Not even Tesla could hope to achieve such a feat. For the next several years the challenge obsessed him. Instinctively

Central to any understanding of electric motors, generators, and transformers is the phenomenon called induction. In a nutshell, magnetic lines of force, as they cut across a conductor (like a copper wire) cause electrons to flow.

Consider two copper wires strung parallel to one another. If a current begins to flow in one, a magnetic field builds around it at right angles to the wire. As the growing field's flux lines cut the second wire, a current

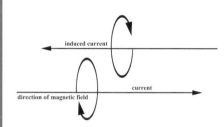

momentarily flows—in the opposite direction. When current is removed from the first wire, its field collapses, cutting through the second wire and again causing a current briefly to flow. This is known as alternating current.

Michael Faraday (1791–1867) discovered and investigated such "induced" currents in 1831. Later experiments proved the remarkable, but quite logical, result that if current in the first wire is made to vary

Michael Faraday

constantly—pumping its own magnetic field up and down—a continuous, varying current flows in the second wire. Energy, thus, is transmitted smoothly and efficiently through empty space.

Faraday discovered and quantified a great deal about the nature of electricity and its dual electric and magnetic nature. A copper disk he caused to spin by means of magnetically induced currents was the world's first electric motor.

---

he knew that the solution lay in electric currents that alternated.

He had no idea how such a machine would work but felt that, somewhere in his mind, the answer already existed. Driven to the extreme and almost unable to sleep, he began to borrow small sums of money that he promptly gambled away. He found that although he was not clever at playing cards, he was highly proficient at billiards. Thus encouraged at the tables, he even borrowed money from his mother and lost it. While on this gambling binge he drank coffee and liquor excessively and chased women, to the deep distress of his religious family. Meanwhile, however, lack of funds forced him to drop out of engineering school.

Tesla's nephew, Nikola Trbojevich, later claimed that the young inventor was "fired" from college because of his irregular life. According to family legend, "his mother got the money together for him to go to Prague, where he spent two years. He might have gone

to the university unofficially, but the records show he was not enrolled in any one of the four universities in Czechoslovakia." Apparently Uncle Nikola, like Michael Faraday, was essentially a self-taught scientist.

While Tesla was living in Prague his father died, forcing him to think seriously about earning a living. Reproached by his mother for his dissolute ways, he resolved to reform and did so at once, as he later said, "without a backward glance." Having observed the newspaper obituaries in Vienna, a city of avid coffee drinkers, he also gave up the stimulant caffeine. Alcohol in small quantities he considered a beneficial tonic, but he soon added smoking to his list of banished indulgences.

With newly installed telephone and telegraph services, the city of Budapest became highly attractive to Tesla. A telephone exchange was opened by a subsidiary of an Edison company. With the help of an uncle, Tesla soon found a job as a draftsman with the Central Telephone Exchange of the Hungarian government. He quickly mastered every aspect of the new technology.

During that time he suffered a strange affliction that, for lack of better knowledge, was thought to be a nervous breakdown. His heart raced and he twitched and trembled for no apparent reason. His normally acute hearing and other senses were preternaturally enhanced: the sound of a ticking watch, or of a fly landing nearby, caused him agony. If he walked in the sun, he felt stunned by the rays beating upon his head. The despairing doctors of Budapest produced no diagnosis, yet told him there was no cure. One physician, however, prescribed heavy doses of potassium (Tesla 1919c).

For whatever reason, and from whatever disease, the self-described "hopeless physical wreck" eventually recovered his health. More than that, he recovered with abnormal vigor. He felt mentally stimulated and discovered "energy to spare." He began taking long afternoon walks with his friend Anital Szigety, sometimes discussing the idea of an alternating current motor, a problem never far from his thoughts.

In Budapest at that time others were also interested in the possibility of an AC motor and the rotational effects associated with alternating currents. In Italy a Professor Ferraris had studied alternating currents and their ability to produce rotation. However, none of these scientists had succeeded in making a functional motor.

The answer came to Tesla:

One afternoon . . . I was enjoying a walk with my friend in the city park and reciting poetry. At that age I knew entire books by heart, word for word. One of these was Goethe's *Faust*. The sun was just setting and reminded me of a glorious passage:

The glow retreats, done is the day of toil;
It yonder hastes, new fields of life exploring;
Ah, that no wing can lift me from the soil
Upon its track to follow, follow soaring!

Tesla in 1879 at age twenty-three

As I uttered these inspiring words the idea came like a flash of lightning and in an instant the truth was revealed. I drew with a stick on the sand the diagram shown six years later in my address before the American Institute of Electrical Engineers. The images were wonderfully sharp and clear and had the solidity of metal. "See my motor here; watch me reverse it" (Tesla 1919c).

Pygmalion, on seeing his statue come to life, could not have been more deeply moved. ⚊

CHAPTER TWO

Geniuses Collide

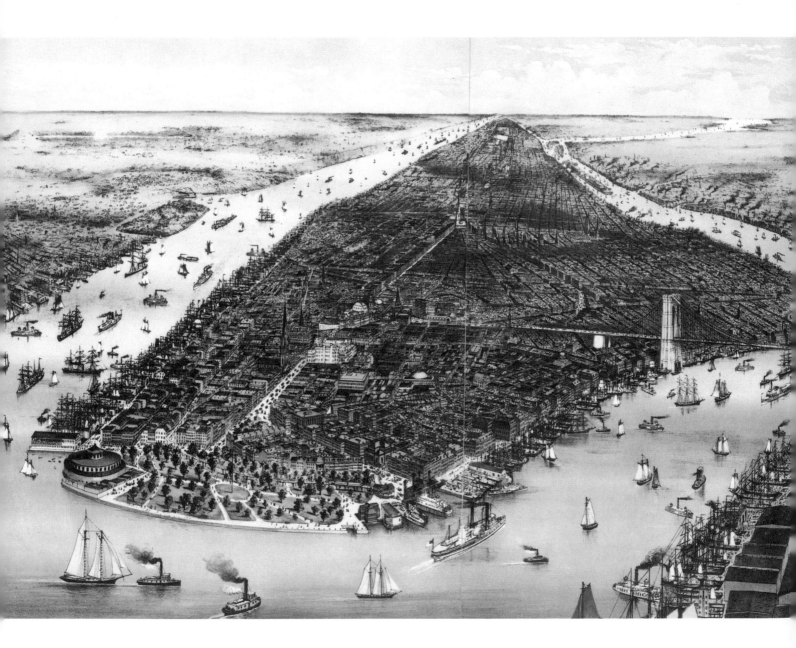

City of New York, 1883 (Courtesy Library of Congress)

THUNDER IS GOOD, THUNDER IS IMPRESSIVE; BUT IT IS LIGHTNING THAT

DOES THE WORK. —MARK TWAIN

Nikola Tesla, immigrant, arrived in New York in 1884 with a letter of introduction to Thomas Edison and very little else. His electrical machines, as yet unbuilt but bright and vivid as solid steel in his mind, were intended to deliver people everywhere from debilitating toil. If the aim seems of immodest size, so was the genius behind it. The ideas Tesla brought with him matured into the motors, transformers, and electrical production and distribution technologies at the base of twentieth-century civilization.

He had yet to learn, however, that sweeping technological change usually fired extremes of both optimism and fear among builders of the Great Capitalist Experiment. This was certainly true of electricity: the President of the United States would not even be allowed to touch the first light switch at the White House.

The eager Serbian immigrant was six and a half feet tall, slim, straight, and twenty-eight, immaculately dressed, and in dire need of a job. Having lost all but a few cents of the travel money lent to him by his uncles (some said lost in a card game), he looked forward to meeting Mr. Edison and persuading him quickly of the wonders of his alternating current motor.

Most electricians of the time were thinking of the mysterious medium in terms of electric lights and trolley cars. Tesla envisioned it as the means to unite cities and distant villages, to span whole continents and ultimately the world. He was laughed at in some circles, partly for being of dark complexion, foreign, and multilingual (fluent in English, French, German, Italian, and Serbian), and partly for dressing "like a Parisian," but he was ridiculed most often for the grandeur of his "impossible" ideas.

During the early 1880s a few inventors and industrialists had forged ahead with efforts to "harness the lightning," undeterred by the obvious fact that streets were being made a nightmare of dangerous overhead wiring. This mostly took the form of direct current electricity. Alternating current was not unheard of, and in fact in 1886 an AC lighting plant had been demonstrated at Great Barrington, Massachusetts, by William Stanley, with the backing

Brush electric arc lights in use on a New York street around 1880. (Courtesy Smithsonian Institution)

Early AC electrical switchboard

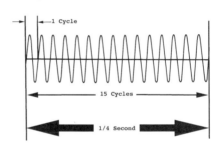

Electrical engineers find it useful to distinguish between two kinds of electron flow: alternating current (AC) and direct current (DC). Direct current moves in one direction only. Electrons from a battery, for example, always flow from its negative to its positive terminal. In an AC circuit electrons are made to move first in one direction and then in the reverse. Ordinary household current in the United States changes direction sixty times per second; it is 60-cycle (or 60-hertz) current.

Tesla understood that advances in power transmission and use depended critically on AC technology because an AC current can easily and efficiently be transformed in its electrical character. That is, an equivalent amount of *power* (in watts) results from any juggling of the *current* (in amperes) and the *potential* (in volts) according to the simple formula: power = current x potential. By contrast, an unvarying DC voltage doesn't possess the constantly expanding and contracting magnetic field of AC; it cannot be modified in a transformer.

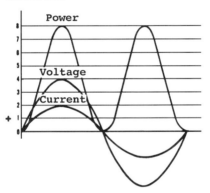

Copper wires carrying current heat up or melt as the number of amperes rises, but maintaining a high potential difference (voltage) doesn't destroy the wire, at least not until extremely high voltages are reached. It makes sense to send power over any appreciable distance with a high voltage and correspondingly low amperage rather than stringing ever thicker, heavier, and more expensive copper wires to accommodate DC.

Much of the nascent electrical industry, and Edison himself, resisted AC from sheer inertia. They understood DC reasonably well and weren't ready for a transition into a more complicated and unfamiliar system. The mathematics of AC isn't quite as straightforward as that of DC. Though Tesla was certainly at ease with the math, his greatest successes appear to have sprung from an apparently innate ability to visualize the forces simultaneously at work in circuits.

of the new Westinghouse Electric Company. But engineers had not begun to solve the basic problems of control and distribution—and as yet, no practical motor using alternating current had been built. Direct current, which was championed by Edison with his usual enthusiasm, was really the only game in New York City when Tesla arrived.

At least twenty electric light and telephone companies competed for markets, using separate wires strung on anything that could be put to use. The *New York Times* reported that all the streets of the lower city were "darkened by wires, carried upon towering structures erected on the roofs of fatuously good-natured owners." A single pole might carry dozens of

crooked crossbeams supporting sagging wires. The precariously exposed electrical wiring and faulty insulation was a constant danger for the tram-pulling horses with metal shoes and the people who drove them, to say nothing of the linemen charged with maintenance. The underwriters' wire approved by insurance companies at the time was itself so poor that cynics referred to it as "undertakers' wire." The general inadequacy of direct current and the city's failure to bury electrical lines caused frequent crises both in homes and on the streets. The Brooklyn Dodgers would later take their name from the citizens who dodged trolley tracks, fearful of electric shock.

Wealthy New Yorkers rushed to have their

Overhead electrical wiring was a hazard and an eyesore for New York residents. (Collection of The New-York Historical Society)

J. Pierpont Morgan (Collection of The New-York Historical Society)

homes wired for electricity. The renowned financier J. Pierpont Morgan, a major investor in the Edison Electric Light Company, was one of the first to have his mansion, at 219 Madison Avenue, illuminated. Mr. Morgan never had to keep up with the Joneses, being always in the vanguard, but he had to live up to his own demanding standards of exclusivity, which is how he found himself involved with electricity.

One of J. P. Morgan's greatest errors was to put money into the Edison venture. Direct current is rapidly diminished by resistance along transmission wires, making it unsuitable for electrification over distances greater than a mile. Few suspected that alternating current would soon become practical.

Morgan's chronic headaches worsened when his carpets and tapestries were singed by short circuits occurring in his mansion. At a time when trained engineers were extremely rare, he employed his very own, who arrived at three o'clock every afternoon to build up steam, and who worked until eleven o'clock at night. Even so, there were many times when the electric lights suddenly flickered out all over the enor-

mous house, most embarrassingly when the host happened to be entertaining important business guests.

Mrs. James K. Brown, a neighbor, complained continuously that the vibrations of Morgan's dynamo made her whole house shake. Morgan, after roaring at Edison, had all of the electrical machinery hoisted up onto thick rubber pads. He even had sandbags piled around the walls of the cellar as if it were a bomb shelter. Mrs. Brown was assuaged for only a short time, for she soon claimed that fumes from the generator were tarnishing her silver. Even though the Morgans switched to another kind of coal, their neighbors remained wary of Edison's electricity. This, it was speculated by enemies, was one of the reasons the financier left so often and so suddenly for long European vacations on his yacht *Corsair*.

Despite the hazards and rude surprises of direct current, however, Mrs. Cornelius Vanderbilt was the sensation of the social season when she swept luminously down the grand staircase at a costume ball as "The Electric Light Bulb." Lusty Manhattan was a city in love with everything new, brash, noisy, crass,

Edison System Central Station on Pearl Street for the distribution of electricity, 1883. (Courtesy Smithsonian Institution)

exciting, and likely to be hazardous to one's health, and lawyers were fewer in those days.

Edison's Pearl Street generating station, in addition to serving the household needs of the wealthy, supplied direct current to industrial plants, businesses, and theaters all over the spreading city. He had just begun to outfit passenger ships with lighting plants, foreseeing that as another source of revenue. The danger of fire at sea made this a particularly challenging undertaking.

On the summer day in 1884 when Tesla, carefully dressed in his bowler hat, striped trousers, and cutaway coat (the whole of his wardrobe), dropped in to see the famous Mr. Edison, there had been an emergency at the Vanderbilt mansion on Fifth Avenue. Two wires had shorted behind a metallic-threaded wall hanging and started a fire. Mrs. Vanderbilt herself had smothered the flames, only to learn that the problem emanated from a steam engine and boiler in her basement. Now the angry socialite was demanding that Edison remove the whole apparatus. No sooner had he rushed back to Pearl Street than the manager

of a shipping firm called to remind him that the SS *Oregon* had been tied up for days awaiting electrical repairs and was losing money by the hour. Unfortunately Edison had no more engineers to assign to the job.

At this juncture he became aware of the tall foreign gentleman hovering politely in the doorway, bowler hat in gloved hand, a letter in his pocket from Charles Batchelor, the English engineer who managed the Continental Edison Company in Europe. Few American colleges then trained electrical engineers, so prospects were good for the rare immigrant who was qualified. But Mr. Edison was not in a congenial mood.

Tesla spoke up, knowing the famous man had a hearing problem, and introduced himself. He produced the brief message from Batchelor. Edison glanced at the few lines and snorted. "I know two great men and you are one of them," Batchelor had written. "The other is this young man!"

Thomas Edison, rumpled, weary, and deeply skeptical, asked Tesla what he could do. While the

Tesla in 1885, at age twenty-nine

Thomas Alva Edison

American inventor was only eight years older than his visitor, and lacked his formal education, he was already world-renowned for his inventions. Tesla recalled their meeting:

> When I saw this wonderful man, who had had no training at all, no advantages, and who did it all himself, and saw the great results by virtue of his industry and application—you see, I had studied a dozen languages . . . and had spent the best years of my life ruminating through libraries. I thought to myself what a terrible thing it was to have wasted my life on those useless things, and if I had only come to America right then and there and devoted all of my brain power and inventiveness to my work, what could I not have done? (Tesla 1919a)

In some awe of Edison, Tesla proceeded to describe the engineering work he had done in France and Germany, and spoke of his plans for induction motors made to run smoothly and powerfully on alternating current. That invention, he reckoned, was worth many fortunes.

Edison knew little of alternating current, chose to believe it the work of the devil, and did not care to learn more about it. Did this dandified "Parisian" realize that what he was suggesting could make a whole industry obsolete? In the past Edison had waged a propaganda war against the gas companies on the grounds that the possibility of explosions made gas too dangerous for human use as a power source. He was therefore experienced in recognizing and heading off any threat of industrial competition.

Tesla, unprepared for the force of Edison's passion, thanked him and turned to leave. As he did so a breathless boy rushed into the plant to report that a junction box at Pearl and Nassau streets was leaking electricity and had injured a carter and his horse. Edison bellowed for his foreman. Then he turned to Tesla and said, "Hold up a minute, Mister. Can you fix a ship's lighting plant?"

Edison jumbo dynamo from Pearl Street

So began this historic collision of geniuses. Eventually it would spark the bitter and long-running "War of the Currents," the taste of which still lingers today in corporate memories. Edison would much later admit that the biggest mistake he ever made was in trying to develop direct current, rather than the vastly superior alternating current system that Tesla had put within his grasp (Josephson 1959).

The two inventors were alike only in that both required few hours of sleep at night. Edison took cat-naps on tables and on an unmade cot in his office. Tesla worked every day from about 10:30 A.M. to 5:00 A.M. In an emergency, both men could and did drive themselves for two or three days without sleep.

But in almost every other respect, they differed strikingly. Tesla suffered from a compulsive fear of germs that goaded him to excessive cleanliness and other eccentric mannerisms. Edison was totally indifferent to such matters, causing his new employee to observe that "he lived in utter disregard of the most elementary rules of hygiene." Had it not been for his wife's constant care, said Tesla in the *New York Times* of October 19, 1931, "he would have died from consequences of sheer neglect."

When a problem had to be solved, Tesla was inclined to approach it mathematically. Edison would simply dive at every possibility, as he had done in seeking his incandescent light-bulb filament. Tesla, who was quite capable of sarcasm, once described this process with amusement:

> If Edison had a needle to find in a haystack, he would proceed at once with the diligence of the bee to examine straw after straw until he found the object of his search. I was the sorry witness of such doings, knowing that a little theory and calculation would have saved him ninety percent of his labor (Josephson 1959, 87–88).

He managed to impress the American inventor, however, by solving the SS *Oregon*'s electrical prob-

Laying the Edison electric mains—the service boxes and expansion joints. (Courtesy Smithsonian Institution)

lems within twenty-four hours, which inspired Edison to overlook his highfalutin' manners and elegant clothing to the extent of offering a regular job. Tesla accepted with pleasure despite his new boss's brusque ways. Legend had it that the American, never having seen the country of Tesla's origin on a map, once asked if he had ever eaten human flesh. Tesla, for his part, observed with dignity that the dynamos at the Edison plant could be made to work much more efficiently, even though they were designed for direct current. He offered to undertake a complete overhaul.

Clearly such a project would take months of work. Edison rashly promised the immigrant $50,000 if he succeeded, perhaps thinking it an impossible undertaking. But the potential of so much money appealed mightily to Tesla, who had by now concluded that he must build his own research laboratory in New York if his alternating current machines were ever to succeed. He drove himself

mercilessly on this job and several months later, to Edison's amazement, announced that the work was successfully completed.

When he asked to be paid, however, Edison seemed astonished. He explained that the offer of $50,000 had been made in jest, saying, "When you become a full-fledged American you will appreciate an American joke" (Tesla 1938). In shock, Tesla threatened to resign. Edison countered by offering him a $10 raise, bringing his salary up to $28 per week, and warned that if he chose to leave, he would have difficulty finding another engineering job in such hard times. Tesla thanked him icily and declared that he would rather take his chances on the streets.

Unable to find employment, the proud immigrant worked for many months at the most arduous hand labor. While digging ditches in the New York streets, he found little comfort in burying electric lines for Edison's direct current system.

Word quickly circulated among the rough-and-

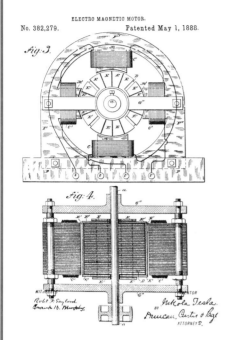

ELECTRO MAGNETIC MOTOR.

No. 382,279.   Patented May 1, 1888.

Fig. 3.

Fig. 4.

Tesla's most famous invention, the AC motor, has been called a technological advance equivalent to the wheel. The analogy is justified by the immense impact the two discoveries had on subsequent technological development. Unlike the wheel, however, the most important moving part of Tesla's AC motor was something invisible and insubstantial: a magnetic field.

All electrical motors, AC and DC, operate on the same basic principle: a magnetized part that turns (rotor) aligns itself with another magnetized part that doesn't turn (stator). Usually both parts are electromagnets, so that their north and south poles can be reversed simply by changing the direction of current running through them. If pole changes are properly timed, the rotor chases around trying to bring itself into alignment with successive stator poles but never catching up. The rotor's own momentum keeps it in the chase, seeking each "next" pole; otherwise it might just twitch back and forth as nearby poles reversed.

Motors before Tesla operated on direct current, and their limitations in commerce and industry had already become troublesome. Because the supply current travels in one direction only, it must be mechanically switched to run first one way and then the other through a motor's pole projections—in DC motors devices called "commutators" do this.

In Tesla's AC motors, by contrast, the field's poles are always in play, moving in steady, invisible arcs around the stator faces. Mechanical contacts, too, can be done away with by using induction to build and reverse the rotor fields. And AC devices operate, of course, without need of converting their source of power.

Tesla didn't merely make AC theoretically feasible, he created a completely operational technology. He patented over a score of designs: motors to overcome high resistance on starting, to run with variable loads, at constant speeds or at variable speeds—anything that might reasonably be asked of electrical engineering. This motor and related AC technology launched modern electrical industry and, essentially, the twentieth-century way of life.

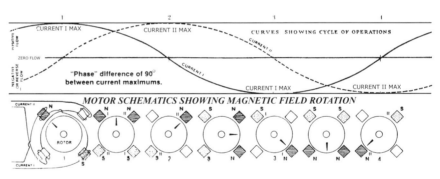

MOTOR SCHEMATICS SHOWING MAGNETIC FIELD ROTATION

ready society of industrialists, engineers, and Wall Street traders that a foreigner of unusual talent was among them. Tesla was soon approached by investors who asked him to design improved arc lighting for the hazardous streets and factories. Although this was not the opportunity he had hoped for, the group was willing to finance a Tesla Electric Light Company at Rahway, New Jersey, with a Manhattan branch office, in April 1887.

In his new laboratory at 89 Liberty Street, Tesla immediately began to build a prototype of the AC motor he had envisioned years before in Budapest. "The motors I built were exactly as I imagined them," he said. "I made no attempt to improve the design, but merely reproduced the pictures as they appeared to my vision and the operation was always as I expected" (Tesla 1919d).

CHAPTER THREE

War of the Currents

"Court of Honor" at the Columbian Exposition in Chicago, 1893.
The age of light that Tesla did so much to bring about was exemplified in
this scene. At nightfall, "stopper" (or Sawyer-Man) lamps by Westinghouse
provided the most spectacular lighting display the world had ever seen.

*I*n November and December of 1887, Tesla filed for seven U.S. patents in the field of polyphase AC motors and power transmission. These comprised a complete working system that included generators, transformers, transmission lines, motors, and lighting. So original were the ideas that they were issued without a successful challenge, and would turn out to be the most valuable patents since the telephone. In all, a total of forty patents were granted.

On May 16, 1888, Nikola Tesla, thirty-one years of age, stood before the prestigious American Institute of Electrical Engineers (later IEEE) at Columbia University. Before him were handwritten notes, jotted hastily in pencil the night before, for a lecture, "A New System of Alternating Current Motors and Transformers." On the table rested a small electrical machine that was about to change the way electricity was generated and utilized. Tesla opened by saying,

> The subject which I now have the pleasure of bringing to your notice is a novel system of electric distribution and transmission of power by means of alternate currents, affording peculiar advantages, particularly in the way of motors, which I am confident will at once establish the superior adaptability of these currents to the transmission of power and will show that many results

heretofore unattainable can be reached by their use (Tesla 1888).

Then, with the flick of a switch, the powerful little motor came to life, and a new era in technology began.

An adventurous and ambitious Pittsburgh industrialist named George Westinghouse, inventor of railroad air brakes, learned about the lecture and demonstration, and knew that this could be the missing link in long-distance power transmission. He came to Tesla's lab prepared to make an offer—one million dollars, according to one story—for all of

One of the two two-phase induction motors demonstrated by Tesla in his historic lecture of May 16, 1888, before the American Institute of Electrical Engineers at Columbia University. The motor developed ½ horsepower and showed that brushes and commutators could be eliminated.

Courts and inventors generally agree, but for different reasons, that patents are a necessary evil—and often an expensive one. When the U.S. Patent Office grants this special protection, it is certifying that its experts, "examiners," deem an invention to be new enough, workable, and genuinely the product of the person applying. The Office does not guarantee its findings will hold up in court, only that the certified inventor has a presumptive priority and claim, and can bring suit on this basis. In fact, American courts have never been entirely comfortable about what is, after all, a monopoly privilege.

In Tesla's day, and until 1995, the exclusive right of a patent ran for a nonrenewable seventeen-year term from date of issue; with some exceptions the term is now twenty

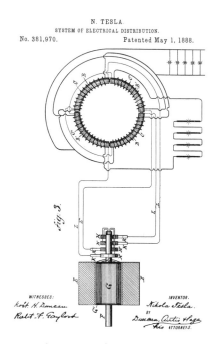

N. TESLA.
SYSTEM OF ELECTRICAL DISTRIBUTION.
No. 381,970.   Patented May 1, 1888.

years from date of application.

Through negotiation, amendment, and redrafts an examiner must be

satisfied of the priority, novelty, and practicality of every point set forth in the "claims." As a result, the inventors often present their case in the broadest terms possible.

Add to this the legal trouble and expense of obtaining the patent, and an inventor's wariness of the process is explained. Tesla's correspondence with the Patent Office (from initial filing to final grant) would often make up a "wrapper" of eighty pages or more. Tesla never felt he had time enough for this long chase. His 111 American patents amount to a fraction of his original and pioneering devices. The most important of them, covering AC power systems and motors, defeated all infringements only because the resources of Westinghouse Corporation lay behind them.

Tesla's AC patents. "Tesla had the answer," he said, "with his induction motor and a complete polyphase system." In actuality, he purchased the patents destined to undergird immeasurable fortunes for $60,000, which included $5,000 in cash and 150 shares of stock in the Westinghouse Corporation. He also agreed to pay royalties of $2.50 per horsepower of electrical capacity sold, which would soon have made Tesla one of the world's wealthiest men (Westinghouse 1888). With more revolutionary inventions in mind, Tesla quickly spent half of his newfound wealth to finance a new laboratory.

Westinghouse had already been skirmishing with Edison over the inadequacies of their respective lighting systems. With the breakthrough provided by Tesla's patents, a full-scale industrial war erupted. At stake, in effect, was the future of industrial development in the United States, and whether Westinghouse or Edison would control the winning technology. Westinghouse recalled:

> I remember Tom telling them that direct current was like a river flowing peacefully to the sea, while alternating current was like a torrent rushing violently over a precipice. Imagine that! Why they even had a professor named Harold Brown who went around talking to audiences...and electrocuting dogs and old horses right on stage, to show how dangerous alternating current was (Ruch 1984).

The development of alternating current was not without its difficulties. Westinghouse hired Tesla and brought him to Pittsburgh to advise in the development of his AC motor for mass production. The troubles began immediately. Tesla had no use for

Top: *The first plant of the Westinghouse Electric Company, on Garrison Alley and Fayette Street in downtown Pittsburgh, had two hundred employees.*

Above left: *George Westinghouse, 1906*

Right: *Early Tesla induction motor manufactured by the Westinghouse Electric Company.*

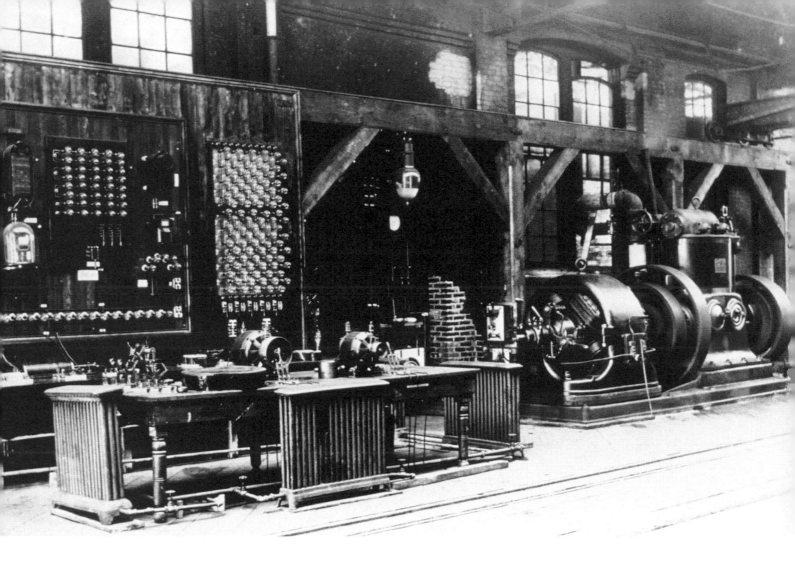

Laboratory where Tesla and Westinghouse engineers developed apparatus for AC systems.

blueprints; he made minute sketches in a palm-sized notepad that he handed off hastily to engineers and mechanics. The chief engineer claimed not to know how the Tesla motor operated, but he knew that it worked when he made it. There were heated arguments over the frequency at which the system would operate. Westinghouse engineers preferred 133 cycles per second, but Tesla insisted on the lower frequency used today—sixty cycles per second.

The Age of Electricity promised the magic of household appliances, horseless trolleys, and skyscrapers with elevators in which to climb them. The new era would bring automobiles, aircraft, nickelodeon moving pictures both spicy and heavily moralistic, and battery-powered magnetic belts that were claimed to have health-enhancing properties. A wealthy man might astound and mystify his family at Christmas with the gift of a double socket. The marketplace would soon boast almost any battery-charged paraphernalia that imagination and the technical genius of the times made possible. Who could reasonably expect that life in this stimulating milieu would be without risk?

No one, therefore, not even the prescient Tesla, foresaw the Great Blizzard of March 11–14, 1888, during which four hundred people perished, many of them electrocuted by the writhing, spitting electric wires that collapsed in the streets of the city amid great hysteria. In the wake of the storm, citizens were infuriated by official delays in removing the overhead electrical danger.

It is strange but true that the introduction of the electric chair in America came purely out of a commercial battle over light bulb sales. Or, more accurately, over what kind of power supply would energize the nation's early lighting. Orders to Edison's lighting companies had fallen behind those for Westinghouse's newer AC systems. With progress marching right past him, Edison and his Wall Street investors opened a delaying campaign to block AC systems in any way possible. The DC interests took up the idea that AC would fail if it was perceived as deadly. One shadowy figure associated with Edison, Harold P. Brown, became a very public advocate of "humane" death—to be inflicted on animals or humans—by AC electricity. Brown electrocuted dogs and horses under questionable experimental conditions. After Edison provided him with research facilities at his West Orange, New Jersey,

Execution of Kemmler from "Tales of Old New York," by Leonard DeGraff.

laboratory, neighbors began to complain of disappearing household pets.

Brown's efforts inspired New York State prison officials to try the idea on a human being. A law was passed in New York (1887) to abandon hanging in favor of electrocution as of January 1, 1889.

Brown, predictably, had a hand in providing apparatus to the state—a 2,000-volt Westinghouse alternator

purchased secondhand—since Westinghouse refused to sell when approached. First to die by the newly prescribed capital punishment was William Kemmler, convicted of killing his wife. He was executed at the Auburn Prison, August 6, 1890. Several jolts were delivered, one for seventeen seconds and another for three and a half minutes. Witnesses reported that the victim's spinal cord burst into flames. The method hasn't worked very predictably, even up to today.

A number of terms were suggested for this new method of execution, including "thanelectrize," "electrophon," "electroctasy," "electrotony," and "fulmenvoltacuss." And why "electrocute," also on the list, should have come to be preferred over the straightforward "electrocize" is anyone's guess. The vested interests in DC current, however, made a point of saying victims of electric shock had been "Westinghoused."

Meanwhile, a murderer was about to be executed in the first electric chair at New York's Auburn State Prison. Professor Harold Brown had succeeded in illegally purchasing a used Westinghouse generator, and hoped to demonstrate once and for all the extreme danger of alternating current. New York State prison authorities looked to electrocution as a more "humane" means of killing human beings. The guinea pig was William Kemmler, a convicted ax-murderer, who died horribly on August 6, 1890, in "an awful spectacle, far worse than hanging." The technique was later dubbed "Westinghousing," in the same manner the guillotine had been named after its inventor. Westinghouse was wryly amused by that use of his moniker.

One of the most important events in Tesla's life took place on July 30, 1891, when he became a citizen of the United States. He often said that he valued his certificate of naturalization above all the honors that subsequently came to him.

Things were happening rapidly to citizen Tesla. His next challenge would be powering and illuminating the Chicago World's Fair, or Columbian Exposition, the first all-electric fair in history. The event celebrated the four hundredth anniversary of Columbus's discovery of America—but one year late, in 1893. The industrial war between backers of Westinghouse's AC and Edison's DC systems was reaching a climax. J. P. Morgan had engineered a

takeover of the Edison Company, the Thompson-Houston Company, and others to form the new General Electric Company.

GE bid a million dollars to provide power and light at the Fair, much of the expense arising from the amount of copper wire necessary to utilize DC power. One set of lines would be required for motors and another for lighting, which required a different level of voltage.

Westinghouse proposed an AC system at nearly half the cost. Better yet, it would be a single "universal system" that could operate motors and lights at the same time. So the only people surprised when Westinghouse got the contract were the backers of General Electric. According to Colonel George R. Davis, Director General of the Fair, the alternating current system saved hundreds of thousands of dollars

worth of copper wire and "what many people deemed a wild experiment became the largest and most satisfactory installation ever made" (Ruch 1986).

GE retaliated by having a court order passed forbidding Westinghouse to use their patented "one-piece Edison lamps of any description." Westinghouse was forced to perfect a two-piece "stopper lamp" by Fair time. Every night of the Fair, lamps that had lost their seals were transported by train to Pittsburgh to be repaired and sent back the next day.

The Columbian Exposition opened on May 1, 1893, as a hundred thousand eager spectators filed into the fairgrounds, awed by the gleaming, neoclassical buildings forming the Court of Honor. Here was something for everyone. Buffalo Bill's Wild West Show gave 318 performances to audiences averaging twelve thousand people a day. American

WESTINGHOUSE ALTERNATING CURRENT SWITCH BOARD

One of the highlights of the Fair was the AC switchboard, with which one man operated forty circuits providing power all over the fairgrounds. It had 1,000 square feet of marble.

Bell Telephone made the first long-distance call from New York to Chicago. Edison's latest phonographs were there as well as the first Kinetoscope, or peep show. Visitors could see the first American-built automobile and the first zipper. They could take a whirl on the first Ferris wheel, with thirty-six cars holding sixty people each, or slip away to see girls from Algiers doing the "Kouta Kouta" dance.

But the greatest spectacle occurred the first evening when President Grover Cleveland pushed a button and a hundred thousand incandescent lamps burst into light. Flags of every nation fluttered in a fortuitous breeze. An orchestra played Handel's *Hallelujah Chorus*, electrically operated fountains shot water skyward, and cannons boomed. This was the "City of Light," the city of the future. Children's author L. Frank Baum was so impressed by the sight

that it became his inspiration for the Emerald City in *The Wizard of Oz.* Another writer declared, "humanity in the Court of Honor became almost a concrete mass...the most spectacular display of lighting the world had ever seen" (Ruch 1986).

This was the work of Tesla, Westinghouse, and twelve new thousand-horsepower AC generation units located in the Hall of Machinery. The Westinghouse central station boasted a huge, forty-circuit switchboard built with a thousand square feet of marble, which provided all the power and light needed for the Fair and required just one operator.

To meet the terms of the contract, each day the management of the Fair counted out silver dollars, half-dollars, and paper currency from the daily receipts and forwarded it in cloth bags to the Westinghouse Company in Pittsburgh. But the most

Above: On display was a Westinghouse generating apparatus for trolleys and city utilities.

Left: Displays by Westinghouse (featuring the Tesla Polyphase System) and General Electric dominated Electricity Hall.

Above: Tesla's exhibit with his "Egg of Columbus," which stood on end when the table it rested on was magnetically excited by AC. Another smaller table with ball can be seen to the left; to the right, an early high-frequency machine.

Opposite page, top: Tesla's sign was made of tinfoil and glass energized with high voltage at a frequency of 40,000 hertz. It produced a lightning-like effect, accompanied by a deafening noise, and it amazed visitors.

Opposite page, bottom: Newspaper caption for this illustration in the New York Sunday World, *July 22, 1894, reads: "Nikola Tesla, Showing the Inventor in the Effulgent Glory of Myriad Tongues of Electric Flame After He Has Saturated Himself with Electricity."*

lasting benefit was in the Great Hall of Electricity, where the Tesla polyphase system of alternating current power generation and transmission was proudly displayed. From that point forward more than 80 percent of all the electrical devices ordered in the United States were for alternating current.

Tesla had his own electrical exhibit at the fair, based on a future that few engineers then understood. The area was uniquely brightened by his latest invention, neon tube lighting, which he himself twisted to form the names of his favorite scientists—Faraday, Maxwell, Henry—and his favorite Serbian poet, Zmaj. To demonstrate the principle of the rotating magnetic field, he created the "Egg of Columbus," a small metallic ovoid on a metal plate, that rose on its end with the pressing of a switch and began to spin rapidly, first in one direction and then in the other, providing smooth and beautiful proof of alternating current's versatility.

Then the tall Merlin-like figure wearing shoes with thick rubber soles stepped onto a stage and allowed two million volts of electricity to pass through his body, creating a halo of electric flames around him. (Readers are warned not to attempt such a performance.) Tesla loved nothing so much as astounding the public and newspaper reporters and baffling his fellow scientists.

For the twenty-seven million people who attended the Fair, it was dramatically clear that the power of the future was AC. Life could not have been sweeter, yet Tesla could scarcely wait to return to New York and continue his experiments. ⤝

CHAPTER FOUR

High Frequency

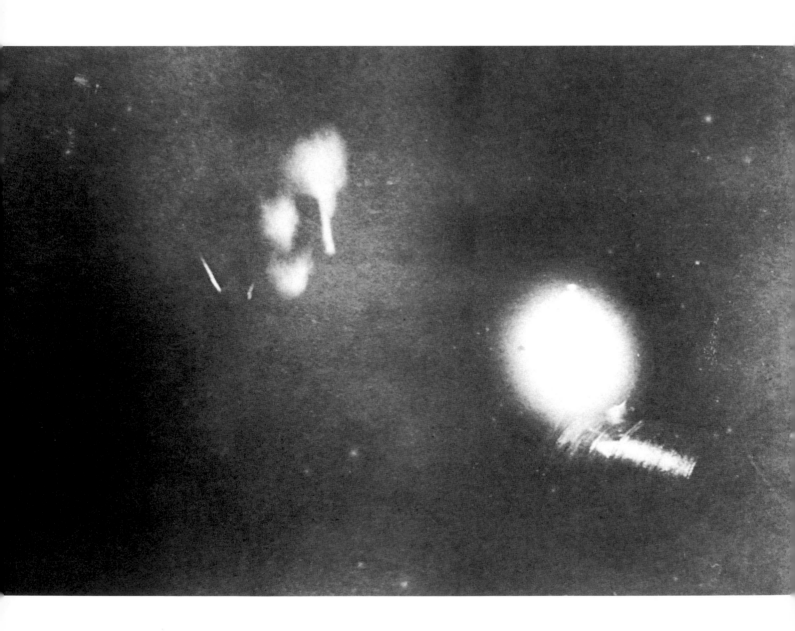

First photograph exposed by phosphorescent light, taken of Tesla in his laboratory. Exposure was eight minutes.

Happily, Tesla's imagination was never constrained by the arbitrary limits of specializing, and he appeared fearless of the dangers of electricity. Basic devices for electrical measurement like the oscilloscope did not yet exist, so the inventor used his body like a sensitive instrument to fine-tune his experiments. In his New York laboratory he was free to dream and probe where the directional signs led him.

In 1873 the Scottish physicist James Clerk Maxwell published a famous *Treatise on Electricity and Magnetism* that suggested light was electromagnetic radiation—electricity vibrating at an extremely high frequency. Using a set of equations described as "elegant," he demonstrated that light, electricity, and magnetism were all properties of the same phenomenon, and all moving at the same speed—the speed of light. He also predicted a wide range of electrical vibrations above and below visible sunlight.

In 1888 Heinrich Hertz of Bonn, Germany, confirmed experimentally that an electric spark propagates electromagnetic waves into space. This discovery set off ripples in scientific circles and prompted intense speculation about new possibilities for electricity.

Tesla began to search for a device that could transport him to this unexplored territory. He knew that higher frequencies would have many technical advantages: lamps could glow brighter, energy could be transmitted more efficiently, and it was less dangerous because it could pass harmlessly across the body.

His initial goal was to approximate the frequency of sunlight and create lamps of revolutionary

Woodcut from Electrical World, *May 20, 1891, showing Nikola Tesla's first of three lectures on currents of high frequency and potential at Columbia College in New York. Delivered in 1891, '92, and '93, the series aroused the technical world to the possibilities of such currents.*

brightness and configuration. This, he hoped, would eliminate Edison's incandescent lamp, which utilized only 5 percent of the available energy. Arthur Brisbane, distinguished journalist for Joseph Pulitzer's *New York Sunday World*, reported in a July 22, 1894, article:

> The light of the sun, according to Mr. Tesla, is the result of vibrations in 94,000,000 miles of ether which separates us from the centre of the solar system. Mr. Tesla's idea is to produce here on earth vibrations similar to those which cause the sunlight, and thus to give us a light as good as that of the sun, with no danger from clouds or other obstructions.

He went on to describe constructing an alternating current machine capable of giving more than two million reversals of current per minute, with the goal of producing a practical and efficient source of light. And "all" he had to do to duplicate the sunlight was

> get this number of vibrations to the second with my machinery on earth. Take a 5 and put after it 14 zeros; then you will have the number of vibrations that occur in the ether every second and which produce light (five hundred trillion). I have succeeded up to a certain point but am still at work on the task.

Tesla began his high-frequency investigations by building rotary AC generators that could run at higher speeds; but as he approached twenty thousand cycles per second, the machines began to fly apart, leaving him far short of his goal of producing artificial sunlight.

The answer came with a remarkable device still known today as a Tesla coil. Patented in 1891, this invention took ordinary sixty-cycles-per-second household current and stepped it up to high frequencies—into the hundreds of thousands of cycles per second. In addition to high frequencies, the coil could

The famous type of step-up transformer associated with Tesla's name first appeared in patent number 454,622 (1891) as part of a high-voltage, high-frequency lighting system. It is actually a two-stage device: a continuous source of alternating current feeding a first set of step-up coils, the output of which, in turn, drives a second step-up device (the Tesla coil itself) in a higher-frequency circuit containing a spark gap and capacitor. The length of the gap across the spark electrodes controls the final frequency because of the time charge takes to accumulate before an arc can jump through the space between them. These discharges may be tuned to take place thousands or hundreds of thousands of times per second.

The Tesla coil was also unique in the way it produced high voltages. Induced waves in the coil vibrate from end to end, each new one augmenting the other through resonant action so that

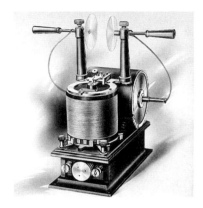

Small Tesla coil designed for use by medical profession, 1897.

their peaks tend to meet and coincide at regular, fixed intervals. These are called standing waves. Their formation depends critically on the coil's length—how many quarter wavelengths of a particular frequency would just fit. Electrical energy builds in this way until it must literally explode from the system.

Tesla was not the first by any means to combine capacitors and coils for calculated effect; nor was he the first to employ a "disruptive discharge." His patent was, however, the first to put them all together to achieve an astonishingly high (for the time) voltage and frequency. This kind of capability leads directly to radio transmission, something Tesla began to explore only a few years later.

---

also generate extremely high voltages. Key to this invention was Tesla's understanding of electrical resonance, in which small electrical vibrations build cumulatively to release tremendous energy.

For the inventor, this coil was like a lamp of Aladdin, transporting him through the electromagnetic spectrum, discovering with each step another phenomenon. When subjected to high-frequency waves, gases such as neon, argon, and xenon would glow. Certain chemicals such as phosphorus responded uniquely to high frequencies, giving off an unearthly light. A piece of iron next to a coil operating at four hundred thousand cycles per second could be brought to white heat by electrical vibrations alone. This process, known as induction heating, is widely used to heat and shape metals today.

Tesla sensed even greater possibilities:

If my memory serves me right, it was in November, 1890, that I performed a labora-

tory experiment which was one of the most extraordinary and spectacular ever recorded in the annals of science. In investigating the behavior of high frequency currents I had satisfied myself that an electric field of sufficient intensity could be produced in a room to light up electrodeless vacuum tubes (Tesla 1919e).

He extended a wire from a coil around the ceiling of his laboratory. He stood in the center of the room with a large vacuum tube in his hand. When a switch was thrown, the tube illuminated brilliantly, the energy being transmitted through the air. "To me," said Tesla, "it was the first evidence that I was transmitting energy without connecting wires in between."

The period between 1891 and 1893 was one of the most fruitful periods in his career. He invented a system of transmitting energy over a single wire, the return circuit occurring wirelessly through space; built the prototypes of four different Tesla coils and many

Above: A bank of industrial lamps driven by one of Tesla's high frequency oscillators, 1898.

Left: Neon lights first displayed at Columbian Exposition, 1893.

versions of them for investigating high-frequency effects and phenomena; and in the final year of this creative period, in which he also discovered such incidental consumer products as neon and phosphorescent tube lighting, he invented the system of wireless transmission that would be known as radio. But all these, as Tesla said, were "merely steps in a certain direction."

In his second lecture to the American Institute of Electrical Engineers at Columbia College, on May 20, 1891, he described and demonstrated his most recent research from a stage illuminated with gas-filled tube lights, some phosphorescent and some made with uranium glass twisted into the names of his favorite poets and scientists.

Then, with hundreds of thousands of volts of high-frequency currents surging across his body, he would hold in his hand a strangely powerful little "carbon-button" lamp. Energy from his body caused gas molecules in the tube to bombard a small button of carborundum until it glowed to incandescence, resulting in a light twenty times brighter than any other lamp in existence. The energy inside the bulb was so powerful that it vaporized diamonds and rubies.

In 1892 Tesla traveled to London and Paris. There, before some of the most prestigious scientists in the world, he demonstrated lights that operated without wire connections; tubes so sensitive as to be able to sense an electronic impulse across the Atlantic; and even a motor that could be powered with a con-

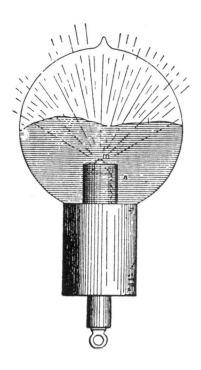

Clockwise from top left: Illustration of carbon-button lamp, in which radiant matter is projected against, or focused upon, a diamond or ruby and rendered incandescent. Demonstrated by Tesla in his lectures of 1891–92.

A replication of a demonstration in Tesla's 1893 lectures showing extremely high-frequency standing waves. "If we succeed in employing the effects of resonance," said Tesla, "the return wire will become unnecessary."

Tesla holds a highly evacuated, gas-filled tube, powered by one of his high-frequency oscillator units. The one-amp tube operated without any connection to wires ("wireless energy") over appreciable distances, which could have been greatly extended with more power. Exposure, two seconds with a lamp of 250 candlepower.

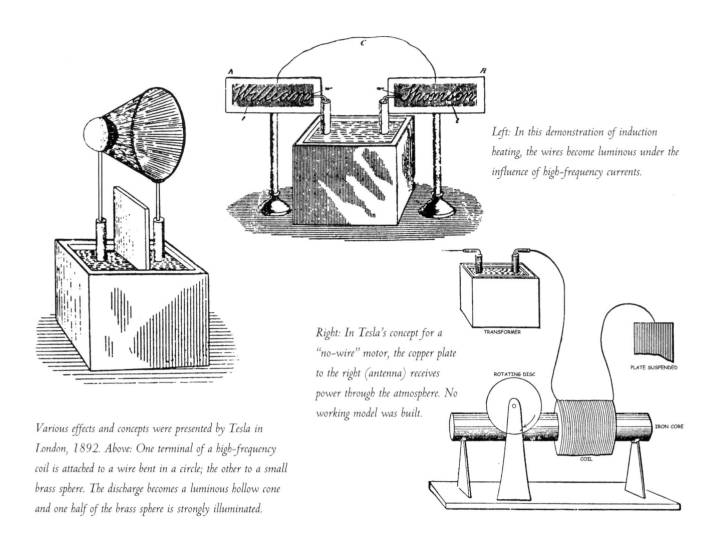

Left: In this demonstration of induction heating, the wires become luminous under the influence of high-frequency currents.

Right: In Tesla's concept for a "no-wire" motor, the copper plate to the right (antenna) receives power through the atmosphere. No working model was built.

Various effects and concepts were presented by Tesla in London, 1892. Above: One terminal of a high-frequency coil is attached to a wire bent in a circle; the other to a small brass sphere. The discharge becomes a luminous hollow cone and one half of the brass sphere is strongly illuminated.

nection to the ground and an antenna. "It is quite possible," he told the Institution of Electrical Engineers in London,

> that such "no-wire" motors, as they might be called, could be operated by conduction through the rarefied air at considerable distances. Alternate currents, especially of high frequencies, pass with astonishing freedom through even slightly rarefied gases. The upper strata of the air are rarefied. To reach a number of miles out into space requires the overcoming of difficulties of merely mechanical nature. There is no doubt that with the enormous potentials obtainable by the use of high frequencies and oil insulation luminous discharges might be passed through many miles of rarefied air, and that, by thus directing energy of many hundreds or thousands of horse-power, motors or lamps might be operated at considerable distances from stationary sources (Tesla 1892).

The distinguished physicist Lord Rayleigh, after watching Tesla's demonstrations, complimented him on a rare talent for discovering fundamental principles, and urged that in the future he concentrate on a "single big idea." This idea would come on a rushed visit to Yugoslavia to visit his mother on her deathbed. "One day as I was roaming in the mountains," he explained,

> I sought shelter from an approaching storm. The sky became overhung with heavy clouds but somehow the rain was delayed until, all of

a sudden, there was a lightning flash and a few moments after, a deluge. It was manifest that the two phenomena were closely related, as cause and effect, and a little reflection led me to the conclusion that the electrical energy involved in the precipitation of the water was inconsiderable, the function of lightning being like that of a sensitive trigger. Here was a stupendous possibility of achievement. If we could produce electric effects of the required quality, this whole planet and the conditions of existence on it could be transformed. We could irrigate arid deserts...provide motive power in unlimited amounts. This would be the most efficient way of harnessing the sun to the uses of man. The consummation depended on our ability to develop electric forces of the order of those in nature (Tesla 1919e).

Thoughts of using electricity to change the weather stayed with Tesla throughout his career. Not everyone was impressed with his wireless energy scheme; least enthusiastic were the large corporations and powerful investors who were even now sinking billions into the power lines that he was suggesting could be eliminated. George Westinghouse himself was reluctant to entertain the idea. But such practical commercial concerns did not deter Tesla:

> In the Houston Street laboratory, I could take in my hands a coil tuned to my body and collect horsepower anywhere in the room without tangible connection, and I have often disillusioned my visitors in regard to such wonderful effects. Sometimes, I would produce flames shooting out from my head and run a motor in my hands or light six or eight lamps (Anderson 1992, 55–56).

To visitors in the 1890s Tesla's lab must have looked like the den of an alchemist. A large coil hummed in constant operation to power wireless lamps mounted on the walls and ceiling. Lab techni-

Tesla's Houston Street laboratory wirelessly illuminated by his efficient phosphorescent lamps. First published in the Electrical Experimenter, *March 1919.*

cians, bathed in eerie blue light, would move from place to place carrying their wireless lamps with them. They recalled the extraordinary sight of Tesla in the darkened laboratory thrusting and parrying at some invisible adversary with his wireless light saber. Though stunning to witness, this magic was only a localized effect created by a strong magnetic field in the room. With modern concerns about the detrimental influence of such fields on human physiology, obtaining power in this way today would not be very popular. Also, the strength of magnetic fields falls off rapidly. Even Tesla was aware that transmission of power over long distances "lay in a different direction."

That direction was suggested one day by a chance observation. While he was working with a coil in the five hundred thousand cycles per second range, a sec-

Above: Movable experimental tuning table (on casters). An ordinary incandescent lamp is lit up at a distance through the influence of "electrified ether-waves."

Left: Tesla with one of his famous "wireless" lamps. Published on the cover of the Electrical Experimenter *in 1919.*

ond coil, unattached and in a distant part of the room, responded sympathetically with a small burst of lightning. These coils were "tuned" to the same frequency. The spark of one coil transmitted radio waves through the air; the other coil received the waves and converted them back into electricity. This was wireless transmission of energy.

Tesla announced his great discovery at a lecture before the Franklin Institute in Philadelphia in February 1893:

> I would say a few words on a subject which constantly fills my thoughts and concerns the welfare of all. I mean the transmission of intelligible signals or perhaps even power to any distance without the use of wires. I am becoming daily more convinced of the practicability of the scheme (Tesla 1893).

A month later, he traveled to St. Louis to speak to a meeting of the National Electric Light Association. In a presentation titled "On Light and Other High Frequency Phenomena," he gave the first recorded description of radio transmission and reception: two tuned electrical circuits, connected to ground and antenna.

To demonstrate the concept, a large coil, conspicuously lacking any wire connections, was moved onto the stage. On top of the coil rested a large vacuum tube. When a second coil was energized backstage, the tube on the coil illuminated brilliantly. Tesla recalled the event twenty-three years later:

> These experiments, I remember, were made in St. Louis. There was a hall with 6,000 or 7,000 people. When I explained how I had shown a phosphorescent bulb to Lord Kelvin in England, and told them that the bulb was going to spring into light, there was a stam-

When you turn on your radio or television, you are receiving all possible signals all the time. Tuning is what happens when some part of its circuitry is adjusted to vibrate in sympathy with a signal of a particular frequency—like a tuning fork sensitive to radio waves. The signal and the circuit "resonate" with one another; other signals, at other frequencies, simply don't excite a reaction and won't be "picked up" in the circuit.

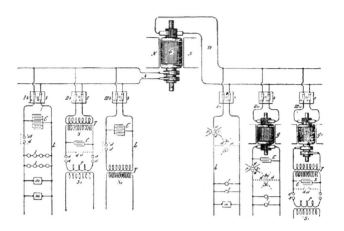

Examples of Tesla's circuits to produce high-frequency electrical vibrations.

One approach to tuning, and historically the first useful method, employs capacitors and coils (inductors), which may act together in a complementary way when alternating (or varying) current is applied. A capacitor is very quick to allow electrons (*i.e.*, current) to surge from one plate to the other through a circuit, but the voltage builds across its plates more slowly, as electrons finally pile up. Inductors are just the opposite: voltage is felt immediately but current has difficulty getting through while the coil's magnetic fields are being built up or collapsing; the passage of current is opposed, or choked, for a time.

If capacitive and inductive properties are exactly matched, a kind of perfectly timed sloshing takes place between them—electrons rush back and forth as voltage peaks first in the condenser and then in the coil. This reciprocating action, or resonance, results in one signal being amplified and the rest being swept away.

pede in the two upper galleries and they all rushed out. They thought it was some part of the devil's work, and ran out. That is the way my experiments were received (Anderson 1992, 87).

But these were merely parlor tricks. "You would think me a dreamer and very far gone if I should tell you what I really hope for," he stated in an article in April 1895 in *Century Magazine*, "but I can tell you that I look forward with absolute confidence to sending messages through the earth without any wires. I have also great hopes for transmitting electric force in the same way without waste."

He knew that higher levels of electrical energy would be necessary to transmit wireless power over long distances, and here again the Tesla coil became a perfect, indispensable instrument. By applying the principles of electrical resonance Tesla was able to reach extremely high voltages, his progress being measured in the length of the blue discharges exploding from the tips of his coils. In 1891 he was able to create sparks five inches long, indicating a potential of about a hundred thousand volts. By modifying and improving his designs, he found that he could generate increasingly higher voltages, with no specific end in sight. "The first gratifying result was obtained in the spring of 1894 when I reached tensions of about 1,000,000 volts with my conical coil."

Century Magazine goes on to describe this new Tesla oscillator:

He connects to the earth, by one of its ends, a coil in which rapidly vibrating currents are produced, the other end being in free space. The purple streamers of electricity thus elicited from the earth and pouring out to the ambient are marvelous.

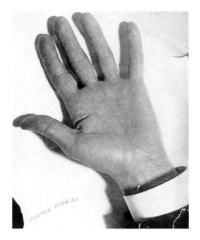

Above: Tesla's hand in a photo exposed with fluorescent lighting. Note cut on palm above thumb.

Left: Tesla experimented with many coil shapes. Here a conical coil, demonstrated in his lab in 1895, is "specially adapted to excite the electrical charge of the earth." The streamers at the top of the coil are of purple hue and several feet in diameter. Tension is about one million volts.

Tesla was becoming a threat to himself and his neighbors, often working late at night to avoid unwanted attention:

> I knew that higher electromotive forces were attainable with apparatus of larger dimensions. I had an instinctive perception that the object could be accomplished by the proper design of a comparatively small and compact transformer . . . with a secondary in the form of a flat spiral. The application of this principle enabled me to produce pressures of 4,000,000 volts, which was about the limit obtainable in my new laboratory . . . as the discharges extended through a distance of 16 feet (Tesla 1919e).

When working with high voltages, Tesla always kept one hand in his pocket to avoid completing a deadly circuit. Still, there was danger enough. A reporter for the *New York Herald* wrote on March 13, 1895, that he came across the inventor in a small café, looking shaken after being hit by 3.5 million volts. "I am afraid," said Tesla,

> that you won't find me a pleasant companion tonight. The fact is I was almost killed today. The spark jumped three feet through the air and struck me here on the right shoulder. I tell you it made me feel dizzy. If my assistant had not turned off the current instantly it might have been the end of me. As it was, I have to show for it a queer mark on my right breast where the current struck in and a burned heel in one of my socks where it left my body.

Fortunately, Tesla survived his high-frequency experiments. Indeed, it was found his resonating electromagnetic coils might produce beneficial effects, as in the case of the medical treatment called diathermy. Today therapeutic use of deep-heating high-frequency currents on the human body is widely known in medicine.

To say that Tesla was ahead of his time is no

The first "extra coil" configuration for Tesla's high-voltage oscillators, in a photo taken at his Houston Street laboratory in October 1898. Streamers are sixteen feet wide and cover an area of two hundred square feet. Estimated pressure is two million volts—prompting him to seek a larger and safer place for his experiments.

exaggeration. Ironically, the Tesla coil is one of his least understood inventions. One past president of the Institute of Radio Engineers remarked that his "contributions to the high frequency field have been remarkably sterile. The young radio engineer of today [1943] may very well complete his formal education without ever having heard of Tesla." But according to Leland I. Anderson, an electrical engineer and leading authority on the inventor,

> Tesla seemed to innately understand the workings of the coil. He knew what to expect. He appreciated the great magnifying aspects of it that were really not understood by his contemporaries, and it's that genius which many of us are just beginning to understand (interview with the authors, 1993).

This helps to explain, although not to justify in the light of today's knowledge, the engineers and physicists who graduate from leading universities without ever having heard of Tesla. Even more, it is hard to believe that a power engineer can obtain a degree with no awareness of Tesla's historic role in developing the AC system, quite apart from appreciating his work in high frequencies.

But the practical applications of his inventions did not hold great interest for Tesla. He saw himself as a discoverer, not merely an inventor of useful devices. "There are some who are artists," he said, "and then there are others." He would be criticized, of course, for having a grasp that exceeded his reach, but the power engineers of today—those who have done their homework—realize what his contemporaries at first failed to understand: why, and how far, and how accurately Tesla was reaching. ◄

CHAPTER FIVE

Lionized and Ionized

Mark Twain and Joseph ("Jo") Jefferson in Tesla's South Fifth Avenue laboratory, 1894, with blurred image of Tesla between.

TESLA HAS CONTRIBUTED MORE TO ELECTRICAL SCIENCE THAN ANY
MAN UP TO THIS TIME. —WILLIAM THOMSON, LORD KELVIN

The inventor's relentless need for research funding, in addition to his love of display, inspired him to invite the wealthy and the famous to his laboratory for after-hours entertainment. Dashing and debonair, he fit well into high-fashion New York society. But his personal side was complex, often as difficult to understand as his electrical inventions.

To Tesla's laboratory came such fabled figures as J. P. Morgan, John D. Rockefeller, Edward H. Harriman, Thomas Fortune Ryan, Jay Gould, the Astors, the Vanderbilts, and later even Henry Ford. Among those who bravely posed with high-voltage sparks pouring from their bodies were the actors Joseph Jefferson and Marion Crawford, the director of the Boston Symphony, celebrated prima donnas, and even occasional kings and queens.

Perhaps Tesla's most famous friend was the writer Mark Twain, with whom the Serb's literary connections went back to childhood. In his autobiography, Tesla describes how Twain helped him recover from a dangerous illness when he was brought the early novels from his local public library and found them "so captivating as to make me utterly forget my hopeless state." He attributed the miraculous recovery that followed to the humorist. Tesla claims that twenty-five years later, when he met Twain in New York, he told him the touching story "and was amazed to see that great man of laughter burst into tears" (Tesla 1919c).

In *Mark Twain's Notebooks & Journals*, the author mentions reading about the sale to Westinghouse of Tesla's electrical patents, "which will revolutionize the whole electric business of the world." Twain had made a bad investment—one of many—in the development of a new DC motor, and was drawn to Tesla for answers. The answer was that this motor had been rendered obsolete by Tesla's polyphase AC. Because this appears to have been the occasion for their first meeting, Twain's tears may have had a more pecuniary cause.

On that basis, the two men became lifelong friends and, incidentally, fellow members of the posh Players Club. Twain later was instrumental in encouraging Tesla to pursue his futuristic weapons for shifting war's destructiveness from men to machines, it

Mark Twain in Tesla's laboratory at 35 South Fifth Avenue, early 1895

Tesla and many of his contemporaries believed in the healthful as well as harmful effects of electricity on the body. The inventor often treated himself with high-frequency electricity to restore his exhausted nervous system. He called it "electrical massage." Early electric parlor games and use of the Tesla coil as a "pleasurizer" eventually gave way to more serious science.

Two pioneer investigators, Arsène d'Arsonval and P. M. Oudin, were intrigued with an electrical current's ability to warm parts of the body. They found that DC currents tended to destroy tissue, but AC a little less so, particularly as the applied frequency rose.

By 1891 Tesla had discovered that in practice the much higher frequencies he achieved transferred more energy to a target part of the body without establishing searing current paths through nerve and muscle. As with any new and potentially hazardous idea he developed, he risked his own body with the prototypes. Fortunately, he found, the action of a current as such is essentially eliminated at or above one megahertz.

Because of other pressing concerns, such as the race to develop radio, he sought no patents for the applied principle or the compact machines he constructed for the purpose. Indeed, he did not trouble to name it either;

"diathermy" wasn't coined until 1909, by the Czech doctor R. von Zeynek.

As a means of alleviating some kinds of pain or promoting certain temperature-dependent processes in the body, the use of radio-frequency heating continues today. Contemporary treatment utilizes ultrasonic or microwave energy, as well as pulses in the 1–1.5 megahertz range.

then being innocently thought that wars would cease when weapons became too horrible to contemplate.

Mark Twain was one of the friends most often invited to Tesla's laboratory for the improvisational shows of fright and delight. On one particular evening Twain himself inadvertently furnished the entertainment when he insisted upon experiencing the gyrations of a platform mounted on an electrical oscillator. Tesla pretended to dissuade him, which of course made Twain all the more desirous of prolonging the test. Once on the machine he kept saying, "More, Tesla, more!" But soon he was crying for help, since an undesired effect of the oscillations on the human body was to create a turmoil in the bowels.

When he was next invited to the laboratory, a wiser Twain wrote: "Friday, Midnight. Dear Mr. Tesla: I am desperately sorry, but a matter of unavoidable business has intruded itself and bars me from coming down. . . . I am very, very sorry. Do forgive me" (Twain n.d.).

Tesla was a frequent guest at the fashionable home of editor and socialite Robert Underwood Johnson and his wife, Katharine. Both of the Johnsons doted on the inventor and Katharine in particular loved him. During evenings at their house at 327 Lexington Avenue he met musicians, actors, writers, dilettantes, and heiresses, as well as industrialists, politicians, and multimillionaires.

Robert Johnson, in his book *Remembered Yesterdays*, describes many of his famous visitors:

A memorable occasion was the first meeting of Tesla and Paderewski, which took place at our table. Two more intellectual or lovable men I have never known. . . . On comparing notes, they discovered that they had both been in Strasburg years before at the same time, Tesla as an electrical assistant on a small salary, and Paderewski as a student in music, and they laughed heartily at the change of their condi-

THE PLAYERS,
16 GRAMERCY PARK.

March 4/94.

Dear Mr. Tesla:
If I can possibly
manage it I'll be there
by 4 p.m., but I am dreadfully
pushed for time, & you
mustn't depend on me.
In haste
Sincerely Yours
S.L. Clemens

Above: Katharine Johnson, Tesla's great admirer

Left: Letter from Twain to Tesla sent from the fashionable Players Club.

tions since that time of storm and stress. The two talked European politics, in which Paderewski would later play a commanding role, representing Poland at the Versailles Peace Conference in 1919 and serving for ten months as premier of a coalition ministry (R. Johnson 1923, 399–402).

Johnson also introduced Tesla to Rudyard Kipling, John Muir, Anton Dvoràk, Helen Hunt Jackson, and others. His countryman, the great physicist Michael Pupin, who came from a Yugoslav background as poor as Tesla's, also was an occasional guest at the Johnsons'.

Tesla could be fun-loving and had a sharp and sarcastic wit. "And you, Mr. Tesla," asked an attractive female guest one evening, "What do you do?" "Oh, I dabble a little in electricity," Tesla said. "Indeed. Keep at it and don't be discouraged," she replied. "You may end by doing something someday."

Johnson considered Tesla one of the few geniuses he had ever met. His deepest regret was that he had not recorded the many prophecies made by Tesla in his house, then thought to be the wildest fancies, but a number of which "materialized."

For example, Tesla had told Katharine Johnson: The time will come when crossing the ocean by steamer you will be able to have a daily paper on board with the important news of the world . . . and by means of a pocket instrument and a wire stuck in the ground, you can communicate from any distance with friends at home through an instrument similarly attuned.

He had told the Johnsons he believed it possible "to direct the movements of an aeroplane or torpedo boat by wireless," and confidently predicted that "some day it would be practicable to run street cars in London with the power of Niagara."

Early in their acquaintance the Johnsons were

Robert Underwood Johnson holding loop with incandescent lamp. Tesla is in the background at the switch.

invited to Tesla's laboratory to observe his high-frequency experiments first hand.

Johnson notes: "I was myself at that time the medium of the passage of an electric current of a million volts of the Tesla system of high frequency . . . and lamps were thus lit up brilliantly through my body" (R. Johnson 1923).

In the early years, when he was lionized by the New York "400," speculation was rife (even in international engineering periodicals) as to why he did not marry. Women whose names were associated with him included the Morgan heiress, Anne, the Dodge heiress, Flora, the pianist Marguerite Merington, and the "incandescent" French actress Sarah Bernhardt.

Tesla first met Bernhardt in Paris in 1892. He was relaxing with friends in a sidewalk café late in the evening when the actress passed by them. In a flirtatious gesture of the times she dropped her handkerchief. Tesla sprang to his feet and returned it to her, and a bond was instantaneously formed between them. Bernhardt is later said to have attended one of his lectures in America, raising speculation among

their friends about a secret tryst. Their meeting was supposedly arranged by—of all people—the celebrated Indian Swami Vivekenanda. Tesla kept the actress's handkerchief for the rest of his life.

As a result of such speculation, Tesla felt compelled to explain the conflict he felt between romance and invention. He did not, however, allude to the inconvenient phobias from which he suffered—his fear of germs in physical contact, an aversion to touching hair and to the sight of earrings, as well as to certain smells. Instead, he stated, "I do not believe an inventor should marry, because he has so intense a nature, with so much in it of wild, passionate quality, that in giving himself to a woman he might love, he would give everything and so take everything from his chosen field." He added, pointedly, "I do not think you can name many great inventions that have been made by married men" (*New York Herald* 1897).

Men also found Tesla striking, in both appearance and personality. Franklin Chester of *The Citizen* declared that no one could look upon the inventor without feeling his force. He was extremely tall, his

From left to right. The heiress Flora Dodge was infatuated with Tesla; the "divine" Sarah Bernhardt (Courtesy Library of Congress); Tesla in 1895 at age thirty-nine.

hair straight and intensely black, brushed sharply back above his ears; his cheekbones were high and Slavic, his eyes blue and deeply set, burning like balls of fire. "Those weird flashes of light he makes with his instruments," Chester wrote, "seemed almost to shoot from them. His head is wedge-shaped. His chin is almost a point. . . . When he talks you listen. You do not know what he is saying, but he enthralls you" (Chester 1897).

Tesla's sex life is a subject of some controversy. In a March 3, 1922 interview with the Serbian-American newspaper *Serbobran* he said, "I destroyed my sexuality at the age of thirty-three because a certain French actress kept coming to me making it impossible for me to concentrate." On another occasion he told a reporter that he "never touched a woman." Whether Tesla was speaking literally or figuratively is a matter of conjecture, as are many other details about the inventor. Some who met him say he spoke with a high, shrill voice; some say soft and low. Some recall a heavy accent; others no accent at all. Unfortunately, no recordings of his voice have ever

been found, though they are said to exist. The exact shades of Tesla's blue (or gray) eyes and even his hair are also subject to disagreement.

The obsessive-compulsive disorders that made him seem so eccentric were manifested in a fear of germs, which caused him invariably to avoid shaking hands and to polish the spotless dishes and silver put before him. His attire was always immaculate and he usually discarded gloves after wearing them for only a week. The thought of touching someone's hair disturbed him greatly, as did the sight of a pearl, a peach, or earrings on a woman. Numbers divisible by three entered into all his calculations, including the number of towels required in his hotel room to serve his excessive cleanliness. If he walked around a block, he would continue until he had circled it three times. Even the number of his hotel room had to be a multiple of three. He said in "My Inventions":

> I counted the steps in my walks and calculated the cubic contents of soup plates, coffee cups and pieces of food—otherwise my meal was unenjoyable. All repeated acts or operations I

Above: Caricature of a "dandified" Tesla

Left: Tesla at a 1910 dinner honoring Henry Clews, newly elected as president of the American Civic Alliance.

performed had to be divisible by three and if I missed I felt impelled to do it all over again, even if it took hours (Tesla 1919a).

Journalists of his own time often wrote of Tesla with florid headlines, as if perhaps describing a new patent medicine, which did little to endear him to competitors and obscured his true nature. In a *New York Sunday World* article of July 22, 1894, Arthur Brisbane drew interesting conclusions about the obvious genius inherent in a person with long thumbs, light-colored eyes (bleached from excessive thinking), and a bulging forehead. An interview between the two at Delmonico's, a fashionable restaurant that Tesla often patronized, lasted from late evening until dawn the following day. The inventor's stature was emphasized by the journalist, who noted, "Mr. Delmonico lowers his voice when he speaks of Mr. Tesla, as Boston cab drivers used to lower their voices when they spoke of [heavyweight champion] John L. Sullivan."

Tesla was not a "regular guy," but could rise to the occasion, as in a game of pool, in which he hustled his companions. Said Delmonico:

> That Tesla can do anything. We managed to make him play pool one night. He had never played, but he had watched us for a little while. He was very indignant when he found that we meant to give him fifteen points. . . . But he bet us all even and got all the money. He studied out pool in his head and then beat us, after we had practiced for years.

Brisbane was evidently unaware that Tesla in his youth had been almost a professional at billiards.

There were also, perhaps unsurprisingly, less attractive aspects of the inventor's personality, among them petty cruelty and snobbery. His secretaries usually suffered the most, and yet his staff remained loyal to him well into old age.

Throughout his career, Tesla was aided by a small

but regular team of workers. George Scherff performed a number of roles including financial support. Kolman Czito was always his main mechanic, and later Tesla was assisted by Czito's son Julius. Also helping periodically were well-known engineers Otis Pond and Fritz Löwenstein.

In the early 1890s Tesla was one of the best known and most admired men in the world. People appreciated the fact that his inventions made their lives better. Everything was looking up for the handsome, brilliant young Serb. His polyphase AC system had just been selected as the means to extract power from the mighty Niagara Falls. His device for wireless transmission of energy was now perfected, with a demonstration planned to transmit signals twenty miles to a boat on the Hudson River. He had demonstrated revolutionary new kinds of lighting. And there seemed to be no limit to the creations that poured from his brain.

Then disaster struck. At 2:30 A.M. on March 13, 1895, fire broke out on the first floor of the building containing Tesla's laboratory. Everything was lost. "The wizard and rival of Thomas A. Edison was burned out," the *New York Times* reported. "His shop, plant, all his apparatus for conducting the scientific experiments on which the gaze of the world is riveted these days, were destroyed, with everything else which the building at 33–35 South Fifth Avenue contained."

The work of half a lifetime was ruined. Nothing was insured. Expensive equipment had collapsed through the floors in molten heaps. Tesla vanished into the streets in a daze, while his friends worried and searched for him. Finally he returned to his room in the Hotel Gerlach, collapsed, and was not heard from for days. When the Johnsons finally made contact, Katharine wrote:

> Today with the deepening realization of the meaning of this disaster and consequently with increasing anxiety for you, my dear friend, I am

FRUITS OF GENIUS WERE SWEPT AWAY.

By a Fire the Noted Electrician, Nicola Tesla, Loses Mechanisms of Inestimable Value.

INVENTIONS IN THE RUINS.

The Workshop Where He Evolved Ideas That Startled Electricians Entirely Destroyed.

YEARS OF LABOR LOST.

New York Herald article on March 14, 1895, reporting the loss of Tesla's laboratory.

even poorer except in tears, and they cannot be sent in letters. Why will you not come to us now—perhaps we might help you, we have so much to give in sympathy (K. Johnson 1895).

Charles A. Dana of the *New York Sun* commented sadly on March 14, 1895:

> The destruction of Nikola Tesla's workshop, with its wonderful contents, is something more than a private calamity. It is a misfortune to the whole world. It is not in any degree an exaggeration to say that the men living at this time who are more important to the human race than this young gentleman can be counted on the fingers of one hand; perhaps on the thumb of one hand. ✒

CHAPTER SIX

Niagara Falls

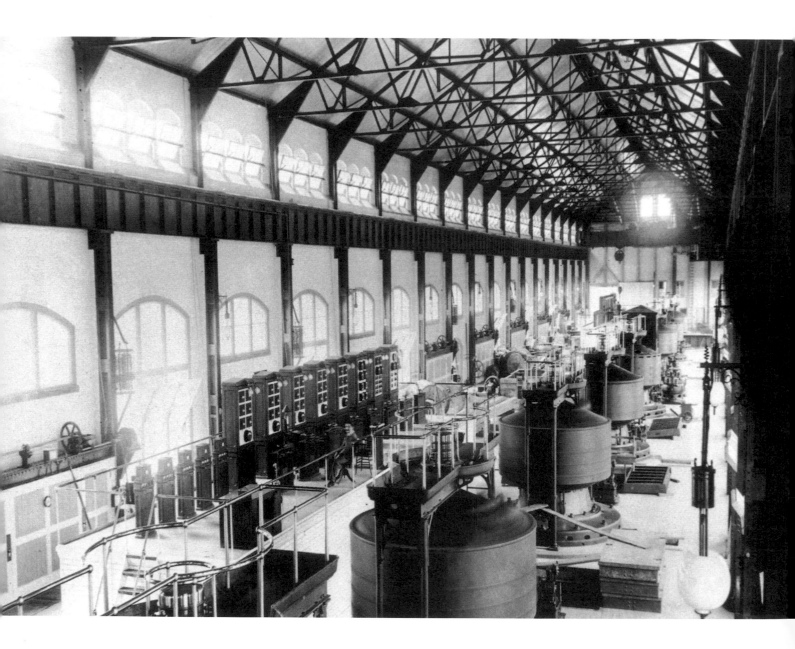

*Interior of Edward Dean Adams power station at Niagara, with
ten 5,000-horsepower Tesla/Westinghouse AC generators—the
culmination of Tesla's dream. (Courtesy Smithsonian Institution)*

The man who came forward to assist Tesla in his time of desperate need was the clever, handlebar-mustached financier, Edward Dean Adams, president of the Cataract Construction Company of Niagara Falls. He had every reason to feel confidence in the inventor. One of the most extraordinary engineering feats in history was nearing completion, and Tesla was the consulting genius.

The building of the Niagara Falls Power Project, begun in 1890, was an act of pure technological optimism. Americans had dreamed of pressing the Falls into "an honest day's work" since the first pioneer sawmill had been built there in 1725. Schemes for extracting power from the Niagara River's precipitous drop in elevation had never been imagined at scales suitable to the Falls' potential—in its latent power it was then equal to all the coal mined in the world each day. Planners had drawn up systems to utilize primitive waterwheels and a few oddities to compress air, pull ropes and chains, or turn Lilliputian DC generators.

What was now proposed was a system of canals and tunnels, diverting the Niagara River down 150-foot wheel pits to turn enormous water turbines. As late as 1893, no one but Tesla had any clear idea or technical means for distributing the energy once captured.

The full hydroelectric concept had not yet been attempted. The earliest power plant of the sort had gone into operation in 1882 at Appleton, Wisconsin, producing a fairly meager 12.5 kilowatts of direct current. Transmission was limited, as in all DC production, to users within a mile or two of the site.

World-famous scientist Lord Kelvin (center) visits the Westinghouse Company, August 1897. At first opposed to AC, he later stated he had become thoroughly convinced that the polyphase transmission scheme was practicable, and that he would recommend it rather than the direct current scheme he had originally advocated.

A Niagara generator under construction at Westinghouse in Pittsburgh in 1894.

Clearly, a breakthrough was called for in power transmission. A distinguished international commission chaired by the celebrated British physicist Lord Kelvin was formed to investigate and receive proposals from all over the world. Eventually seventeen plans were submitted by firms located in six countries, but all were rejected. Just six of them described electrical means of distribution, and only one of these was based on alternating current. The plan cited Tesla's motors, there being no other AC successes worth considering.

But the triumph of alternating current at the 1893 Chicago World's Fair, vividly displayed by Tesla and Westinghouse, had clinched the wavering confidence of investors. Lord Kelvin had shared with Edison the view that alternating current was the work of the devil—right up until the Chicago exhibition, when he made an about-face.

The War of the Currents had come to a close, but not without leaving a residual bitterness in the corporate world. Stockholders had been cheated by insider manipulations during the General Electric takeover of Edison, Thompson-Houston, and other companies. More rancor than harmony continued to plague the growth of the infant prodigy, electricity. Enough stability was restored, however, to enable the two gigantic corporations to bid on and win contracts and even work together on construction of the Niagara Project.

In October 1893 the Niagara Falls Commission awarded Westinghouse a contract to build the powerhouse at the Falls, to be outfitted with the first two of ten generators that Tesla had designed. Those dynamos of five thousand horsepower were the largest ever built thus far. General Electric, licensing certain of Tesla's patents, was awarded a contract to build

The process of making electricity usually involves conversion of either heat or mechanical energy. By far the most abundant and reliable form of mechanical energy on earth comes from flowing water. Thus began the development of waterwheels, which extract energy easily from the environment.

Mill ponds and water dropping through a few feet supplied energy as fast as waterwheels could transform it into shaft rotation, ultimately to drive lathes, drophammers, millstones, and the like. A really spectacular water source like Niagara Falls wasn't of much practical use before the end of the nineteenth century because no way existed to harness or distribute even a fraction of the Falls' power.

Two technological advances changed this: the Pelton wheels (introduced in 1884) and Tesla's AC system of electrical generation and

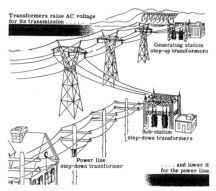

Transformers raise AC voltage for its transmission . . . . .

Generating station step-up transformers

Sub-station step-down transformers

Power line step-down transformer

. . . . and lower it for the power line.

transmission (1888). At Niagara, specially designed Pelton wheels were built, 5½ feet in diameter, and placed at the bottom of 140-foot water shafts supplied by a large canal from the upper river. Water rushing through propeller-like blades trades gravitational, kinetic energy for rotation. The turbine's shaft, through constant-speed gearing and a governor, in turn drives an electric generator, thus translating mechanical energy into electrical. Generator output, today

usually three-phase AC, is stepped up in voltage with transformers to tens or hundreds of thousands of volts and distributed on power lines throughout its service region. Users at the network's many endpoints use transformers again to "step down" their electrical power before plugging in. (High transmission voltages require extraordinary insulation and are dangerous to use.) Most households receive power at 120 volts, with perhaps a 240-volt line for heavy electrical appliances.

Hydroelectric generation today at Niagara Falls captures a usable two gigawatts out of a theoretical three gigawatts of water energy flowing over the cataracts. As momentous a beginning as the first Niagara plan was (seventy-five megawatts, with all of the contributing installations), it tapped only 4 percent of the mighty Falls' potential.

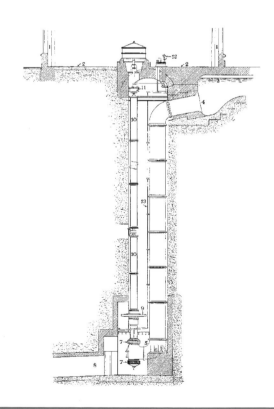

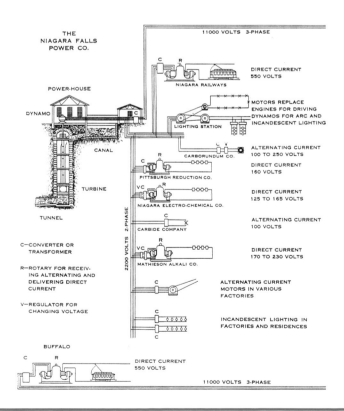

THE NIAGARA FALLS POWER CO.

POWER-HOUSE

DYNAMO

CANAL

TURBINE

TUNNEL

C—CONVERTER OR TRANSFORMER

R—ROTARY FOR RECEIVING ALTERNATING AND DELIVERING DIRECT CURRENT

V—REGULATOR FOR CHANGING VOLTAGE

BUFFALO

2200 VOLTS 2-PHASE

11000 VOLTS 3-PHASE

DIRECT CURRENT 550 VOLTS
NIAGARA RAILWAYS

MOTORS REPLACE ENGINES FOR DRIVING DYNAMOS FOR ARC AND INCANDESCENT LIGHTING
LIGHTING STATION

ALTERNATING CURRENT 100 TO 250 VOLTS
CARBORUNDUM CO.

DIRECT CURRENT 160 VOLTS
PITTSBURGH REDUCTION CO.

DIRECT CURRENT 125 TO 165 VOLTS
NIAGARA ELECTRO-CHEMICAL CO.

ALTERNATING CURRENT 100 VOLTS
CARBIDE COMPANY

DIRECT CURRENT 170 TO 230 VOLTS
MATHIESON ALKALI CO.

ALTERNATING CURRENT MOTORS IN VARIOUS FACTORIES

INCANDESCENT LIGHTING IN FACTORIES AND RESIDENCES

DIRECT CURRENT 550 VOLTS

11000 VOLTS 3-PHASE

Benjamin G. Lamme, chief
Westinghouse engineer, had the
difficult task of constructing Tesla's
generators and motors on an
enormous scale.

Edward Dean Adams station at Niagara Falls during construction, 1895. The first Niagara
generator had a stationary internal armature and a revolving field for cooling.

twenty-two miles of transmission lines to Buffalo. Tesla's polyphase system would be used throughout the project, its flexibility demonstrated by the fact that GE was able to transform two-phase current from the generators into three-phase distribution lines.

The construction period was traumatic for engineers, mechanics, and workers, but it undoubtedly weighed most heavily on the head of lawyer Edward B. Rankine, the young director of the project, and on the investors. In addition to Edward Dean Adams, backers of the project included several of the wealthiest men of America and Europe. J. P. Morgan signed the first subscription, and it was said that he never wavered during the dark nights of doubt. Other investors included John Jacob Astor, Lord Rothschild, and W. K. Vanderbilt. Lord Kelvin, following his conversion, was at all times an ardent supporter. The "patience and aggressive faith" of

director Rankine, who was said to have been "repulsed here and laughed at there," was often credited with standing between the original project and failure. He and Tesla gave each other respect and mutual support, even when capitalists faltered.

By contemporary standards the Westinghouse generators were behemoths, with electrical outputs at the extreme end of the spectrum of sane engineering imagination. Yet a completed machine already sat on the factory floor when the commission made a fact-finding visit.

The commissioners turned to Tesla in New York for reassurance throughout the months before the first test; his buoyant optimism was always restorative, though no one had a clue if he could do what he said. Seeing much farther than the first delivery of power to Buffalo, he promised, "If the company will put 400,000 horsepower upon a wire, I will deliver it

To make AC power into working machinery requires a "system": generators, transformers, transmission wires, and motors, all meshing in an efficient electrical way. Polyphase current is, today, part of routine electrical practice, but when Tesla first introduced its principles and devices, the concept was somewhat mind-wrenching. Tesla made one of those rare leaps in the way of thinking about things, moving without pause past the still-novel, single alternating current to the hybrid magnetic fields of many currents acting simultaneously.

Ordinary household AC has the form of a smooth sine wave; voltage builds

to a positive peak and then to a negative maximum. One complete cycle is said to be a full 360°.

Two equal AC voltages of exactly opposite phase (180° away from one another) have the effect of doubling the voltage, but they are still in step, both peaking at the same time. Household 240 VAC is created this way, by wiring to two 120 VAC leads that are 180° out of phase. Nonetheless, it's still called "single-phase 240"—motors don't have to be constructed much differently than for a single 120 VAC supply.

Tesla went beyond this simple combination of 180°-opposed currents.

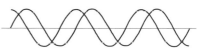

In *two-phase* voltage—his earliest polyphase system—the voltage in one wire, or "leg" of the system, is a quarter of a cycle (90°) ahead of the other. The poles in a two-phase motor must be spaced to accommodate the separation between those peaks.

But a further development of the polyphase concept, *three-phase* voltage, proved to be the most efficient for power transmission and for heavy-duty motors. In the three-phase system, the current in each leg is a third of a cycle (120°) removed from the others.

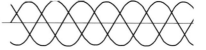

at a commercial profit in the city of New York" (Rankine 1926, 28–30).

Rankine, too, was thinking far ahead:

If it be practicable to transmit power at a commercial profit in these moderate quantities to Albany, the courage of the practical man will not halt there, but, inclined to following the daring promise of Nikola Tesla, would be disposed to place 100,000 horsepower on a wire and send it 450 miles to New York in one direction, and 500 miles in the other to Chicago—and supply the wants of these great urban communities.

McClure's magazine of October 1894 reported that the commissioners' anxieties were not allayed until "Nikola Tesla, that illuminating wizard of electricity, persuaded these capitalists that he had discovered, and to a great measure perfected, mechan-

ical applications which would make it possible to deliver the electric current, under complete control, and without costly loss from waste, at long distance." However,

They would not know until the turbine wheels were actually started, the colossal power delivered to the dynamos, and after being by them converted, and the electricity conveyed thence to the testing points. The scientific world is awaiting these experimental tests, and the worlds of commerce and manufacturing with no less interest.

The project was finally approaching completion after a nightmare of doubt and financial crises. The planners, builders, and bankers had worried through five years of uncertainty. They—but never Tesla—were not at all sure the system would work. And even if it performed as planned, would the hydroelectric

Above: The first three Niagara AC generators go on line November 16, 1896. (Courtesy Hagley Museum and Library)

Left: Air-blast transformers built by the General Electric Company for the first Buffalo transmission line, November 1896. (Courtesy Hagley Museum and Library)

High-tension lines to Buffalo, and eventually New York City. (Courtesy Hagley Museum and Library)

Enormous Tesla polyphase AC motors ready for service. (Courtesy Hagley Museum and Library)

power be commercially competitive with coal and steam? In the midst of all this doubt, Tesla's laboratory had been destroyed by fire, and the only man who seemed to have the answers was lying in his bed, speaking to no one—utterly distraught.

Tesla was still shaken and ill when he was persuaded to visit Niagara Falls four months before the project was to go on line. A *Niagara Falls Gazette* reporter wrote on July 20, 1896, that

> his hands trembled, but his face was earnest and his eyes fairly ablaze as he said, "There is no obstacle in the way of the successful transmission of power from the big power house you have here. The problem has been solved. Power can be transmitted to Buffalo as soon as the Power Company is ready to do it."

The machines may have been running smoothly in Tesla's three-dimensional imagination, but to investors, they were still unproved and expensive. The worries were unwarranted. When the switch was thrown, the first power reached Buffalo at midnight, November 16, 1896. The *Niagara Falls Gazette* reported that day, "The turning of a switch in the big powerhouse at Niagara completed a circuit which caused the Niagara River to flow uphill."

The Ninth Ward Polish-American gun squad fired a twenty-one-gun "national" salute.

The first one thousand horsepower of electricity surging to Buffalo was claimed by the street railway company, but already the local power company had orders from residents for five thousand more. Within a few years the number of generators at Niagara Falls reached its planned complement of ten, and by 1900 the little town of Niagara was thriving with industry, while power lines were electrifying New York City. Soon Broadway was ablaze with lights; the elevated street railways and subway system rumbled; and even the Edison systems converted to alternating current, either by operating substations or by changing over.

One of the earliest and most important power customers was the Pittsburgh Reduction Company, predecessor of the Aluminum Company of America. In a mere half-dozen years, power stations and transmission lines were being built across America, bringing electric light, heating, manufacturing, and hundreds of new labor-saving appliances.

A financial reporter for the *New York Times* wrote lyrically on July 16, 1895, about Tesla's part in the unrivaled engineering triumph of the nineteenth century: Perhaps the most romantic part

George and Marguerite Westinghouse at Niagara Falls in the mid-1890s.

of the story of this great enterprise would be the history of the career of the man above all men who made it possible ... a man of humble birth, who has risen almost before he reached the fullness of manhood to a place in the first rank of the world's great scientists and discoverers—Nikola Tesla.

The wonders of Niagara are first that it worked, and second that the commission dared to inaugurate the idea on such a grand scale. Their adoption of an AC generator and distribution system was a leap into new technology, and at untried power levels. Charles F. Scott, distinguished past president of the AIEE, commented in 1943,

> The evolution of electric power, from the discovery of Faraday in 1831 to the initial great

installation of the Tesla polyphase system in 1896, is undoubtedly the most tremendous event in all engineering history (Scott 1943).

It was now some thirty years since a schoolboy in faraway rural Austria-Hungary had expressed his dream of harnessing Niagara Falls, and the vision had become reality. Even Tesla confessed to marveling at "the unfathomable mystery of the mind" that allowed such hopes to come true. Later he would write:

> The possibilities of will power and self-control appealed tremendously to my vivid imagination ... until finally my will and wish became identical. They are so today, and in this lies the secret of whatever success I have achieved. My imaginings were equivalent to realities (Tesla 1915a).

But there were complications. Both the Westinghouse and General Electric corporations were morally and financially drained by the War of the Currents. Years of litigation, the absorption of Edison's company and others by professional managers at GE, and the financial teetering of Westinghouse all contributed to a takeover. This was the era of the robber barons, and one of the biggest was ready to make his move. J. P. Morgan, hoping to bring all hydroelectric power in the United States under his control, now proceeded to manipulate stock market forces with the intention of starving out Westinghouse and buying the Tesla patents. Thanks in part to Tesla, this did not happen.

George Westinghouse called on the inventor, pleading that he could not pay the liberal royalties on his system as provided in their contract. Tesla, in a magnanimous and history-making gesture, tore up the contract. He was, after all, grateful to the one man who had believed in his invention. And he was convinced that greater inventions lay just ahead. Thus the Westinghouse Electric Company was saved for future triumphs.

Tesla, although sharing the glory, was left forever afterward in recurring financial difficulties that he did not fully comprehend. Unfortunately, most Americans continued to think he was enriched by fabulous royalties. Tesla did not attend the opening celebrations at Buffalo. He returned to Niagara Falls, however, on January 12 of the following year and was honored at a "power banquet" attended by four hundred of the important bankers, engineers, lawyers, mechanics, and others who had helped to create what was now seen as an unqualified triumph. Tesla's reception at Buffalo's Ellicott Club was described as one of "enthusiastic pandemonium." The *Niagara Falls Gazette* reported on January 12, 1897:

> The guests sprang to their feet and wildly waved napkins and cheered for the famous scientists.... The undisputed highlight of the

dinner was the speech given, albeit reluctantly, by Nikola Tesla, who given the cause for this gathering, was indeed the hero of the day.

After waiting out several minutes of applause, Tesla described Niagara as "a monument worthy of our scientific age, a true monument of enlightenment and of peace." He said, "It signifies the subjugation of natural forces to the service of man, the discontinuance of barbarous methods, the relieving of millions from want and suffering." He declared Niagara Falls "a signal for the utilization of water power all over the world, and its influence upon industrial development is incalculable." But his speech was abruptly cut by the sponsors of the dinner. Having read the text beforehand, they were dismayed to see that Tesla intended to announce a new discovery that would make the power lines at Niagara obsolete.

> I have devised means which will allow us the use of electromotive forces much higher than those practicable with ordinary apparatus. In fact, fresh progress in this field has given me hope that I shall see fulfillment of one of my fondest dreams, namely, the wireless transmission of energy (Tesla 1897).

Niagara Falls was built by many gifted scientists and engineers and thousands of workers, but it could not have happened without Tesla. Today the system employed at Niagara remains largely unchanged. As one physicist has said, it "is so important technologically, it's like asking who invented the paper clip." Nothing but AC made any industrial sense after the success of Tesla's system. But in the way that popular impressions occasionally distort history, Thomas Edison would be credited with the achievement. Another great irony was that Tesla, though famous, was almost penniless and without a laboratory. ⤴

CHAPTER SEVEN

Who Invented Radio?

Tesla in a thoughtful pose in front of his "web" coil, May 1896.

Tesla emerged from the destruction of his laboratory a more cautious man. He turned down an offer he distrusted to capitalize a new company with $100,000 in stock, choosing instead to accept a $40,000 "no-strings" loan from Edward Dean Adams. Finding a suitable building at 46 East Houston Street, he hurriedly began to rebuild his laboratory and resume his work.

Urgent letters and phone calls arrived almost daily at the Westinghouse Corporation from the inventor, in a great state of anxiety to replace lost equipment. "You will greatly oblige me if you will do whatever is in your power to ship what is required with the least possible delay," he wrote to general superintendent Albert Schmid in Pittsburgh. "Let me know immediately what is the smallest size rotating two-phase transformer you have in stock." He urged that it be sent by express rather than freight, adding, "Please, do not spare any pains of expense. I shall rely as to the price entirely on the fairness of the Westinghouse Company. I believe that there are gentlemen in that company who believe in a hereafter" (Tesla 1895).

There was good reason for concern. The international race to invent wireless communication was attracting many contenders. In 1895, Sir Oliver Lodge of Oxford, England, managed to send and receive a telegraphic signal about 150 yards. Soon after, Guglielmo Marconi built a system that could transmit and receive a Morse signal over a distance of one and a quarter miles. In June of 1896, he applied for and received a British patent. Both were using the spark-gap system employed by Heinrich Hertz, which was limited in effectiveness and range. Some more powerful means was needed to transmit signals over greater distances, and to allow them to be sent and received selectively.

The questions of who invented radio, and when, and what defines the invention, have sparked fierce debates that still continue. It was assumed, after James Clerk Maxwell's discovery in 1873 of a vast range of electromagnetic vibrations above and beyond visible

Sir Oliver Lodge

Marchese Guglielmo Marconi

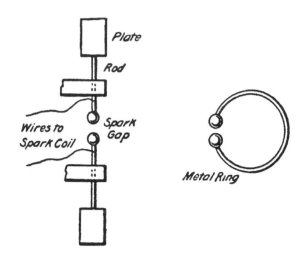

Above: Hertz's famous oscillator and receiver of "radio" waves. The sender (left) was a spark gap loaded with two metal plates that acted like a condenser. Sparks in the gap radiated high-frequency waves. When the second spark gap (right) and the ring were of the right size, the spark was reproduced without any wire connection.

Left: Heinrich Rudolf Hertz (Courtesy Library of Congress)

light, that a massless medium, the ether, was the carrier of light waves. Tesla also believed that the "luminiferous ether" filled all unoccupied space in the universe and transmitted electromagnetic radiation. But little or nothing was understood about the propagation of waves in this medium.

Germany's Heinrich Hertz had verified the existence of radio waves in the years 1878–88, during the same period when Tesla was developing his AC power system. The unit of electrical frequency, the hertz, was named for him, and for a number of years radio waves were called Hertzian waves. According to Dr. David Goodstein of the California Institute of Technology,

> Hertz had tested Maxwell's theory and incidentally, in the course of verifying it, created the first radio transmitter and the first receiver. He had shown that you could create an electrical signal in one place and detect it in

another place with nothing in between (interview with the authors, 1996).

But the apparatus used by Hertz, Lodge, Marconi, and others was not what we call radio today. Tesla, in fact, thought that Hertz had misinterpreted the results of his experiment. Tesla believed that radio signals were induced by earth currents, not air waves. "I considered this so important," he said,

> that in 1892 I went to Bonn, Germany, to confer with Dr. Hertz in regard to my observations. He seemed disappointed to such a degree that I regretted my trip and parted from him sorrowfully (Tesla 1919g).

Another important contributor to the nascent art of wireless communication was Sir William Crookes, the discoverer of radiant energy. Tesla had befriended Crookes while he was in England, and was heavily influenced by his thinking—particularly the idea of tuning electrical circuits to resonance. As Crookes said,

On his London trip of 1892, Tesla befriended Sir William Crookes, the discoverer of radiant matter. Crookes and other Victorian scientists were interested in the phenomenon of telepathy and concluded that certain sensitive people could communicate with high-frequency brainwaves. They were "tuned" to resonate at the same frequency. Tuning is at the heart of radio and television transmission.

"A sensitive," Crookes said, "may be one who possesses the telepathic transmitting or receiving ganglion in an advanced state . . . or who, by constant practice, is rendered more sensitive to these high-frequency waves. . . . In this way . . . the transmission of intelligence from one sensitive to another through long distances, seems to come into the

Sir William Crookes

domain of law, and can be grasped" (Crookes 1896).

Crookes's ideas had a powerful influence on Tesla. One night in his hotel room he had a vision that his mother came to him on an angelic cloud. "In that instant," he said, "a certitude, which no words can express, came upon me that my mother had just died. And that was true" (Tesla 1919f).

From the experience, he concluded "it should be possible to project on a screen the image of any object one conceives and make it visible. . . . I am convinced this wonder can and will be accomplished in time to come" (Tesla 1919a).

Throughout his life, Tesla considered himself a "perfect receptor" of these cosmic waves.

Any two friends living within the radius of sensibility of their receiving instruments, having first decided on their special wavelength and attuned their respective instruments to mutual receptivity, could thus communicate as long and as often as they pleased by timing the impulses to produce long and short intervals in the ordinary Morse code (Crookes 1897).

At this point, the question of who invented radio becomes both legal and technical. It is a matter of record that in St. Louis in 1893 Tesla demonstrated a system with all the fundamental components of modern radio communications: (1) an antenna or aerial wire, (2) a ground connection, (3) an aerial-ground circuit containing inductance and capacity, (4) adjustable inductance and capacity (for tuning), and (5) sending and receiving sets tuned to resonance with each other (Quinby 1977).

The young Marchese Guglielmo Marconi had

taken out the first wireless telegraphy patent in England on June 2, 1896. His device had only a two-circuit system, as did another patent he attempted to register in the United States in 1900, with which "he could not have transmitted across a small pond," in the opinion of one contemporary radio expert. Later he set up longer demonstrations, apparently using the Tesla oscillator to transmit a signal across the English Channel in 1899.

Tesla filed his basic radio patent applications—number 645,576 ("System of Transmission of Electrical Energy") and number 649,621—on September 2, 1897. They were granted in 1900. Marconi's first patent application in America, number 763,772, was filed on November 10, 1900, a few months after Tesla's had been granted. The Marconi application was turned down, and during the next three years he filed revised applications for wireless, which were repeatedly rejected because of the priority of Tesla, Lodge, and the German experimenter Carl F. Braun. The Patent Office made the following comment on October 15, 1903:

> Many of the claims are not patentable over Tesla patent numbers 645,576 and 649,621, of record, the amendment to overcome said references as well as Marconi's pretended ignorance of the nature of a "Tesla oscillator" being little short of absurd. Ever since Tesla's famous lecture on alternating current of high frequency, delivered before the American Institute of Electrical Engineers in 1891 and repeated in 1892 before the Institute of Electrical Engineers and the Royal Institution in London, the Société Internationale des Électriciens, and the Société Française de Physique, Paris, which lectures have been widely published in all languages, the term "Tesla oscillator" has become a household word on both continents (Anderson 1980).

A factor then intervened that is all too familiar to struggling inventors, even today: the crushing influence of a monopoly or big corporation. In 1900, Marconi's first British company became the Marconi Wireless Telegraph Company, Ltd., which developed a branch in the United States, the Marconi Wireless Telegraph Company of America, and both firms thrived on the stock markets. British Marconi stock soared from $3 to $22 per share and the glamorous young Italian nobleman was internationally acclaimed. Both Edison and Andrew Carnegie invested in Marconi; Edison and Michael Pupin became consulting engineers of American Marconi. J. P. Morgan and all of Wall Street welcomed this merging of old and new venture capital. On December 12, 1901, Marconi for the first time transmitted and received signals across the Atlantic Ocean, and ticker tape snowed from New York windows.

Otis Pond, an engineer then working for Tesla, said, "Looks as if Marconi got the jump on you."

Tesla replied, "Marconi is a good fellow. Let him continue. He is using seventeen of my patents" (Duncan 1972). But the patents were not as safe as he thought. In 1904 the U.S. Patent Office suddenly and surprisingly reversed its previous decisions and gave Marconi a patent for the invention of radio. The reasons for this have never been fully explained, but there is little doubt that the decision was influenced by the powerful financial backing for Marconi in the United States. Tesla was embroiled in other problems at the time, but when Marconi won the Nobel Prize in 1911, he was furious. He sued the Marconi Company for infringement in 1915, but was in no financial condition to litigate a case against a major corporation.

Commander E. J. Quinby, USN (retired), was a pioneer in radio engineering who remembered the early days of commercial radio in America. He said,

> While others fought bitter word battles in our courts over whose patents were really valid on the all-important system of tuning to avoid wholesale radio interference, nobody seemed to recall that Tesla had covered the subject back before the turn of the century with his comprehensive and fundamental patent on tuning of electrical circuits to resonance. Without this feature, today's ever-expanding radio service would be utter chaos (Quinby 1977).

Eventually the U.S. government took notice of Tesla's assertions when Marconi sued the U.S. Court of Claims, alleging "infringement" of his patent rights by the U.S. military forces. Finally the government, no doubt acting in its own best interests, vindicated radio's nearly forgotten inventor.

In 1943 the United States Supreme Court named Tesla as the primary inventor of radio. The Court determined that Tesla's patent number 645,576 had anticipated the fundamental radio patents of all other contenders. Unfortunately, the historic decision took place a few months after Tesla died. Essentially the

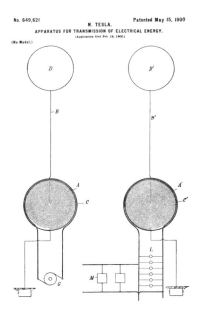

Above: Tesla's U.S. patent number 649,621 is still the fundamental means for transmitting and receiving radio waves.

Right: Tesla demonstrates "wireless" power transmission in his Houston Street laboratory in March 1899.

Below: Marconi sits in receiving room at his station in Glace Bay, Nova Scotia, site of the first transatlantic radio transmission, 1901. (Courtesy Smithsonian Institution)

Radio transmission, as we know it, basically requires a regularly rising and falling source of electric energy (an oscillator) and a way of boosting that vibrating source to power levels that will carry from an antenna to distant receivers. Radio reception calls for a similar pair of stages: a sensing circuit (with an antenna), tuned to the expected transmission frequency, and a circuit for enlarging, or amplifying, the weak signal in the sensing circuit.

Thus, when controversy arose in court cases over priority in radio invention, the legal wrangling focused on "two tuned circuits each at transmitter and receiver, all four tuned to the same frequency." From the history of such litigation, it is far from certain that the judges understood the electrical nuances involved. The U.S. Supreme Court eventually found (in 1943) that Tesla's U.S. patent number

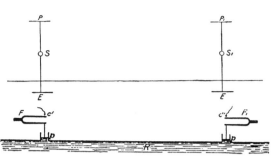

Tesla's "wireless" telegraphy mechanically illustrated.

645,576 (filed in September 1897) was the first to contain these elements.

The antenna is the actual transmitting part. Rapidly varying currents (at the transmission frequency) running up and down its length induce a correspondingly varying magnetic field to radiate away from it at right angles. That field, though much weakened by its spreading through space, must be sufficient to induce detectable currents

in a reception antenna as the field lines cut across it.

To send information with such elementary equipment requires breaking up the transmission into dots and dashes, for example, and finding some way of discovering the signal at the receiving end. Flashing lights or metal-powder "coherers" were early means.

Better signaling—sending voice or music—needs a smoother oscillator and a way of combining (or "modulating") the oscillator frequency with much lower-frequency electrical waveforms of voice and music. At the receiving end the radio "carrier" frequency must be stripped away, leaving the original content to be reproduced through a speaker or headphone. All of this became possible with quartz crystal oscillators and diodes and De Forest's invention (1906) of the vacuum tube triode.

---

case finally answered the question of who invented radio, but how many children or teachers know that answer today?

The inventor's posthumous victory was hailed by influential radio pioneers, including J. S. Stone, who declared:

> Among all those [Tesla, Lodge, Marconi, and Thomson], the name of Nikola Tesla stands out most prominently. Tesla, with his almost preternatural insight into alternating current phenomena that enabled him...to revolutionize the art of electric-power transmission through the invention of the rotary field motor, knew how to make resonance serve, not merely the role of a microscope, to make visi-

ble the electric oscillations, as Hertz had done, but he made it serve the role of a stereopticon. ...It has been difficult to make any but unimportant improvements in the art of radio telegraphy without traveling, part of the way at least, along the trail blazed by this pioneer who, though eminently ingenious, practical and successful in the apparatus he devised and constructed, was so far ahead of his time that the best of us then mistook him for a dreamer (Anderson 1986).

Tesla scholar Leland Anderson, in a monograph on the invention of radio, writes that some confused the argument over the principles of transmission and reception of radio signals with the important inven-

U.S. Navy shipboard transmitter manufactured by the Löwenstein Radio Company. This was a 5-kilowatt set capable of 1,500-mile transmission used during World War I. A handwritten caption by Nikola Tesla reads: "Apparatus installed under my patents on many war vessels which according to Secretary Daniels is 'superior' to any other."

tion by Lee De Forest of the audion, or triode vacuum tube, which put voice in the wireless. The definition of radio that finally evolved from depositions by many technical radio experts and scientists boiled down to this: "A radio communication system requires two tuned circuits each at the transmitter and receiver, all four tuned to the same frequency." It does not, Anderson adds, include the variable modulation through which voice and music can be transmitted. Nor does it address the mode of electromagnetic propagation—that is, ground wave and/or sky wave and their effects. "It does, however, implicitly describe the deliberate, selective transmission of a specific frequency and the selectable reception at that same frequency" (Anderson 1980).

And yet the argument over who invented radio continues. The truth is not nearly as complicated as the mythology would indicate: patents were registered, adjudicated, and readjudicated over many years. But always the winding path discloses that Tesla (not Marconi) was the inventor of radio, as we describe it today.

Unfortunately the influential Smithsonian Institution has done no favor to students of the history of technology. Bernard S. Finn, Curator of Electrical Collections at the National Museum of American History, while granting Tesla's genius, wrote in a 1996 analysis of his contributions that, because he was a loner, "the unfortunate consequence ... was that his impact on practical technical develop-

Announcer at the first commercial radio station, KDKA Pittsburgh, in the early 1920s. Westinghouse owned the company.

ments was severely impaired." This, says Finn, means that "we should be careful in what we claim were the consequences of his activities" (Finn 1996). It is common knowledge that if "loners" were excluded from the categories of invention and discovery, they would be lonely fields indeed.

The Smithsonian Institution has yet to properly credit Tesla for his work in electrical power and radio. And because of the time lag involved in correcting misinformation in encyclopedias and textbooks, versions of the Smithsonian tilt continue to this day as a major flaw in most reference books. Some confusion may also have resulted from the fact that Tesla regarded his patented wireless system as merely one aspect of a vast global and interplanetary design for conducting both information and electric power.

Marconi, for all his charm, prestige, and industrial success, appears on the record to have been a

patent pirate. None would ever question, however, that he did a first-rate job in commercializing the inventions, not just of Tesla, but of others as well.

Robert H. Marriott, first president of the Institute of Radio Engineers, commented that Marconi had

> played the part of a demonstrator and sales engineer. A money-getting company was formed, which in attempting to obtain a monopoly, set out to advertise to everybody that Marconi was the inventor and that they owned that patent on wireless which entitled them to a monopoly (Marriott 1925).

Long before anyone else, Tesla had described in print radio as we know it today—not just the sending of a message from one point to another, but the entire broadband transmission of intelligence. According to Dr. David Goodstein,

> Various people in various different countries had the idea of exploiting this as a means of communication. But I think Tesla was the one with the real vision—the vision that described the system that we have today—in which you would broadcast not simply signals, but signals on...many different carrier frequencies, so that you could broadcast many signals at the same time, and then you would have a series of antennas in places where there were receivers, and the antennas would be coupled into what are called resonate circuits, that were sensitive to one frequency only, tuned to a certain frequency, and would detect one of this babble of frequencies that were going out over the airwaves. It would detect just one of these signals and make an intelligible transmission. I think that Tesla envisioned that, just the way he had earlier envisioned the power grid, the alternating current power grid, and once again, his vision described the world that we live in (interview with the authors, 1996).

Second banquet meeting of the Institute of Radio Engineers (now part of the Institute of Electrical and Electronics Engineers) at Luchow's in New York City, April 24, 1915. Many prominent figures in the development of radio attended. Nikola Tesla is standing at back, seventh from the right.

Tesla was confident that his contributions to science would eventually be recognized. One day in January 1927 the inventor, then seventy-one years old, was lunching with a young visitor from Yugoslavia when the guest asked him about the patent wars that still simmered in the courts. He paused, smiled, and said, "Let the future tell the truth and evaluate each one according to his work and accomplishments. The present is theirs, the future for which I really worked, is mine" (Petković 1927).

CHAPTER EIGHT

X-rays, Earthquakes, and Robots

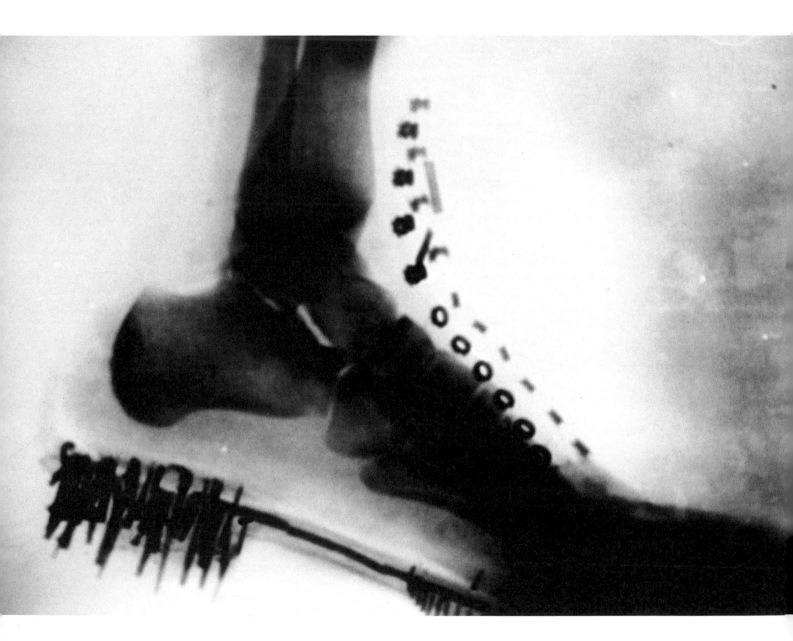

One of the first X-ray photographs—an accidental exposure (possibly of Tesla's foot) made shortly before the destruction of his laboratory by fire.

In the midst of the race for wireless communication, Tesla scarcely needed the sudden controversy and excitement generated when Wilhelm Roentgen announced his discovery of the X-ray on December 28, 1895. According to Michael Pupin, every physicist worth his salt "dropped his own research problems and rushed headlong" into X-ray work (in some cases heedless of the dangers involved). Many American experimenters were consumed with a risky desire to see their own brains.

Roentgen, working in Germany with the cathode-ray ultra-vacuum tube developed by Sir William Crookes, noticed that if a current passed through the tube, a nearby piece of paper painted with a barium substance appeared to fluoresce brightly. He demonstrated that this effect was caused by invisible rays capable of passing through opaque bodies and exposing photographic plates. Roentgen dubbed his discovery "X-rays," and showed how it could revolutionize diagnostic medicine, making it possible to photograph organs and bones.

Tesla, while experimenting with his molecular-bombardment or "carbon-button" lamp, as reported in his lectures of 1892, had detected "visible light, black light and a very special radiation." With the radiation, he had made shadowgraph pictures on plates inside metal containers. Late in 1894 he had carried out experiments with a Manhattan photographer, Tonnele & Co., on the radiant power of phosphorescent bodies. A great number of the photographic plates showed "curious marks and defects" that he was preparing to investigate further when the fire in his laboratory took place. When Roentgen announced the discovery of X-rays, Tesla could only send him congratulations and a few shadowgraph pictures recovered from the rubble and ash. Roentgen replied at once that he found them "very interesting. If you would only be so kind as to disclose the manner in which you obtained them" (Roentgen 1897).

Many scientists in Europe and America soon tried to patent devices similar to Roentgen's, or otherwise rushed to commercialize X-rays; both Edison and Pupin were among them. Inventors A. E. Kennelly and Edwin J. Houston joined competitors in the race to utilize X-rays, employing a simple version of the Tesla coil to create Roentgen rays.

In the popular imagination, the hoped-for potential

Wilhelm Konrad Roentgen (Courtesy Library of Congress)

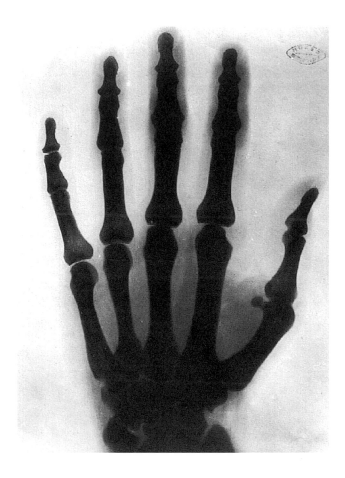

Early "shadowgraph" taken in Tesla's lab.

of the X-ray was not limited to medicine, but stirred a multitude of less worthy appetites including voyeurism, greed, and trendy frivolity. Medical charlatans claimed the invisible rays would cure blindness, but Tesla quickly spoke out to discourage such cruel deceptions.

In a series of articles published in the electrical press in 1896, he warned of the potential dangers of X-rays—long before anyone was aware of the side effects—and suggested means for their safe operation. He knew what he was talking about. His high-tension coils were capable of showing the shadow of a hand on a phosphorescent screen at the incredible distance of fifty feet. One day he placed his hand directly in front of a powerful cathode ray tube; the hand turned black and was covered with blisters in a few moments. The reaction was so violent that he came to the conclusion

that rather than radiation, a "material stream" of particles had passed through his skin.

The *New York Times* reported on March 12, 1896,

> the results of the experiments of Nikola Tesla in radiography have excited a great deal of interest in the medical profession. His conclusions were to the effect that the X-rays were of a nature of a stream of material particles which strike the sensitive plate with great velocities. Sometimes a particle larger than an electron, would break off from the cathode, and pass out of the tube. He said he felt a sharp, stinging pain where it entered his body, and again at the place where it passed out.

> It has been demonstrated by Mr. Tesla to his satisfaction that small metallic objects or bony or chalky deposits can be infallibly detected in any part of the human body. He also gives it as his opinion that it might be possible by the use of the X-rays to project a suitable chemical into any part of the body, which would make it a valuable therapeutic agent.

A glass blower now became a permanent member of Tesla's staff, and the lab was cluttered with hundreds of different tubes for experiments. Of particular interest were the tubes first created by Phillipp Lenard in Germany, which contained a thin aluminum window opposite the cathode. Tesla and others had observed that the cathode ray actually passed a few centimeters through the aluminum window into the surrounding air. As the power of the ray was increased, the window became unnecessary, as it burned a hole through the glass wall of the tube, which resealed itself when the ray was deactivated. Tesla observed

> that the glass bulges out and the hole, through which the streamer rushes out, becomes so large as to be perfectly discernible to the eye. As the matter is expelled...the streamer

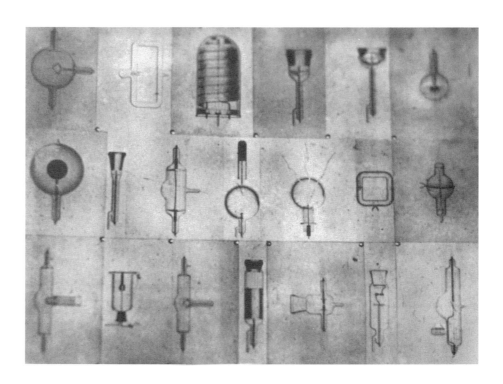

Above: Tesla displayed drawings of some 120 vacuum tubes and bulbs, from which hundreds of devices were produced, to illustrate his lecture on X-rays and high-frequency apparatus at the New York Academy of Sciences, April 6, 1897.

Left: Original reciprocating steam engine, later fitted with coils and magnetic fields to produce currents of precisely constant frequency.

becomes less and less intense, whereupon the glass closes again, hermetically sealing the opening. . . . Here, then, we have positive evidence that matter is being expelled through the walls of the glass (Tesla 1896a).

These were the seminal experiments for what would later be called Tesla's death beam.

Roentgen gave us a gun to fire—a wonderful gun indeed, projecting missiles of a thousand-fold greater penetrative power than that of a cannon ball, and carrying them probably to distances of many miles, with velocities not producible in any other way we know of (Tesla 1896b).

It was not the only unusual subject that Tesla was investigating at the time. He had also become interested in mechanical vibrations, hoping to find a way to produce perfectly periodic or isochronous waves. In the early days of electrical power transmission the frequency of alternating current was not as precise as it is today. "We were driving for perfection," Tesla said, as he began to construct an ingenious device called a mechanical oscillator. Inside this little cast-iron "engine" was a piston driven by compressed air that produced extremely precise mechanical vibrations—so precise that he was able to create the first electric clocks that ran on alternating current. He said these clocks "will show correct time. The vibrations obtained in this way would not vary one-millionth of a second in a thousand years" (Anderson 1992, 39).

As he experimented with his new device, interesting phenomena began to appear. At a certain periodic-

Tesla had an uncanny understanding of the energy that could be released through resonance. A few amperes built to high potential through resonant reinforcement in a Tesla coil, for example, becomes a megawatt discharge when released across the space of a few nanoseconds. With mechanical vibrations the same principle operates. The isochronous ("equal time") mechanical oscillator patented by Tesla in 1893 was occasionally used by its inventor as a resonant "tickler" to inject energy, an additive train of timed blows, into various structures. It is possible thus to determine a structure's characteristic resonant frequency, or even to cause a catastrophic failure, by stressing it in this way. (By his own accounts, he narrowly averted destroying his lab in the course of one such experiment.)

As for the limits of energy through resonance, Tesla imagined none. In 1935 he announced that the earth

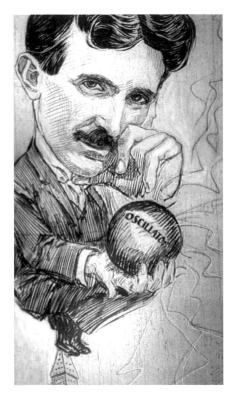

itself could be split with patient application of small taps at the right frequency. In truth, as he doubtless

knew, materials are seldom uniform enough or efficient enough as resonators to perform in ideal ways. Beneath the hyperbole, however, lay some solid claims. He saw utility in sending vibrations through the earth to investigate, among other things, the planet's composition, and coined a term—telegeodynamics—for the new science.

In the late 1930s, he submitted a proposal to Westinghouse and several large oil companies to replace the dangerous technique used in oil exploration of setting off deep dynamite explosions and interpreting them seismically. A comparable amount of energy, he calculated, could be imparted to bedrock with his relatively small oscillating machine. He received no takers for the idea, but the method of prospecting by isochronous oscillation was adoped only a few years later. Tesla has not been sufficiently credited for the invention.

ity of vibration, the glass in the laboratory windows would rattle and shake. As the period was changed, machines and other objects in the room began to shudder, some tumbling off workbenches to the floor.

Out of curiosity, he attached the oscillator to one of the iron support pillars in the laboratory and set the machine to vibrating. Then he sat in a chair and began carefully noting his observations. Unknown to him, the vibrations were being transmitted from the pillar into the sandy subsoil beneath the building. As the vibrations increased, they sent shock waves out through the neighborhood. Nearby buildings began to tremble, tables began to shake, plaster fell from ceilings, and windows shattered in the miniearthquake.

The local police, now familiar with Tesla's antics,

descended on the laboratory. Throwing open the door, they beheld an amazing sight—a tall, dapper figure smashing a small mechanical device with a sledgehammer. According to biographer John J. O'Neill the vibration immediately ceased, and Tesla announced to the police:

> Gentlemen, I am sorry, but you are just a trifle too late to witness my experiments. I found it necessary to stop it suddenly and unexpectedly and in an unusual way just as you entered. . . . Now you must leave, for I have many things to do. Good day, gentlemen (O'Neill 1944, 164).

It is difficult to prove that this event took place, or that a minor earthquake actually resulted (there is

The first practical remote-controlled robot. The crewless boat shown in this promotional illustration contained its own motive power, propelling and steering machinery, and numerous other accessories, all of which were controlled without wires from a distance.

no record of it in the newspapers), but Tesla mentioned it at several points in his life in reference to what he called the art of "telegeodynamics."

In May of 1898, the USS *Maine* exploded somewhat mysteriously in Havana Harbor. The United States declared war against Spain. Trains were crowded with troops being rushed to Cuba.

For Tesla, the timing was propitious. On July 1, 1898, he filed patent number 613,809, "Method of and Apparatus for Controlling Mechanism of Moving Vessels or Vehicles." It was granted on November 8 of that year, "but only after the Examiner-in-Chief had come to New York and witnessed the performance for what I claimed seemed unbelievable" (Tesla 1919f).

One month later, at the first Electrical Exhibition in Madison Square Garden, audiences were amazed and bewildered to see the world's first remote-controlled vessel on display. Everyone

expected surprises from Tesla, but few were prepared for the sight of a small, odd-looking iron-hulled boat scooting around in a pond especially built for it in the great auditorium, and equipped, as Tesla described it, with "a borrowed mind."

"When first shown . . . it created a sensation such as no other invention of mine has ever produced," he wrote in his autobiography. As happened fairly often with his inventions, many of those present were unsure how to react, whether to laugh or take flight. He had cleverly devised a means of putting the audience at their ease, however, encouraging them to ask questions of the boat. For instance, in response to the question "What is the cube root of 64?" lights on the boat would flash four times. In an era when only a handful of people knew about radio waves, some thought that Tesla was controlling the small ship with his mind.

"I conceived the idea of constructing an automaton which would mechanically represent me, and

Tesla's U.S. patent number 613,809 describes the first device anywhere for wireless remote control. In 1898 he operated a three-foot model boat demonstrating both radio control and robotry in one incredible presentation.

His working model, or "teleautomaton," responded to signals of only one frequency. This scaled-down ship used a device called a coherer (the "sensitive device" of his patent) that relies on a metal oxide powder to conduct when its grains draw together in the presence of a magnetic field. With a signal applied from a reception antenna, the powder grains suddenly "cohere" and the circuit is completed. The boat was powered by large batteries inside its hull. Only the instructions came by radio.

To perform numerous functions, Tesla had a geared mechanism shift a disk with many sets of electrical contacts laid out on it. Each advance of

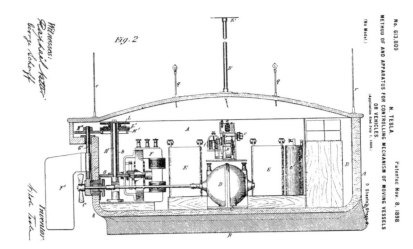

Sectional view of tele-mechanical vessel

the disk slid into place a different combination of connections for the operating state of rudder, motor, and lighting. The operator had to be versed in the switching sequence, advancing the contact disk by the right number of transmissions to control the craft's steering, propulsion, and lighting.

Tesla did not limit his method to boats, but generalized the invention's potential to include vehicles of any sort and mechanisms to be actuated for any purpose. He envisioned one operator or several simultaneously directing fifty or a hundred vessels or machines through differently tuned radio transmitters and receivers.

which would respond, as I do myself," Tesla later explained.

Such an automaton evidently had to have motive power, organs for locomotion, directive organs, and one or more sensitive organs so adapted as to be excited by external stimuli. A storage battery placed within it furnished the motive power. The propeller, driven by a motor, represented the locomotive organs. The rudder, controlled by another motor likewise driven by the battery, took the place of the directive organs (Tesla 1900a).

Radio waves were received by a thin metal antenna on the boat. Two small electric lamps were mounted on the stern, and within the hold was a mechanical "brain," along with a radio receiving set and various

other tuned devices enabling the robot to obey orders. It executed movements in all directions to the utter astonishment of spectators and reporters. Signals were sent with a small box with a lever and a telegraph key.

When a *New York Times* writer suggested that Tesla could make the boat submerge and carry dynamite as a weapon of war, the inventor himself exploded. Edison had recently designed an electric torpedo that derived its power by a cable from the mother ship. Tesla quickly corrected the reporter: "You do not see there a wireless torpedo, you see there the first of a race of robots, mechanical men which will do the laborious work of the human race" (O'Neill 1944, 169).

Perhaps naïvely, Tesla believed that with devices of this nature, war could become a "mere" contest of machine against machine.

So long as men meet in battle, there will be bloodshed. Bloodshed will ever keep up barbarous passion. To break this fierce spirit, a radical departure must be made, an entirely new principle must be introduced, something that never existed in warfare—a principle which will forcibly, unavoidably, turn the battle into a mere spectacle, a play, a contest without loss of blood…machine must fight machine. But how accomplish that which seems impossible? The answer is simple enough: produce a machine capable of acting as though it were part of a human being—no mere mechanical contrivance, comprising levers, screws, wheels, clutches, and nothing more, but a machine embodying a higher principle, which will enable it to perform its duties as though it had intelligence, experience, reason, judgment, a mind (Tesla 1900a).

The military thought the machine looked too fragile to serve any useful purpose in warfare and objected that there was no way to prevent an enemy from interfering with the signals. Tesla, in his zeal to astound, had again overwhelmed the public and most of his colleagues at Madison Square Garden. His demonstration of wireless alone would have been impressive enough in 1898. Automation, however, represented a plunge into the future for which industry and the U.S. War Department were unprepared. This was unfortunate, because he was once again broke and unable to continue research. His efforts to interest financiers in automated mechanisms failed. Even after he developed a fully submersible version of the craft, and a unique process called "individualization," which made the vessel "deaf and unresponsive like a faithful servant, to all calls but that of its master," he could find no takers. He later wrote:

I remember that when later I called on an official in Washington with a view of offering the invention to the Government, he burst out in

A larger model of Tesla's remote-controlled boat, photographed with its deck removed.

laughter upon my telling him what I had accomplished. Nobody thought then that there was the faintest prospect of perfecting such a device…my boats were controlled through the joint action of several circuits and interference of every kind was excluded (Tesla 1919f).

Submergible version of Tesla's remote-controlled craft

Few computer scientists are aware, says Leland Anderson, that when certain computer manufacturers tried to patent digital logic gates after World War II, the Patent Office pointed to Tesla's priority in the electrical implementation of them for secure communications, control systems, and robotics. Because of this, new patents could not be obtained and the technology for digital logic gates remained in the public domain (interview with the authors, 1998).

The U.S. government did not officially take up the development of remote-controlled devices until 1918. Ironically, Tesla's patents had expired.

In 1898 Tesla also proposed to automobile manufacturers the building and public exhibition of an automobile which would perform a great variety of operations involving something akin to judgment.

"But my proposal was deemed chimerical," he said, "and nothing came from it" (O'Neill 1944, 175).

His friend, mining engineer John Hays Hammond, Jr. (who had advanced $10,000 to finance the wireless and robot demonstration at Madison Square Garden), used Tesla's patent to build an electric dog on wheels that followed him around. He also guided a yacht by remote radio control in Boston harbor and brought it back safely to its slip. Eventually he received a large government contract to develop remote-controlled craft, but not a penny went to the idea's originator.

Tesla's life at this point must have seemed to him a mockery. His bank account was bare from the years of costly radio and robot research, from the expensive equipment, and from patent lawyers' fees. His inventions would help to introduce a world revolution in communications (the Information Age), a future whose blessings he clearly visualized—yet strange to say, he could see no income on the horizon to help him get on with his work. Later he asserted, "Money does not represent such a value that men have placed upon it. All my money has been invested into experiments with which I have made new discoveries enabling mankind to have a little easier life" (Petković 1927).

Success in his next venture, Tesla believed, would be the greatest gift he could possibly make to humanity. ⚘

Tesla in his Houston Street laboratory. Caption for this photo in Electrical Review, *March 29, 1899, reads:*
"The operator's body, in this experiment, is charged to a high potential by means of a coil responsive to the waves
transmitted to it from a distant oscillator."

CHAPTER NINE

Colorado Springs

*This publicity photo taken at Colorado Springs was a double exposure.
Tesla poses with his "magnifying transmitter" capable of producing millions
of volts of electricity. The discharge here is twenty-two feet in length.*

In January 1898 Tesla once again invited the examiner-in-chief of the U.S. Patent Office in Washington, D.C., to travel to New York for an unusual demonstration. In a patent filed the previous year, "System of Transmission of Electrical Energy" (number 645,576), he claimed, "it has become possible to transmit through even moderately rarefied strata of atmosphere electrical energy to practically any amount and to any distance." Sending power through the upper atmosphere was such an extraordinary claim that it required a demonstration.

Awaiting the examiner in Tesla's lab was a system of two tuned coils, similar to those in his radio patent, connected by fifty feet of glass tubing. The tubing was evacuated to simulate atmospheric conditions four to five miles above the earth's surface. "When I turned on the current," said Tesla, "I showed that through a stratum of air at a pressure of 135 millimeters, when my four circuits were tuned, several incandescent lamps were lighted" (Anderson 1992, 127). Tesla came to the conviction "that it would be ultimately possible, without any elevated antenna— with very small elevation—to break down the upper stratum of the air and transmit the current by conduction."

A friend and patent lawyer,

Leonard E. Curtis, on being advised of Tesla's scheme, offered to find land and provide power for his research from the El Paso Power Company of Colorado Springs. The next supporter to come forward was Colonel John Jacob Astor, who owned the Waldorf-Astoria Hotel that Tesla had patronized for many years. With $30,000 from Astor, the inventor prepared at once to move to Colorado and begin building a new experimental station near Pikes Peak. He was joined by a gifted young engineer, Fritz Löwenstein, along with a mechanic, Kolman Czito, and a few other assistants.

Tesla wrote to Curtis: "This is a secret test.... My work will be done late at night when the power load will be least." Curtis wrote back, "All

View of Colorado Springs, Colorado, around 1900 with Pikes Peak in the distance. (Courtesy Pikes Peak Library District)

Tesla's Colorado Springs laboratory in late summer of 1899. Handwritten caption on photo reads: "Experimental Station built to obtain Engineering Data for 'World System Plant.'"

things arranged, land will be free. You will live at the Alta Vista Hotel. I have interest in the City Power Plant so electricity is free to you" (Hunt 1976).

Arriving at Colorado Springs in May 1899, Tesla went to inspect the acreage. It was some miles out in the prairie, east of a school for deaf and blind students. Local folk were curious to know why the world's most famous electrical inventor had come to their neck of the woods. He told reporters that he intended to send a radio signal from Pikes Peak to Paris, but furnished no details.

Moving into the Alta Vista Hotel, he chose room 222 (divisible by 3), which had a clear view of majestic Pikes Peak. The hotel staff was prepared to supply him with any amount of clean linen, the manager saying, "It is good to have a clean gentleman in the hotel." The elite of Colorado Springs, awed by the

legendary presence, entertained him with a welcoming dinner at the local gentlemen's club.

Tesla had left his ever-anxious accountant, George Scherff, in charge of the New York laboratory, which quickly became a staging area for a great many expensive mechanical devices, all needing to be shipped at once, by railway express if possible. Shipments soon began arriving: thousands of feet of wire, copper bars, generators and motors, even specially fabricated balloons for high-altitude work.

The laboratory that began to rise from the prairie floor was both wired and weird, a contraption with a roof that rolled back to prevent it from catching fire, and a wooden tower that soared up eighty feet. Above it was a 142-foot metal mast supporting a large copper ball. Inside the strange wooden structure, technicians began to assemble an enormous

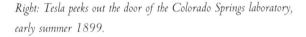
Above: Early coil configuration discharging.

Right: Tesla peeks out the door of the Colorado Springs laboratory, early summer 1899.

Tesla coil. The primary coil had a diameter of fifty-one feet and consisted of only a few turns of heavy-gauge wire. The secondary coil within it was ten feet in diameter, with a hundred turns of wire. This enormous air-core transformer could deliver a current of 1,100 amperes (Quinby 1983). The configuration would also contain a mysterious "third coil" that magnified electrical effects through resonance. The existence of this coil was not known until the 1970s.

Builders erected a high fence around the site, and signs appeared on every post—KEEP OUT. GREAT DANGER—in hopes of keeping the curious at a distance. Fritz Löwenstein could not resist posting at the door another sign, quoting Dante's *Inferno:* "Abandon hope, all ye who enter here." It was to be one of the most powerful radio transmitters ever built, designed to generate millions of volts. (One million volts is generally considered the threshold energy of lightning.)

The experimental station was situated 6,037 feet above sea level. Tesla knew that with the powerful currents he was about to generate, something unusual was certain to take place. He also knew that Colorado was famous for displays of electric force. "Lightning discharges are . . . very frequent and sometimes of inconceivable violence," he wrote. At one point, he calculated that some twelve thousand discharges had occurred in two hours, and within fifty kilometers from the laboratory. "Many of them resembled gigantic trees of fire with the trunks up or down."

In the midst of these incredible natural displays, Tesla would sit taking measurements. He soon found the earth to be "literally alive with electrical vibrations." At times his measuring devices were more

Tesla's large-scale oscillating apparatus. Coil at left, fifty-one feet in diameter, formed part of the magnifying transmitter. Published June 1900 in Century Magazine.

affected by discharges taking place at great distances than those nearby. "The strange actions did not stop then, but continued with undiminished force. No doubt whatever remained," said Tesla, "I was observing stationary waves" (Tesla 1904a).

Tesla was able to calculate that these waves propagated from one antipode of the earth to the other in a frequency between four and twelve hertz. They are known today as ELF, or extra-low-frequency waves. Tesla wrote:

> Impossible as it seemed, this planet, despite its vast extent, behaved like a conductor of limited dimensions. The tremendous significance of this fact in the transmission of energy by my system had already become clear to me. Not

only was it practicable to send telegraphic messages to any distance without wires, as I recognized long ago, but also to impress upon the entire globe the faint modulations of the human voice; far more still, to transmit power in unlimited amounts to any terrestrial distance and almost without any loss.

Electromagnetic waves at extremely low frequency have a remarkable ability to propagate in the space between the earth's surface and the ionosphere. These waves are also able to propagate several hundred feet through the earth and to moderate depths in the ocean, in spite of high absorption in sea water. Estimating accurately the resonant frequency of the earth-ionosphere cavity in 1899 was an act of genius in its

Tesla, among the first to achieve any kind of radio signaling through the atmosphere, became rather quickly intrigued with the transmission possibilities of the earth itself.

Because Tesla's first high-energy experiments with radio took place at the base of the Rockies, in Colorado Springs, his observations may indeed have been aided by a fairly conductive geology. Certainly, he produced and measured ground wave disturbances, and recognized their decay with distance. His hope, however, was to find that he could resonantly reinforce them—as in his famous Tesla coil—and keep a system of waves in play inside the earth. Patent number 1,119,732 (1914) envisioned several such generators setting up a grid of intersecting waves by which global position might be known, to a ship at sea for example, or even motion detected from afar by plotted patterns

of reflection. In principle he anticipated such navigation aids as LORAN and VOR—but through the grander concept of earth-girdling transmission rather than atmospheric, regional broadcasts.

His further hope, to inject currents in the earth carrying useful amounts of electrical power, failed on the difficulty of finding a way to direct or focus it: all but the tightest, in-step waves—like

laser or maser beams—spread too quickly to carry power very far. Tesla proposed that the earth itself might be charged relative to its upper atmosphere and provide an unlimited source that need only be redistributed through earth waves (whose efficiency would then be irrelevant). Alas, this does not seem to be a workable idea.

Printed in the Electrical Experimenter, *February 1919.*

own right. Today that discovery is seen as the first disclosure of a phenomenon now known as the Tesla-Schumann cavity. Not until the late 1950s did the U.S. Navy rediscover the phenomenon while looking for a way to send radio messages to submerged submarines. Only in the 1990s was Tesla's name added.

To test his theory, Tesla had to become the first man to make electrical effects on the scale of lightning. The giant transmitter was arranged accordingly. On the evening of the experiment, he dressed for the occasion in a Prince Albert coat, white gloves, and derby hat. To avoid electrocution, he took the precaution of wearing shoes with four-inch cork soles. One of his assistants described him as looking like a "gaunt Mephistopheles."

Each item of equipment, every wire and connection, had been carefully checked. Tesla instructed his mechanic, Czito, to open the switch for only one second. The secondary coil began to sparkle and crack and an eerie blue corona formed in the air around it. Satisfied with the result, he ordered Czito to close the switch until told to cease. Huge arcs of blue electricity snaked up and down the center coil. Exploding discharges could be heard outside (Cheney 1981, 135).

Bolts of man-made lightning more than a hundred feet in length shot out from the mast atop the station. The commotion could be heard in the mining town of Cripple Creek, fifteen miles away. Tesla thrilled to the sight of great rods of flame. Then suddenly the lightning stopped. The experimental

Tesla's assistant prepares to close switch—a very brave man.

station went black. He shouted to Czito to turn the power on again, but nothing happened. His experiment had burned out the dynamo at the El Paso Electric Company. Not only Tesla, but the entire city had lost power. The power station manager was livid and the local population began to have second thoughts about the famous inventor. But about a week after the blackout, both Tesla and the power station were back in business. However, Tesla received no more free power.

Soon word came to him through the newspapers that Marconi had just sent a wireless signal across the English Channel. Concerned that the Italian inventor might be using his patents, Tesla wrote to his friend Robert Johnson on October I, 1899: "I have made splendid progress in a number of lines, but how grieved I was to find that a number of my confreres in wireless telegraphy—of the syndicating kind—have been indulging in an awful lot of lying!" (Tesla 1899a).

For nine months Tesla conducted experiments at Colorado Springs. Though he kept a day-to-day diary that was rich in detail, the results of his experiments are not clear. One question has never been answered definitively: Did Tesla actually transmit wireless power at Pikes Peak? Tesla's first biographer, John J. O'Neill, concludes that he did:

It appears evident that Tesla . . . tested his power-transmission system at a distance of twenty-six miles from his laboratory and was able to light two hundred incandescent lamps, of the Edison type, with electrical energy

Above: Caption in Century Magazine, June 1900, *reads: "The photograph shows three ordinary incandescent lamps lighted to full candle-power by currents induced in a local loop consisting of a single wire forming a square of fifty feet each side, which includes the lamps, and which is at a distance of one hundred feet from the primary circuit energized by the oscillator."*

Right: Discharge from ball connected to secondary coil at the Colorado Springs laboratory.

Experiment to illustrate the transmission of electrical energy through the earth without wire. Printed in Century Magazine, *June 1900, the caption reads: "The coil shown in the photograph has its lower end or terminal connected to the ground, and is exactly attuned to the vibrations of a distant electrical oscillator."*

extracted from the earth while his oscillator was operating. These lamps consumed about fifty watts each; and if two hundred were used in the test bank, the energy consumed would be 10,000 watts, or approximately thirteen horsepower (O'Neil 1944, 197).

But there is no evidence of this claim and the results have not been duplicated since.

Contemporary electrical engineers Robert Golka and Will Mische have attempted to replicate Tesla's Colorado Springs work in separate experiments. Even though they used comparable components and power levels, they were unable to transmit useful levels of power in the kilowatt range by radio waves.

What of Tesla's scheme to transmit electrical energy through the upper atmosphere—the very idea that brought him to the foot of Pikes Peak? His diary notes that among the items rushed to him by express were four double-focus Roentgen tubes with thick platinum targets. Was this the means of transporting energy to a high altitude? An entry reads: "Arrangements with single terminal tube for production of powerful rays. There being practically no limit to the power of an oscillator, it is now the problem to work out a tube so that it can stand any desired pressure" (Tesla 1899b, 29).

With such a device, Tesla later claimed he could send a conducting beam into the atmosphere and transmit enough energy to create an effect in the sky like the aurora borealis. In the *New York Herald Tribune* of June 5, 1935, he described the process as follows:

The principle is this: A ray of great ionizing power is used to give to the atmosphere great powers of conduction. A high tension current of 10,000,000 to 12,000,000 volts is then passed along this ray to the upper strata of the air, which strata can be broken down very readily and will conduct electricity very well.

Again, his extensive Colorado Springs notes do not record the results of any such experiments. In later years a son of Fritz Löwenstein who also worked for Tesla stated that while at Colorado Springs, his father observed Tesla's experiments with a beam device of this nature (Litt 1940).

Another unusual occurrence at Colorado Springs was the formation of small, glowing spheres of

Above: The experimental station in December 1899

*Right: An anteroom off the experimental area in Tesla's station at
Colorado Springs, 1899. An X-ray photographic cabinet together
with a Geissler and X-ray tube lie on the table, underneath an
electric heater.*

To the
American Red Cross
New York City.

The retrospect is glorious, the prospect is inspiring: much might be said of both. But one idea dominates my mind. This — my best, my dearest — is for your noble cause.

I have observed electrical actions, which have appeared inexplicable. Faint and uncertain though they were, they have given me a deep conviction and foreknowledge, that ere long all human beings on this globe, as one, will turn the eyes to the firmament above, with feelings of love and reverence, thrilled by the glad news: "Brethren! We have a message from another world, unknown and remote. It reads: one ... two ... three ...."

Christmas 1900

Nikola Tesla

Above: Caption in June 1900 Century Magazine *reads: "The picture shows a number of coils, differently attuned and responding to the vibrations transmitted to them through the earth from an electrical oscillator."*

Left: Tesla's letter to the American Red Cross announcing he had received an extraterrestrial communication.

electricity, darting around Tesla's equipment. Known today as "ball lightning," it is one of nature's most mysterious phenomena. Interrupted in its path, it can explode, as Tesla put it, "with inconceivable violence."

On a summer night in 1899, Tesla became aware of strange rhythmic "counting codes" on his low-frequency radio receiver. He later wrote:

My first observations positively terrified me, as there was present in them something mysterious, not to say supernatural, and I was alone in my laboratory at night.... Although I could not decipher their meaning, it was impossible for me to think of them as having been entirely accidental. The feeling is constantly growing on me that I had been the first to hear the greeting of one planet to another. A purpose was behind these electrical signals.

When the newspapers picked up this information, the so-called Martian Messages created a

firestorm of debate. No one had ever heard regular signals from space, and Tesla concluded that they must be from living creatures on a nearby planet, such as Mars or Venus. The *Colorado Springs Gazette* of March 9, 1901, had a field day:

If there are people in Mars, they certainly showed most excellent taste in choosing Colorado Springs as the particular point on the earth's surface with which to open communications. . . . It is a good rule in inventional science, "When you're going to tell one, tell a good one," and men have become great by observing the rule.

Just how far-fetched was Tesla's assertion that he had received a communication from space? Says noted physicist Dennis Papadopoulos of the University of Maryland, a specialist in wave propagation and a Tesla admirer:

I believe that Tesla could have gotten these

Ball lightning is an unexplained phenomenon of nature. It usually occurs during lightning storms and appears as spheres of plasma (the same state of energy as lightning) one to twelve inches in diameter. Ball lightning can float through the air and bounce along the ground, and has even been seen to pass undisturbed through sheets of glass and the walls of airplanes and submarines.

Tesla first noticed spherical discharges in arcs from his large coil at Colorado Springs. These, he reasoned, might be dust particles instantly vaporized in the bolts from his machine. He claimed he was able to generate them with some consistency in high-voltage discharges that manifested the "interaction of two frequencies," one of them a stray, or parasitic, oscillation present in the coil.

More recently, experimenters attempting to confirm Tesla's observations reported similar "plasmoids" when operating two closely spaced coils of different resonant frequencies. Until a convincing theory produces ball lightning that doesn't extinguish itself in the blink of a camera shutter, it remains an open question whether such laboratory phenomena are essentially the same as natural fireballs.

Tesla's description of ball lightning fascinated military scientists during the Cold War era. The distinguished Russian physicist Peter Kapitsa investigated its possible utility for destroying enemy planes and submarines. In recent decades the U.S. government has spent a considerable sum to investigate the plasma-physics that underlie this phenomenon.

Small glowing nodules appearing in streamers may be ball lightning.

signals from space, though not from alien civilizations. That's what radio telescopes do today, receive signals from space—from the sun and from the stars. The sun sends a lot of high frequency waves, at 20 megahertz. There is absolutely no reason that Tesla could not have had a sensitive enough device to really measure waves which were above the iono-spheric cut-off, which is around three mega-hertz (interview with the authors, 1998).

Thus, in addition to his many other achieve-ments, Tesla may have built the first radio telescope.

The experimental station at Colorado Springs had served its purpose, rewarding him more richly than he had hoped. His final entry in his journal, on January 7, 1900, noted further improvements he wished to make in his oscillator for future research.

Then the laboratory was closed down forever. Returning to New York in 1900, he wrote:

> While I have not as yet actually effected a transmission of a considerable amount of energy, such as would be of industrial importance, to a great distance by this new method . . . the practicability of the system is thoroughly demonstrated (Tesla 1900a).

He may have been mistaken. ⤴

CHAPTER TEN

Wardenclyffe Tower

Tesla's Wardenclyffe tower and power plant at Shoreham, Long Island, as it looked in 1904.

EVEN THE GODS OF OLD, IN THE WILDEST IMAGININGS, NEVER UNDER-
TOOK SUCH GIGANTIC TASKS OF WORLD-WIDE DIMENSION AS THOSE
WHICH TESLA ATTEMPTED AND ACCOMPLISHED. —JOHN O'NEILL

When Tesla returned to New York City from Colorado Springs it was a brand new century. Only five years had passed since the Niagara project went on line and it was already clear that his polyphase AC system was transforming civilization. Now a cheap and abundant supply of power was within almost everyone's reach. New York was becoming, quite literally, the world's most powerful city.

Huge buildings surged toward the sky. Automobiles appeared in the city streets. Excavation was under way for the new subway system. In more and more industries, AC motors were turning the wheels. Every night countless incandescent lights glowed with energy supplied by a waterfall hundreds of miles away. But these miracles would soon be taken for granted.

The air hummed with talk of wireless communication. The British Marconi Company was already advertising in America. "The Marconi system is endorsed by such men as Andrew Carnegie and Thomas A. Edison, and by the press of the entire world," their notice read. "Edison, Marconi, and Pupin are the consulting engineers of the American company." Tesla was so convinced of his own imminent suc-

cess in this new technical area that he seemed unconcerned by Marconi's advances. Assuming that he would soon be rich again, he took up suites in the first Waldorf-Astoria on Fifth Avenue, one of the most expensive hotels in town.

Again he was a welcomed guest in the lively home of Robert and Katharine Johnson, with whom he discussed his adventures at Colorado Springs. Robert was so impressed by what he heard that he invited the inventor to write an article for *Century Magazine*. What evolved was a futuristic treatise published in July 1900 titled "The Problem of Increasing Human Energy." In it Tesla predicted an extraordinary future based on electric power.

Herald Square looking north in the early 1900s. (Courtesy Smithsonian Institution)

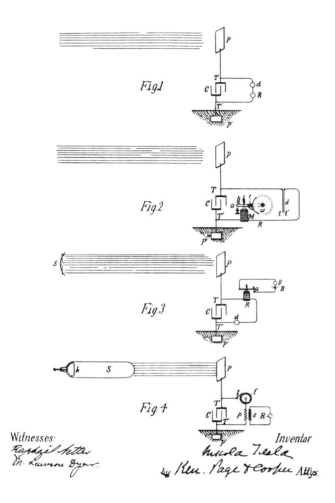

Witnesses:

Randzil Sittle
M. Lawson Dyer

Inventor

Nicola Tesla

by Kerr, Page & Cooper Att'ys.

Above: Wall Street financier J. Pierpont Morgan invested $150,000 in Tesla's broadcast center on Long Island, but held 51 percent of Tesla's radio patents as security. (Collection of The New-York Historical Society)

Left: Tesla's "Apparatus for Utilization of Radiant Energy," patented in 1901.

He wrote of broadcasting the human voice and likeness for the first time, of directly harnessing the energy of the sun and the planets, of machines capable of thinking. He thought artificial lightning might be used to modify the weather and predicted machines that could even eliminate warfare between nations.

This was heady stuff in 1900; the article caused a sensation. To heighten the effect, Tesla included astonishing photographs of some of his experiments in Colorado Springs that did not bear a direct relationship to the text. One photo portrays him sitting beneath huge streamers of deadly electricity, calmly reading a book (see page 84). The photograph is actually a double exposure, but Tesla did nothing to discourage the illusion. According to historian Thomas Hughes,

Here is a man who is moving out of the con-

ventional realm of invention into one that is more dramatic, heroic, and in a way tragic; where he's playing with the fire of the gods . . . almost a Prometheus trying to steal the fire of the gods. . . . Because of this he lost his way as an inventor. He became a heroic experimenter in search of the unknown (interview with the authors, 1997).

Tesla's article caught the attention of one of the world's most powerful men, J. P. Morgan. Under Morgan's influence American investors were in a falsely bullish mood. The financier had just purchased the Carnegie Steel Company from Andrew Carnegie at a much inflated price. He was in the process of creating a billion-dollar U.S. Steel trust, acquiring iron fields and shipping lines from John D. Rockefeller. The memory of Tesla's successes at

Tesla's "World System" was an astonishingly accurate prediction of the electronic world we live in today, but in 1906 it could scarcely be believed. His promotional brochure stated that the system would possess the following features:

(1) The interconnection of the existing telegraph exchanges or offices all over the world;

(2) The establishment of a secret and noninterferable government telegraph service;

(3) The interconnection of all the present telephone exchanges or offices on the globe;

(4) The universal distribution of general news, by telegraph or telephone, in connection with the press;

(5) The establishment of intelligence transmission for exclusive private use;

(6) The interconnection and operation of all stock tickers of the world;

(7) The establishment of a "World System" of musical distribution, etc.;

Promotional illustration for Tesla's "World System"

(8) The universal registration of time by cheap clocks indicating the hour with astronomical precision and requiring no attention whatever;

(9) The world transmission of typed or handwritten characters, letters, checks, etc.;

(10) The establishment of a universal marine service enabling the navigators of all ships to steer perfectly without compass, to determine the exact location, hour, and speed to prevent collisions and disasters, etc.;

(11) The inauguration of a system of world printing on land and sea;

(12) The world reproduction of photographic pictures and all kinds of drawings or records.

"Besides these I referred to," Tesla added, "other and incomparably more important applications of my discoveries will be disclosed at some future date" (Tesla 1919e).

Niagara Falls had taught Morgan how rudely a new technology could shake up the economy. He knew that if Marconi did not make the breakthrough with wireless, it would be Tesla.

A guest in Morgan's home, Tesla proposed a scheme that must have sounded like science fiction: a "world system" of wireless communications to relay telephone messages across the ocean; to broadcast news, music, stock market reports, private messages, secure military communications, and even pictures to any part of the world. Tesla wrote:

> When wireless is perfectly applied the whole earth will be converted into a huge brain, which in fact it is, as all things being particles of a real and rhythmic whole. We shall be able

to communicate with one another instantly, irrespective of distance. Not only this, but through television and telephone we shall see and hear one another as perfectly as though we were face to face (Tesla 1900).

While this was a little beyond anyone's comprehension, Morgan did like the prospect of being able to communicate swiftly and securely with the stock exchanges and banks of the world. That alone would be worth an investment. He offered Tesla $150,000 to build a transmission tower and power plant. A more realistic sum would have been $1,000,000, but Tesla took what was available and went to work immediately. But he kept his trump card concealed: the purpose of the tower was not just to transmit

Massive Wardenclyffe tower, plant, and laboratory under construction in 1902.

messages. It was to make a grand demonstration of wireless power transmission.

Tesla turned to James D. Warden, manager and director of the Suffolk Land Company of Long Island, for the needed land. Warden made available two hundred acres of isolated farming country near Shoreham, Long Island, which offered the necessary amenities of a nearby railroad. Situated near the cliffs overlooking Long Island Sound, the site was called Wardenclyffe.

Tesla again encountered Stanford White, the talented, scandal-prone society architect, famed designer of the Washington Square Arch among other New York landmarks, at the home of the Johnsons. White, who had designed the Niagara powerhouse, was excited by the new project and offered his services gratis.

W. D. Crow, a well-known engineer who was White's associate, also joined the Wardenclyffe team. In addition to a powerhouse and transmitting tower, the architectural plans included four or five additional buildings, as well as a real estate development named Radio City, to house the hundreds of people who would be employed by the world's first broadcasting facility (Anderson 1968).

During the development phase, Tesla was an occasional guest at the Morgan residence. He became acquainted with Anne Morgan, the dark-eyed, strong-willed twenty-seven-year-old daughter of J. P. and Frances Morgan. Like Tesla, Anne Morgan thought and wrote constantly about the advancement of civilization, and worked diligently to advance her ideas. She and Tesla became casual friends, Anne enlisting him occasionally in her social causes and he counting on her to insure the continued goodwill of her father.

By 1901 the Wardenclyffe project was under construction, the most challenging task being the erection of an enormous tower, rising 187 feet in the air and supporting on its top a fifty-five-ton sphere made of steel. Beneath the tower, a well-like shaft plunged 120 feet into the ground. Sixteen iron pipes were driven three hundred feet deeper so that currents could pass through them and seize hold of the earth. "In this system that I have invented," Tesla explained, "it is necessary for the machine to get a grip of the earth, otherwise it cannot shake the earth. It has to have a grip . . . so that the whole of this globe can quiver" (Anderson 1992, 203).

A winding stairway descended into the center of the shaft, through which enormous current would be passed. This complex electromagnetic oscillator could be tuned to emit a wide range of extra-low and high frequencies. The hemispheric globe on top was designed to store electrical energy that could be released as needed, like a gigantic capacitor. The tower was built of special fir timbers, "prodigiously strong and very highly insulating," in such a way that

The railroad station across from Nikola Tesla's Wardenclyffe plant in a photo taken from the tower around 1914.

every piece could be removed at any time and replaced if necessary. The design was an octagonal pyramid, built for strength and to prevent the globe on top from succumbing to the gale-force winds that blew in from the ocean. Tower and powerhouse were connected by two channels—one carrying compressed air and water to the tower, the other for electric mains (Anderson 1968).

Every day Tesla arrived by train from the Waldorf-Astoria Hotel in Manhattan. He debarked at Shoreham at about 11:00 A.M., accompanied by a Serbian manservant carrying an enormous hamper of food. For a time he returned to New York each mid-afternoon, but after the laboratory and machine works were completed he rented a cottage near the Long Island shore and roughed it for a year. Soon the fan-

tastic structure could be seen rising through the tree-tops from across the Sound in New Haven, Connecticut. Shoreham residents watched its growth with awed anticipation and believed that their town was about to become another wonder of the world, like Niagara Falls.

White designed the brick powerhouse as a simple rectangle—a one-story building divided into four large rooms with a central brick chimney. The tower was 350 feet from the building, a distance necessary to protect workers in the plant from errant bolts of lightning from the antenna. By November 1901 the steam boilers and engines had arrived and were being installed.

Almost immediately it became apparent that either the design for the magnificent tower must be scaled down or more funds must be raised. Tesla

Above: Wardenclyffe machine and glass-blowing shop (side away from tower)

Left: Wardenclyffe plant building, designed by Stanford White, as seen from the tower in 1914.

Opposite: Large mercury interrupter devised by Tesla for handling fifty horsepower of electrical energy at a rate of 100,000 breaks per second. Stairway to tower tunnel can be seen in the background.

wrote to Stanford White on September 13, 1901, seven days after President McKinley had been mortally wounded by an assassin:

> I have not been half as dumfounded by the news of the shooting of the President as I was by the estimates submitted by you. . . . One thing is certain; we cannot build that tower as outlined. I cannot tell you how sorry I am, for my calculations show that with such a structure I could reach across the Pacific (Tesla 1901a).

Tesla had planned to demonstrate the operation of his radio-controlled boat at the Paris Exposition of 1900 from his office in New York, but the Exposition opened and closed without him as more pressing problems demanded his attention.

Morgan was habitually slow in sending money. After the first year Tesla was forced to move back to Manhattan and to open offices at the Metropolitan Tower to increase both his visibility and his income. He resumed his pleasant habits, dining—on credit—at the Waldorf-Astoria and mingling with other distinguished gentlemen at the Players Club.

His attempts to find investors other than his friend Colonel Astor were unsuccessful. Astor had bought five hundred shares of stock in the Nikola Tesla Company and cheerfully covered Tesla's hotel bills at the Waldorf-Astoria. George Westinghouse

Tesla's tower with dome frame, completed in 1904.

The Marconi demonstration, which stirred universal excitement, was more damaging than Tesla cared to admit. J. P. Morgan, among others, could no longer understand why the inventor needed that great expensive plant. Other scientists, inventors, and businessmen, nursing jealousy over his victory in the War of the Currents, were not averse to making damaging statements. Tesla's own countryman, the inventor Michael Pupin, called the Wardenclyffe scheme an expensive waste of money. Edison said that he did not believe in Tesla being able to talk around the world, but that he thought that Marconi would, sooner or later, perfect his system (Edison 1905).

Stress and constant financial pressure were beginning to take their toll. Both Tesla and George Scherff, who tried to help in any way he could, came close to having serious accidents. Tesla, who once worked without sleep for eighty-four straight hours, was experimenting, for unknown reasons, with small jets of water moving at high velocity and under pressures of ten thousand pounds per square inch. The high-pressure stream caused a cylinder to explode, and a cast-iron cap crashed through the ceiling after narrowly passing his face. As for Scherff, his eyes were injured in an explosion of hot liquid metal he was pouring, and it was feared at first that he had been blinded.

Early in 1902 the tower was nearing completion, except for the giant globe or hemispheric electrode at the top. The plan was to cover the frame with stainless steel sheeting, but it was never accomplished due to a shortage of money. Tesla had ordered specially designed generators and transformers from Westinghouse, and even the company he helped to create was demanding payment. Tesla would wake Scherff, his loyal assistant, in the middle of the night and they would walk the beach for hours as Scherff took shorthand notes in the dark. "I swear! If I ever get out of this hole nobody will ever again catch me without cash," Tesla told him (Anderson 1968).

turned down an opportunity to invest in the project, thinking the economy too volatile for such a plunge. Despite his respect for Tesla's genius, he was not convinced of the practicability of so grandiose a scheme.

George Scherff was again urging Tesla to manufacture small diathermy machines based on the Tesla Pad, which doctors were recommending for arthritis patients. Instead the inventor published a handsome brochure describing his "world system."

Then on December 12, 1901, the world awoke to the news that Marconi had signaled the letter "S" across the Atlantic from Cornwall, England, to Newfoundland.

Tesla's experiments at Colorado Springs may have left him with a mistaken estimate of the earth's conductivity. But his larger objective of wireless power transmission need not be dismissed on that score. The views he proposed simply outdistanced by several decades the necessary science to investigate them.

Tesla did not know of the complex interaction of solar wind and earth's magnetic field that creates the ionosphere, which is an excellent conductor. But he supposed an upper, conductive layer did exist, and that the earth and its upper atmosphere could be treated as plates of an enormous condenser. Having proposed this model, the great problem for him was to measure these planet-wide electrical properties and discover a way to use them. Emphasis shifted back and forth in his design from using the earth as conductor to using the upper atmospheric channel. An interesting fact is that his first radio patent really

From the Electrical Experimenter, *June 1919.*

describes power transmission; radio signaling is specified simply as one useful employment of the principle. Establishing a link between upper atmosphere and earth was the great obstacle. He reckoned that bringing one end of a large (man-made)

condenser to an altitude of, say, thirty thousand feet would be sufficient—at high enough voltage—to create electrical contact.

When designing the Wardenclyffe facility at sea level it appears he sought to tunnel upward from its globe-shaped tower top (one plate of the condenser) with a high-frequency signal and a bank of ultraviolet lights, acting much as the leader stroke in a lightning discharge. The other terminal of this great capacitor was taken over a hundred feet into the ground, down a specially lined access shaft beneath the tower and then through several hundred feet more of pipe driven into the earth from the shaft's floor. He spoke of trying to shake the earth with his signal, that is, to impress electrical impulses on the planet and build their strength through resonance.

To his dying day Tesla insisted that his wireless power scheme was feasible, but no one has been able to produce the results he anticipated.

To make matters worse, there was a panic on Wall Street, brought on by Morgan's attempts to manipulate the market. Tesla wrote to Morgan for desperately needed funds:

> You have raised great waves in the industrial world and some have struck my little boat. Prices have gone up in consequence twice, perhaps three times higher than they were (Tesla 1903a).

Tesla was forced to reveal his hand.

> Mr. Morgan, what I contemplate and what I can certainly accomplish is not a simple transmission of messages without wires to great distances; it is the transformation of the entire globe into a sentient being, as it were, which can feel in all its parts and through which thought may be flashed as through a brain. . . . From one single plant thousands of trillions of instruments could be operated, each costing no more than a few dollars, and situated in all parts of the globe. Will you help me or let my great work—almost complete—go to pot? (Tesla 1903b)

Morgan replied coldly: "I have received your letter . . . and in reply would say that I should not feel disposed at present to make any further advances" (Morgan 1903). Word soon spread that the financier had backed out of the deal. Tesla was financially and

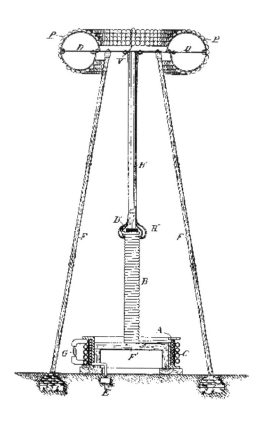

Tesla's patent, "Apparatus for Transmitting Electrical Energy," was applied for in 1902 at Wardenclyffe, but was not granted until 1914.

emotionally shattered. He wrote to Morgan angrily:

> Have you ever read the book of Job? If you will put my mind in place of his body, you will find my sufferings accurately described.... There has hardly been a night when my pillow was not bathed in tears, but you must not think me a weak man for that. I am perfectly sure to finish my task, come what may. What chance have I to land the biggest Wall Street monster with the soul's "spider thread"? You are a big man but your work is wrought in passing form. Mine is immortal (Tesla 1904b).

Beginning at midnight on July 15, 1903, and for several succeeding nights, residents of Shoreham reported strange activities at the Wardenclyffe facility. The *New York Sun* reported on July 16, 1903:

> Natives hereabouts are intensely interested in the nightly electrical display shown from the tall tower where Nikola is conducting his experiments in wireless telegraphy and telephony. For a time, the air was filled with blinding streaks of electricity traveling through the darkness on some mysterious errand.

Tesla gave no explanations.

Even electrical engineers who have studied Tesla's work are not sure how the system at Wardenclyffe was to operate. It is not known whether Tesla intended to test his wireless power concept using the "conduction" technique to send a current through the ionosphere, or the "stationary wave" technique, using the earth itself to transmit energy. Both are mentioned in his patent number 1,119,732, applied for in January 1902.

Tesla biographer John O'Neill described a large circular hole, five feet in diameter, at the top of the Wardenclyffe cupola, designed to allow rays from a bank of ultraviolet lights to go upward to the sky. This, he conjectured, was for the purpose of ionizing the air to create a conducting path to the stratosphere (O'Neill 1944, 149). Tesla alluded to such experiments as well:

> I made tests on a large scale with the transmitter referred to and a beam of ultra-violet rays of great energy, in an attempt to conduct the current to the high rarefied strata of the air and thus create an aurora display such as might be utilized for illumination, especially of oceans at night (Tesla n.d.).

Wardenclyffe remains a mystery to this day. Years of inflation sent Tesla's costs skyrocketing. Then came the heartbreaking time when he could no longer pay his workers or even afford coal to fire up the boilers. Flocks of bill collectors harassed him until he could no longer continue. The tower that was meant to fulfill his dreams had become his greatest nightmare. He wrote to Scherff, "The Wardenclyffe specters are hounding me day and night.... When will it end?" (Anderson 1968).

On July 4, 1917, the Wardenclyffe tower was dynamited and razed by the mortgage holder, the proprietor of the Waldorf-Astoria Hotel, to make the property more salable. Tesla had been unable to satisfy hotel bills amounting to $20,000.

Unable to overcome his financial burdens, he was forced to close the laboratory in 1905. Occasional visitors were amazed to see the intricate mechanisms: glass-blowing equipment, X-ray devices, many varieties of high-frequency coils, a radio-controlled boat, exhibit cases with at least a thousand bulbs and tubes, an instrument room, electrical generators and transformers, wire and cable, library and office—all seemingly deserted. The *Brooklyn Eagle* reported on March 26, 1916: "It is not too much to say that the place has often been viewed in the same light as the people of a few centuries ago viewed the dens of the alchemists or the still more ancient wells of the sorcerers."

To guarantee payment of $20,000 in hotel bills, Tesla gave two mortgages on Wardenclyffe to George C. Boldt, proprietor of the Waldorf-Astoria. Unable to make a single payment, Tesla turned the deed over to the Waldorf-Astoria in 1915.

Though the tower is long gone, the deserted Wardenclyffe laboratory still stands on Long Island, a haunting memory of Tesla's plans for wireless energy transmission. "It was not a dream," he declared, "but a simple feat of scientific electrical engineering, only expensive—blind, fainthearted, doubting world" (Tesla 1905). ✎

CHAPTER ELEVEN

Powerhouse in a Hat

Tesla in his office in 1916, demonstrating an electrical apparatus.

*I*n 1904, one year after the Wardenclyffe debacle, the U.S. Patent Office suddenly and surprisingly reversed itself, giving Marconi a patent for the invention of radio. The courts later corrected the injustice, but not until after Tesla's death. The patent examiner's action was followed by the revelation that Morgan and Edison had joined others as major investors in Marconi America (later RCA).

The following year, Tesla's patents on the AC induction motor expired. The genius who had helped create billion-dollar corporations was struggling to pay the rent on his small office at 165 Broadway, just across from the New York Public Library. His enemies had been so successful in representing him as a poet and visionary that it was absolutely imperative for him to put out something commercial without delay.

A unique idea had been taking shape in his mind, inspired by the waterwheels he had played with as a child. In an article published on his fiftieth birthday in 1906, Tesla announced something entirely new to the world—a revolutionary prime mover called the bladeless turbine. He wrote,

> A long time ago I became possessed of a desire to produce an engine as simple as my induction motor; and my efforts have been rewarded. No mechanism could be simpler, and the beauty of it is that almost any amount of power can be obtained from it. In the induction motor I produced the rota-

tion by setting up a magnetic whirl, while in the turbine I set up a whirl of steam or gas (Tesla 1906a).

The invention was based on two principles of fluid dynamics, long known to engineers. "I felt certain there must be some means of obtaining power that was better than any now in use," Tesla explained in the *New York Herald Tribune* of October 15, 1911, "and by vigorous use of my gray matter for a number of years I grasped the possibilities of the

The experts laughed—at first—when told this Tesla turbine of 200 horsepower ran 16,000 revolutions to the minute. The upper part of the casing is removed to show the rotor, which is eighteen inches in diameter and measures three inches on edge.

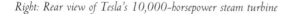

Above: Tesla turbine of 110 horsepower, small enough to fit in a hat.

Right: Rear view of Tesla's 10,000-horsepower steam turbine

principles of the viscosity and adhesion of fluids and conceived the mechanism of my engine."

The first tiny bladeless rotary turbine was built in 1906 by Julius C. Czito, the son of Tesla's assistant at Colorado Springs and other laboratories. The shaft held eight very thin disks of German silver; the rotor attained tremendously high speeds, averaging thirty-five thousand revolutions per minute. At this speed, said Czito, "the centrifugal force generated by the turning movement was so great it appreciably stretched the metal in the rotating disks" (O'Neill 1944, 222). The small motor weighed less than fifty pounds and could deliver 110 horsepower. In a letter to a friend, Tesla described it as "a powerhouse in a hat."

From the outset, Tesla's disk turbine commanded immediate worldwide excitement. He was lauded in engineering and scientific journals, with only occasional cautionary warnings that his claims in the past had not always materialized. Many well-known engineers were impressed. Yet almost from the begin-

ning, it could be seen that Tesla was traversing an old and unhappy path.

His new invention was unwelcome because it represented the threat of yet another technological struggle, a "war of the turbines." By the turn of the century both the General Electric and Westinghouse corporations had already invested millions in the Curtis and Parsons bladed turbine designs. Neither company was interested in having its investment undermined. Historian Thomas Hughes has stated that Tesla's creativity may have been his undoing. "Industrialists invest money, learning and skill in a system, and this gives the system a momentum, a motion that tends to continue," said Hughes. "Tesla was a radical inventor, highly imaginative, who wished to introduce new systems, not improving upon other people's work. And for this reason, he was not appreciated by his peers" (interview with the authors, 1997).

The Tesla turbine had many distinct advantages over conventional bladed designs, in which a series of

Turbines are generally machines that go around because a driving fluid strikes various parts and forces them, through reaction or deflection, into rotation. In a Pelton wheel, for example, a high-pressure stream of water runs into scooplike arms around the wheel's circumference. Its principle of action, impulse, is self-explanatory.

A much more complex and versatile type, the Parsons turbine, utilizes the energy of expanding gases, like steam or ignited fuels. It has many rotors, all studded with directional vanes that are deflected, like a propeller, by gases rushing through. Jet engines are descended from this design idea.

In 1913 a completely different principle for a turbine was advanced by Tesla. Startlingly simple in design, it consisted of only a stack of closely spaced flat disks fixed to a shaft. The assembly was contained within a cylindrical casing provided with an inlet for any high-pressure fluid and an outlet.

High-velocity fluid entered the casing at a tangent and was directed around the outer perimeter of the disks and cylinder wall. In accordance with principles of fluid mechanics, gases and steam literally adhered to the disks and propelled them forward at a high rate of speed. The path of the fluid is an inward spiral. Arriving at the inner region of the disks, spent fluid finally flows out of the turbine through cutouts near the center.

The basic concept strained engineering credulity. Nothing in this turbine was actually driven—deflected or pushed—by the fluid. A physicist today would speak of a "no-slip" condition at the disk surface and a sub-boundary layer separation between disks.

"No-slip" simply expresses the fact that fluids in contact with solid surfaces will have, where they meet, a thin outer layer moving at the same speed as the surface. In motion, the fluid's contacting layer will try to bring the surface—the disk—up to speed.

Beyond this very thin region, fluid is trying to rush on at full speed; there is a "boundary layer" between the no-slip surface and the fuller flow—like the broad central current away from the banks of a river. But by spacing the disks closer together than the width of the full boundary layer (a matter of millimeters), the fluid is prevented from establishing any free-flow path to carry itself and its energy away unconnected to the disks. In this way, all the energy of the fluid is imparted to the disks.

Tesla, as it happened, filed his patent in two ways: first, for a device that transforms fluid velocity into mechanical rotation (as discussed here); and second, the other way around—feeding water or air, for example, into an externally driven turbine and accelerating it, pumping it, with the same disks. The drawings, unsurprisingly, are nearly identical; it is an invention with a beautiful mechanical symmetry.

There were problems, however. In higher-power, higher-speed versions, the turbine failed. Extremely high rotational velocities at the disks' perimeter caused failure in alloys then available.

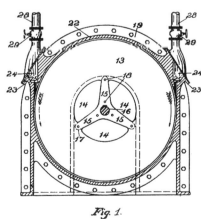

Left: Tesla turbo pump

Fig. 1.

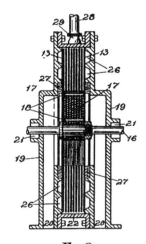

Fig. 2.

Sketch of Tesla's concept for a turbine-powered automobile.

blades or buckets capture the energy imparted by fluids or gases. Bladed turbines are high-precision machines built to very close tolerances, and thus expensive to construct and operate. Another unique feature of Tesla's turbine was that it was completely reversible, making it ideal for use aboard seagoing vessels that required two separate conventional turbines for forward and reverse operations, or a cumbersome set of reverse gears. Slightly modified, the turbine also became a highly efficient pump, so rugged in design it could operate even in mud. "As an air compressor," Tesla wrote, "it is highly efficient. . . . Refrigeration on a scale hitherto never attempted will be practical, through the use of this engine in compressing air, and the manufacture of liquid air commercially is now entirely feasible." Most important was his astonishing claim that his turbine, operating on steam, could achieve 95 percent efficiency when fully staged. Even today, bladed turbines still operate at about 60 to 70 percent efficiency (Hayes 1993).

The invention also presented extraordinary possibilities for automobiles. First, it required no transmission, and reached maximum RPM almost instantaneously. It had no pistons or crankcase and therefore required no oil to operate. With only one moving part, almost no maintenance was required. In terms of

efficiency, Tesla believed the turbine would make it possible to travel across the country on a single tank of fuel, which also meant that it generated virtually no exhaust to pollute the air.

The basic patents were granted in 1913, as "Fluid Propulsion" patent number 1,061,142 and "Turbine" patent number 1,061,206. Of the turbine Tesla said:

> This is the greatest of my inventions . . . take my rotating field. . . . There are millions invested in it already. Well, that is a very useful thing, but the field is limited to dynamos and motors. . . . Here you have a new power for pumps, steam engines, gasoline motors, for automobiles, for airships, for many other uses, and all so simple (Stockbridge 1911).

In 1910 and 1911 tests of several Tesla turbines ranging from one hundred to five thousand horsepower were conducted at the Edison Waterside Power Station in New York City. Here, Tesla was definitely in unfriendly territory. Edison still harbored resentment toward his former employee. The AC power system invented by Tesla had cost him a fortune and he was not about to let it happen again. Edison engineers were not fond of Tesla, either. The inventor did little to ingratiate himself with the staff, regularly arriving at the power station at the five o'clock quitting time and insisting that his favorite men remain into the night on overtime pay. Like Archimedes, lost in his circles, he was oblivious to the ill will surrounding him.

During one of the tests, there was actually laughter when Tesla told a panel of experts that the turbine was running at sixteen thousand RPM. All doubts evaporated, however, when a tachometer was placed on the shaft and Tesla's claim was confirmed.

In spite of positive reports, the Edison staff declared the turbines unsatisfactory, and circulated the story that the turbine was a complete failure. Westinghouse also turned down an invitation to develop Tesla's turbine commercially, and asked him

Tesla's experimental installation at the Edison Waterside Station, New York City, in 1912. Shown are a propulsion turbine on the left and a brake turbine on the right.

to return equipment borrowed for the tests at Waterside Station. Tesla realized what he was up against:

> My turbine is an advance of a character entirely different. It is a radical departure in the sense that its success would mean the abandonment of the antiquated types of prime movers on which billions of dollars have been spent. Under such circumstances the progress must needs be slow and perhaps the greatest impediment is encountered in the prejudicial opinions created in the minds of experts by organized opposition (Tesla 1919e).

He turned next to the Allis Chalmers Manufacturing Company of Milwaukee, builders of reciprocating engines and turbines. The company agreed to build 200- and 675-horsepower versions of his steam turbine. But engineering problems soon appeared, as reported by Hals Dahlstrand, consulting engineer for Allis Chalmers. The most serious was the charge that when the unit was dismantled, "the disks had distorted to a great extent and the opinion was that these disks would ultimately have failed if the unit had been operated for any length of time." The final complaint was that Tesla had not given the engineers sufficient information. At this point, the inventor simply walked out, saying only, "They would not build the turbines as I wished" (O'Neill 1944, 227).

Still convinced that his turbine had valuable commercial applications, he introduced a gasoline version in 1920. He especially hoped to capture the attention of automobile and airplane manufacturers. "I had particular designs on that man from Detroit," he said, referring to Henry Ford, "who had the uncanny fac-

Nothing upset Tesla more than the sight of smoke belching from the chimneys of power plants. To reduce pollution he suggested a number of environmentally friendly alternatives that are considered cutting-edge technology today.

WIND POWER

"The power of the wind has been overlooked. Some day it will be forcibly brought to the position it deserves through the need of a substitute for the present method of generating power. Given a good breeze, I have estimated that there is as much as half a horsepower to every square foot of area exposed. The contrivance that has been at the disposal of mankind from all time, the wind-mill, is now seen in the rural districts only. The popular mind cannot grasp the power there is in the wind."

SOLAR POWER

"The sun's rays falling upon the earth's surface represent a quantity of energy so enormous that but a small part of it could meet all our demands. By normal incidence the rate is mechanically equivalent to about 95 foot pounds per square foot per second, or nearly 7,300 horsepower per acre of ground. The energy of light rays, constituting about 10% of the total radiation, might be captured by a cold and highly efficient process in photo-electric cells which may become, on this account, of practical importance in the future."

GEOTHERMAL POWER

"Another way of getting motive power without consuming any material would be to utilize the heat contained in the earth, the water, or the air for driving an engine. The difficulties of sinking shafts and placing boilers at depths of, say, twelve thousand feet, corresponding to an increase in temperature of about 120° C, are not insuperable, and we could certainly avail ourselves in this way of the internal heat of the globe. [The] internal heat of the earth is great and, in comparison with the demands which man can make upon it, is practically

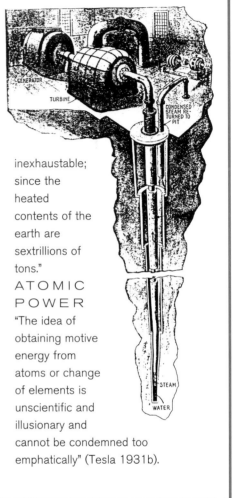

inexhaustible; since the heated contents of the earth are sextrillions of tons."

ATOMIC POWER

"The idea of obtaining motive energy from atoms or change of elements is unscientific and illusionary and cannot be condemned too emphatically" (Tesla 1931b).

---

ulty for accumulating millions." Naturally, he was thrilled when representatives of the Ford Motor Company came calling. But joy turned to anger when he learned that the reason for the visit was to ask him to join a psychological society for the investigation of psychic phenomena (Tesla 1919f).

In 1918, the National Advisory Committee for Aeronautics (later NASA) took serious interest in Tesla's gasoline turbine and requested a proposal and technical information. "Machines of this kind can be produced that will develop 10 horsepower for every pound of weight," said Tesla, "while the lightest engines of the present day give only about one horse-power for each two pounds of weight, or one twentieth of the power developed by my turbine. I have no doubt that is the engine of the future" (Tesla 1906a). But the proposal never came and, like so many of his later ideas, the project never got off the ground.

John C. Whitesell, a young engineer who worked with Tesla on the gasoline turbine at the Budd Company in Philadelphia, summarized the problem:

As I look back, the only metal he had to use was Monell and the 10″ rotor grew 1/16″ in diameter at 30,000 revolutions per minute. Should Tesla have had metals then as are available today [1963] to take over 3,000 degrees,

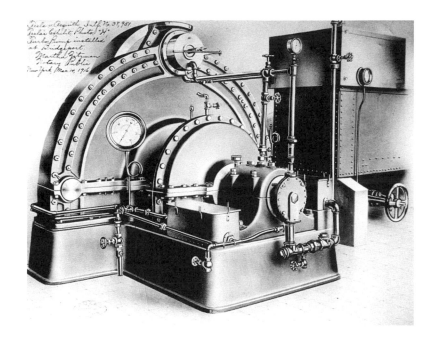

Large Tesla turbo pump

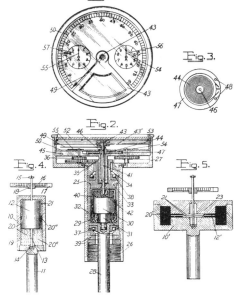

Tesla's patent illustration for an automobile speedometer, 1918

the turbine would have been a success, as the principles are the same (Whitesell 1963).

Again, Tesla was ahead of his time.

Unfortunately, very little research has taken place to test whether Tesla's claims could be better substantiated with the engineering and metallurgy available today. Professor Warren Rice of the University of Arizona conducted extensive tests of Tesla-type turbines (multiple-disk rotating devices) for the U.S. Navy in the 1950s and 60s. Rice reported that the engine performed at 41 percent efficiency, approximating Tesla's results, but falling far short of Tesla's claim of 97 percent. Rice explained:

> The really hard questions concern economic viability and details of materials use and of constructions. . . . I think that these practical problems remain with us today, and were largely dismissed by Tesla as details. His thinking seems to have been so innovative and so creative that he relegated problems that he regarded as mundane or routine to others who would follow him (Rice 1980).

Tesla's turbo-pump has had a different history. Since the 1980s, the bladeless Tesla pump has been in widespread commercial use in mines, oil fields, and elsewhere, being far more resistant to corrosives and particulate damage than conventional pumps. Texaco was one of the first large companies to put it to use.

Tesla had invested nearly twenty years of his life in the turbine and all he had to show for it were piles of scrap iron, financial problems, and an even more damaged reputation. In order to survive, he filed a group of patents for devices based on the same fluid propulsion principles as his turbine. One of these was an automobile speedometer, which he sold to the Waltham Watch Company. The invention was a tremendous success, yet he somehow lost money in its development. He also invented a frequency meter, an electric water fountain, a ship's log, and a flow meter—all successful in their own right, but not the kinds of innovations he had in mind. "If I truly have a gift for invention," he said, "I will not squander it on small things" (Tesla 1917).

Honors, Welcome and Otherwise

Tesla working in his office at 8 West 40th Street.

As a matter of history it is the Tesla principle and the Tesla system which have been the directing factors in modern electrical engineering practice. —Charles F. Scott

When Wardenclyffe passed from his hands, Tesla no longer had a laboratory. He continued to keep a small office in the Metropolitan Tower, offering his services as a consulting engineer. Routinely on entering his office he had the blinds drawn by two attendant secretaries, as he preferred to work in low light; "a notorious sun-dodger," one reporter called him.

The blond, sensitive Miss Dorothy Skerritt had joined the firm in 1912 at 8 West 40th Street, across from the New York Public Library. She was devoted to Tesla, regarding him as a saint who appeared to possess mind-reading powers. The competent young Muriel Arbus, who had preceded her, became a feminine success story during World War II as director of Arbus Machine Tool Sales.

During lightning storms Tesla would sit in his office on a black mohair couch and applaud the spectacular performances outside his picture window. The master of lightning was now merely a spectator. He still slept only a few hours each night, and was tormented by dreams of his mother's death

and that of his older brother, Dane. Aloof and self-absorbed, he was occasionally seen sitting in parks, writing in his journal and feeding the pigeons. His employees and friends feared he might become so distracted that he would step in front of a taxicab.

Money continued to be his greatest problem. In 1915, he filed a lawsuit against Marconi, stating the obvious—that the Italian inventor had infringed on Tesla's radio patents. "The process is universally adopted; everybody uses it," he said to his attorney. "There are millions and millions involved in it."

Marconi won the Nobel Prize in 1909, a fact Tesla resented. (Courtesy Library of Congress)

If I could only get one cent for every apparatus that is manufactured in accordance with my invention, I could erect a building like the Woolworth and not feel the expense. Everybody uses it, but nobody says thanks (Anderson 1992, 33).

Tesla had an office in the Woolworth Building in 1914, but he fell behind in the rent. In the end, when he could not even afford to push his case against Marconi, he withdrew more deeply into his private world.

His losses with the passing years began to include old friends. In 1906 Stanford

Top: Tesla's greatest patron, George Westinghouse, died in 1914 and is buried in Arlington National Cemetery.

Right: Katharine Johnson wrote to Tesla, "We shall soon be far away from you, but then you would never know it. You don't need anybody, inhuman that you are. How strange it is that we cannot do without you" (K. Johnson 1905).

White, who had blueprinted both the Niagara Falls and Wardenclyffe powerhouses, was murdered by Harry K. Thaw. Apparently resentful of White's former friendship with his showgirl wife Evelyn Nesbit, Thaw fired three shots into the architect on the roof of Madison Square Garden.

John Jacob Astor, one of Tesla's closest friends and financial backers, went down on the *Titanic*. After his death, it was discovered that he still held five hundred shares of stock in the Nikola Tesla Company that he did not carry on his books.

Another dear friend, Mark Twain, died in 1910. Like Tesla, he had also suffered severe financial setbacks. In his old age, the humorist became more pessimistic about mankind. His last work, a novella titled *The Mysterious Stranger*, is thought to have been inspired by Tesla's childhood in Austria-Hungary.

In 1913 J. Pierpont Morgan died in Rome during a spiritual journey. News of his death was relayed by coded telegram, to be broken gently on Wall Street. Tesla, despite his cruel disappointments with Morgan, continued to hold the Morgan dynasty in high regard. Dorothy Skerritt remembered, "When Morgan, Sr., was living, Tesla could get money from him just by asking for it" (Skerritt 1955). A month after Morgan died, Tesla wrote to J. P. Morgan, Jr., for an appointment. The immediate result was a loan of fifteen thousand dollars; but it was the last money he would receive from the Morgan Company. George Westinghouse died the following year and Tesla was left without powerful financial supporters.

Life was not going well for Tesla's intimates, Katharine and Robert Johnson. A scandal that remained an undisclosed secret had erupted at *Century Magazine* in spring 1913, threatening Robert's position. Tesla tried to help his friend, but without success. In time the "little embarrassment" led to Johnson's resignation as editor; the nature of

Tesla advocated exercise and good nutrition long before such ideas were fashionable. In his beliefs he was more like a New Age spiritualist:

> Everyone should consider his body as a priceless gift from one whom he loves above all, a marvelous work of art, of indestructible beauty, and mastery beyond human conception, and so delicate that a word, a breath, a look, nay a thought, may injure it (Tesla 1900a).

The inventor was in excellent health until his eighties. This he attributed to a lack of social vices. "Even smoking, snuffing or chewing tobacco will eventually impair the health," he said, "though not quite so much as chewing gum, which, by exhaustion of the salivary glands, puts many a foolish victim into an early grave" (Tesla 1932a).

He also abstained from eating meat:

Many races living almost exclusively on vegetables are of superior physique and strength. In view of these facts every effort should be made to stop the wanton and cruel slaughter of animals, which must be destructive to our morals.

His early experience with cholera influenced his thinking about water:

> The majority of people are so ignorant or careless in drinking water, and the consequences of this are so disastrous.... It should be made a rigid rule—which might be enforced by law—to boil or to sterilize otherwise the drinking-water in every household and public place.

One vice Tesla did not eschew was a glass of whiskey each day. "It is not a stimulant," he said, "but a veritable elixir of life" (Tesla/Viereck 1935).

Tesla on the cover of the Electrical Experimenter, *1917*

---

the scandal was never disclosed. He became permanent secretary of the American Academy of Arts and Letters, living thereafter on a reduced income. Tesla and Johnson settled into a pattern of borrowing small sums of money from each other to cover bank overdrafts from their respective little "financial fainting spells." The inventor and his friends continued to live as well as they could manage, which, in the case of the Johnsons, still included European holidays. Katharine often pleaded with Tesla to visit her. "I want to see if you have grown younger, more fashionable, more proud. But whatever you may be you will always find me the same" (K. Johnson n.d.).

He spent his usual Thanksgiving holiday with the Johnsons and teasingly asked her in his thank-you note not to despise millionaires, since he was about to become one. Tesla's optimism was inexplicable. She invited him again for Christmas, adding, "when I wrote you last Sunday morning I sent you my first thoughts out of sleep. I knew that you were depressed but did not know why. Please let me have a word dear Mr. Tesla that I may have something to count on, something to expect." Until her death, Katharine maintained her infatuation for Tesla. "I think I would be happier if I knew something about you," she wrote. "You, who are unconscious of everything but your work and who have no human needs."

Through the years, the Johnsons had confidently expected that their friend and favorite inventor would become a Nobel laureate, at least for the invention of radio. It had been a blow to them, therefore—as it had been to Tesla himself—when the 1909 Nobel

Tesla's technological contributions are not always fully appreciated, but he did receive a number of awards and recognitions during and after his lifetime. He held high offices in numerous engineering and scientific societies. In the 1890s, when Alexander Graham Bell served as president of the Institute of Electrical Engineers (now the IEEE), Tesla was vice president. Both men later received the highest award of that organization, the Edison Medal. The Franklin Institute awarded him the Elliot Cresson Gold Medal in 1894. He also received at least thirteen honorary academic degrees from universities in the United States and Europe, including Yale and Columbia, as well as universities in Paris, Vienna, Prague, Grenoble, and Belgrade.

Governments also recognized Tesla. He received the Order of St. Sava from Yugoslavia and the Order of the White Lion from the Czechoslovak government. In Strasbourg, France, his name is displayed with other great scientists including Einstein, Bohr, Rutherford, Plank, and Laplace at the Électricité de Strasbourg building. The City of Philadelphia awarded him the John

Scott Medal in 1934. In 1975 he was inducted into the National Inventors Hall of Fame.

A block of the "American Inventors" U.S. commemorative stamps was issued in 1983 for Steinmetz, Armstrong, Tesla, and Farnsworth. Today the IEEE, the National Rural Cooperative Electric Association, and the Tesla Memorial Society give annual awards in his name. But to Tesla, all the honors he received paled in significance to his American citizenship papers. These were always kept in a safe, he said, while all his orders, diplomas, degrees, gold medals, and other distinctions were packed away in old trunks.

Prize in physics went to Carl F. Braun of Germany and Guglielmo Marconi of Italy for their "separate but parallel development of the wireless telegraph." Tesla shrugged and went for a long walk, carrying breadcrumbs and grain for the pigeons of Manhattan, particularly those inhabiting Bryant Park behind the New York Public Library. He once said to a reporter, "These are my sincere friends." That location, which is also near a former office of Tesla's, now bears the street sign "Tesla Corner."

Then, for a change, came good news. On November 6, 1915, the *New York Times* announced that Nikola Tesla and Thomas Edison were to share the Nobel Prize in physics. The Johnsons and other friends rejoiced, but Tesla, who had mixed feelings, said he had received no official notice. Undoubtedly the idea of sharing the prize with Edison did not please him. He told the press, however, that the award might have been based on his discovery of a means of

transmitting energy without wires. The original item, based on a Reuters News Service dispatch from London, drew the comment from Edison that he, too, had had no official advice of the award. Rumors at once began to spread that the two old competitors had declined to share the prize.

Meanwhile the story appeared worldwide in leading journals and newspapers. All of this was very odd, because the Nobel Prize Foundation announced on November 14 that in fact the prize for physics had been conferred upon two English scientists, Professor William H. Bragg of the University of Leeds and his son, W. L. Bragg of Cambridge University, for their work in determining the structure of crystals. The Nobel Foundation described as "ridiculous" the idea that an award would be changed simply because a recipient did not wish to accept it. No further amplification was ever given.

It was not the last of Tesla's flirtations with the

THE NEW YO

TESLA'S DISCOVERY NOBEL PRIZE WINNER

Transmission of Electrical Energy Without Wires, Which Affects Present-Day Problems.

TO ILLUMINATE THE OCEAN

Scientist Says Collisions Will Be Avoided and Unlimited Water Drawn to Irrigate Deserts.

Nikola Tesla, who, with Thomas A. Edison is to share the Nobel Prize in Physics, according to a dispatch from London, said last evening that he had not yet been officially notified of the honor. His only information on the matter was the dispatch in THE NEW YORK TIMES.

"I have concluded," he said, "that the honor has been conferred upon me in acknowledgment of a discovery an-

"AMERIC

Joseph H. paredness
PITTSFIEI
H. Choate,
Britain, desc
one of the
tions in the
paredness a
chusetts brai
League tonig
ion that we
not for war
the close of
he said, a
desire to i
would have
diers availat
try would b
The Amer
inferior to
Nations in
and is lacki
the Army, s
quire half o
fend our for
he asserted,
Navy, as e
experts in
regarded by

FLED FR

She Was L
Shor
Women fle
the waiting

Above: Tesla in 1915, at age fifty-nine

Left: New York Times, *November 7, 1915*

Swedish medal and its big cash award. In recent years it has been learned that he was also nominated for an undivided Nobel Prize in physics in 1937. The nominator was Felix Ehernhaft of Vienna, who had nominated Albert Einstein for the prize in 1921. But the winners that year were Clinton J. Davisson of the United States and George P. Thomson of Great Britain for their discovery that subatomic particles, particularly electrons, might under certain circumstances act as waves rather than as material bodies. Tesla found a way to rationalize his loss.

> In a thousand years, there will be many recipients of the Nobel Prize, but I have not less than four dozens of my creations identified with my name in technical literature. These are honors real and permanent, which are bestowed, not by a few who are apt to err, but by the whole world which seldom makes a

mistake, and for any of these I would give all of the Nobel Prizes during the next thousand years (Tesla 1915b).

Tesla's life might have been more productive and the world richer had he actually received the Swedish award. His sisters, uncles, aunts, nieces, and nephews in Yugoslavia were extremely proud of him and wrote often with news of their increasingly extended and ambitious family. Usually regarded as the rich and famous uncle in America, he was often called upon to assist in family emergencies or to help young relatives with educational costs. Several members of the younger generation were named Nikola. Occasionally, however, it was the wealthy uncle who asked for help.

Tesla's finances became a matter of public record when the *New York Times* reported his bankruptcy on March 18, 1916:

Testimony given by Nikola Tesla, the electrical inventor, in a supplementary proceeding begun by the city to collect a judgment for $933 for personal taxes, was filed yesterday. ...Mr. Tesla said under oath that he was penniless, and had been living on credit. His home is the Waldorf.

Asked how he lived, he said, "Mostly on credit. I have a bill at the Waldorf that I have not paid for several years." To the question of whether there were other judgments against him, Tesla replied, "Scores of them." He testified that no one owed him money. Asked if he owned any jewelry, he said, "No sir; jewelry I abhor." All of his stock in the Nikola Tesla Company had been pledged since 1902, and his income at the time was just $350 to $400 a month. His company had started with two hundred patents, he said, but all except a few had expired or been lost for nonpayment of patent fees. The court appointed a receiver for his earnings.

Tesla's awkward situation began to weigh on those other members of his profession who still remembered him. For this reason, the prestigious American Institute of Electrical Engineers decided to nominate him for their highest award—the Edison Medal, of all things. When his colleague the distinguished engineer B. A. Behrend visited to give him the news, he flew into a fit of indignation. Any other engineer in the country would have been delighted to receive it, but Behrend understood the irony and injustice of the situation.

Behrend argued that the prestige of receiving the Edison Medal could help Tesla continue his work, but he refused to accept it. He urged Behrend to forget the whole matter, saying,

I appreciate your good will and your friendship, but I desire you to return to the committee and request it to make another selection. . . . It is nearly 30 years since I announced my rotating magnetic field and alternating-current system before the Institute.

I do not need its honors, and someone else may find it useful (O'Neill 1944, 232).

Behrend refused to give up, which brought a retort from Tesla so scathing that it seemed to express the injuries of decades:

You propose to honor me with a medal which I could pin upon my coat and strut for a vain hour before the members and guests of your Institute. You would decorate my body and continue to let it starve for failure to supply recognition of my mind and its creative products which have supplied the foundation upon which the major portion of your Institute exists. And when you would go through the vacuous pantomime of honoring Tesla you would not be honoring Tesla but Edison, who has previously shared unearned glory from every previous recipient of this medal.

Although Behrend's mission seemed hopeless, he continued to visit Tesla at his office on many occasions, always urging the importance of the medal for his work. Finally, after heroic efforts, Tesla agreed to accept. Plans were made for the presentation, and Behrend believed that the worst of his trials were over.

On the evening of May 18, 1917, a tall, dignified Tesla in white tie and tails attended the banquet at the Engineers Club, talking and joking charmingly through dinner. When it came time for the guests to cross the street to the auditorium of the United Engineering Societies building for formal addresses, however, the guest of honor went missing. Behrend and the committee fanned out in panic to search both buildings, the nearby sidewalks, and finally, on an inspiration, Bryant Park. There Behrend saw a small crowd gathered about a tall man in evening dress, his arms raised aloft like Saint Francis, in a smothering of pigeons. Tesla smiled at him, bade his sincere friends good evening, dusted his hands and coat with a silk handkerchief, and accompanied Behrend to the auditorium to be greeted by a standing ovation from the

Above: Bryant Park, behind the New York Public Library, where Tesla frequently fed the pigeons. (Collection of The New-York Historical Society)

Right: Nikola Tesla "blue" portrait by the Princess Vilma Lwoff-Parlaghy, first exhibited in March 1916 at a reception given at the Princess's studio in New York City. The portrait measures 48 by 53 inches and was intended to be shown under blue illumination. It was sold at auction on April 19, 1924, after the artist's death. The present owner is unknown.

anxious engineers. Behrend set the tone of the meeting:

> Were we to seize and eliminate from our industrial world the results of Mr. Tesla's work, the wheels of industry would cease to turn, our electric cars and trains would stop, our towns would be dark, our mills would be dead and idle.

W. W. Rice, Jr., president of the AIEE, reminded those present of Tesla's contribution to radio: "His work...antedated that of Marconi and formed the basis of wireless telegraphy...throughout all branches of science and engineering we find important evidence of what Tesla has contributed."

Finally, stepping to the podium, Tesla began his acceptance speech. Though it probably pained him, the guest of honor found words with which to paint the virtues of Thomas Edison (who did not attend the ceremony) as a man who had achieved wondrous

things despite little education. After a long and somewhat fantastic presentation during which he even described a machine that could change the weather, Tesla announced that his lifelong dream of wireless energy transmission had just become a reality.

"Recently," he said, "I have obtained a patent on a transmitter with which it is practicable to transfer unlimited amounts of energy to any distance. . . . To conclude, gentlemen, we are coming to great results" (Tesla 1917). Tesla kept his Edison Medal in his safe for the rest of his life, one of his most treasured possessions. After his death, it mysteriously disappeared and has never been recovered. ✒

CHAPTER THIRTEEN

War by Electrical Means

Tesla in 1916 pointing to the discharge in a photograph taken at Colorado Springs in 1899.

World War I was sparked by a bloody incident in Tesla's homeland—the assassination of Austrian Archduke Francis Ferdinand in Sarajevo by a Serbian nationalist named Gavrilo Prinzip. On December 20, 1914, Tesla published an article in the *New York Sun* titled "Nikola Tesla looks to Science to End the War." He postulated that war was a physical process whose duration could be determined by a simple mathematical equation. "War is essentially a manifestation of energy involving the acceleration and retardation of a mass by a force," he explained. "Translated into popular language this means that the period of duration of an armed conflict is theoretically proportionate to the magnitude of the armies or number of combatants." Tesla calculated that World War I would last five years. He also concluded that the duration of war could be reduced to zero with a weapon of sufficient magnitude.

As early as December 8, 1915, a *New York Times* story had reported his invention of a superweapon:

Nikola Tesla, inventor, winner of the 1915 Nobel Physics Prize [*sic*], has filed patent applications on the essential parts of a machine, the possibilities of which test a layman's imagination and promise a parallel of Thor's shooting thunderbolts from the sky to punish those who had angered the gods. Dr. Tesla insists there is nothing sensational about it, that it is but the fruition of many years of work and study. He is not yet ready to give the details of the engine which he says will render fruitless any military expedition against a country which possesses it. Ten thousand or a thousand miles would be all the same to the machine, said Tesla. A man in a tower on Long Island could shield New York against ships or army by working a lever, if the inventor's anticipations become realizations.

All of this was little consolation to the soldiers who were dying on the battlefields of Europe. Contrary to popular thinking, new technology was only adding to the savagery. Trench warfare with bayonets and rifles was made more lethal by the introduction of machine guns, poison gas, flame throwers, and a German artillery gun of

Tesla resided at the finest hotel in town, the Waldorf-Astoria, from 1900 to 1920. (Collection of The New-York Historical Society)

Tesla envisioned war in the future as a "mere contest" between machines. This concept was illustrated by Paul Frank and appeared in *Science and Invention*, February 1922. The caption read:

> War of the future as it will be conducted from the viewpoint of Dr. Tesla: Machines of destruction will be more terrible than anything concocted by the masterminds behind the "World War." Armies and navies will sail under the ocean and through the skies with not a man on board. According to Tesla, these death-dealing monsters of the sea and air will be controlled and directed from distant points hundreds or even thousands of miles away by radio waves of the proper sequence and frequency. The tower-like structures seen on the land in the accompanying picture are transmitting radio-electric power for operating and controlling the sea and air defense craft. . . . Man will be the mastermind behind the future war, but machines only will meet in mortal combat. It will be a veritable war of "Science."

incredibly long range known as "Big Bertha." A rumbling, lumbering land battleship called a tank, an idea first conceived during the Renaissance by Leonardo Da Vinci, was introduced. Its invention had been delayed mainly by the lack of propulsive power. Flimsy airplanes of the French and German forces quickly became both hero-makers and widow-makers, yet Americans joined up eagerly to fly them. It was the first war in which heroes were to be overwhelmed by brute mechanical force and technological innovation.

So opposed were Americans to entering World War I that General John Pershing's troops were vaguely and euphemistically described as an Expeditionary Force on a sort of exploration or excursion, beginning with an Atlantic cruise. Tesla had no illusions; he had been kept vividly aware of the slaughter in the First and Second Balkan Wars (1912–13) via letters from his family.

Electricity was having a profound effect on the conduct of warfare. "I have not thought it hazardous to predict," Tesla said, "that wars in the future will be waged by electrical means" (Tesla 1915c). Radio was one of the most important innovations. Troops could now communicate over longer distances, enlarging the scope and scale of battle. Telegraphy was an obvious advantage aboard naval vessels. The earliest on-board sets, based on Marconi's design, were limited in range to about sixty miles and operated on a single frequency, which made it extremely easy for an enemy to eavesdrop.

In this regard, the U.S. Navy had a secret weapon. Since 1912, Tesla had licensed his associate, Fritz Löwenstein, to supply the Navy with radio communication apparatus based on his fundamental radio patents. A five-kilowatt set was capable of sending messages as far as fifteen hundred miles. In addition, the transmitters contained a unique arrangement of circuits that permitted secret communications.

The German threat officially arrived in America in 1915. Dr. Heinrich F. Albert, the secret head of German propaganda in the United States, forgot his briefcase one afternoon on a New York elevated train. A U.S. Secret Service agent who had been tailing him grabbed the briefcase and made a hurried escape. Inside were found numerous documents marked "strictly private," which provided the details of an extensive network of German spies in the United States.

Before the war, a German firm had been licensed to use Tesla's wireless patents to build a radio station for the U.S. Naval Radio Service on Mystic Island near Tuckerton, New Jersey. The system far surpassed the single-channel transatlantic cable, since it was built to operate on several adjacent-frequency channels and to transmit in multiplex mode. Chief engineer Emil Mayer reported to Tesla that messages from the station were being received at a distance of

French army radio intercept station, 1918 (Courtesy National Archives)

nine thousand miles. For two years, Tesla received royalties of about $1,000 per month for these patents. But when war with Germany became inevitable, the Tuckerton Radio Station was closed by the government, for fear that submarines could use it as a navigational beacon.

On April 2, 1917, two weeks after German U-boats torpedoed three American ships suspected of carrying arms for the British, President Wilson persuaded Congress to declare war on Germany. The best minds in the country were assembled to help win the war with technology. Tesla rose to the occasion with an interview in the *Electrical Experimenter* in August 1917 titled "Tesla's Views on Electricity and the War." Here the inventor provided the first technical description of what would later be known as radar:

> The method of locating such hidden metal masses as submarines by an electric ray.... That is the thing that seems to hold great promise. If we can shoot out a concentrated ray comprising a stream of minute electric

THE ELECTRICAL EXPERIMENTER

H. GERNSBACK EDITOR
H. W. SECOR ASSOCIATE EDITOR

Vol. V. Whole No. 52   August, 1917   Number 4

Tesla's Views on Electricity and the War

By H. WINFIELD SECOR
Exclusive Interview to THE ELECTRICAL EXPERIMENTER

NIKOLA TESLA, one of the greatest of living electrical engineers and recipient of the seventh "Edison" medal, has evolved several unique and far-reaching ideas which if developed and practically applied should help to partially, if not totally, solve

interview and some of his ideas on electricity's possible rôle in helping to end the great world-war are herein given:

The all-absorbing topic of daily conversation at the present time is of course the "U-boat." Therefore, I made that subject my opening shot.

pacity of chief electrician for an electric plant situated on the river Seine, in France, I had occasion to require for certain testing purposes an extremely sensitive galvanometer. In those days the quartz fiber was an unknown quantity—and I, by becoming specially adept, managed to pro-

Nikola Tesla, the Famous Electric Inventor, Has Proposed Three Different Electrical Schemes for Locating Submerged Submarines. The Reflected Electric Ray Method is Illustrated Above; the High-Frequency Invisible Electric Ray, When Reflected by a Submarine Hull, Causes Phosphorescent Screens on Another or Even the Same Ship to Glow, Giving Warning That the U-boats Are Near.

the much discust submarine menace and to provide a means whereby the enemy's powder and shell magazines may be exploded at a distance of several miles.

There have been numerous stories bruited about by more or less irresponsible self-styled experts that certain American inventors, including Dr. Tesla, had invented among other things an *electric ray* to destroy or detect a submarine under water at a considerable distance. Mr. Tesla very courteously granted the writer an

"Well," said Dr. Tesla, "I have several distinct ideas regarding the subjugation of the submarine. But lest we forget, let us not underestimate the efficiency of the means available for carrying on submarine warfare. We may use microphones to detect the submarine, but on the other hand the submarine commander may employ microphones to locate a ship and even torpedo it by the range thus found, without ever showing his periscope above water.

"Many years ago while serving in the ca-

duce an extremely fine cocoon fiber for the galvanometer suspension. Further, the galvanometer proved very sensitive for the location in which it was to be used; so a special cement base was sunk in the ground and by using a lead sub-base suspended on springs all mechanical shock and vibration effects were finally gotten rid of.

"As a matter of actual personal experience," said Dr. Tesla, "it became a fact that the small iron-hull steam mail-packets (ships) plying up and down the river Seine

Article from the Electrical Experimenter, *August 1917, in which Tesla proposes three different electrical schemes for detecting submarines.*

charges vibrating electrically at tremendous frequency, say millions of cycles per second, then intercept this ray, after it has been reflected by a submarine hull for example, and cause this intercepted ray to illuminate a fluorescent screen (similar to the X-ray method) on the same or another ship, then our problem of locating the hidden submarine will have been solved.

Meanwhile Tesla's old nemesis, Thomas Edison, had gone to Washington as head of the Naval Consulting Board. His assignment was to develop new technology for the Navy, but he had no time for visionary dreamers like Tesla. "I don't look for electricity to play such an important part in this newer slaughter. It's going to be a struggle of explosives. That will be the all-important element" (Edison 1915).

It would take twenty more years for Tesla's concept of radar to be perfected. In 1934 Dr. Emile Girardeau led a French team that built rudimentary radar both on ships and ashore, "using precisely apparatuses conceived according to the principles stated by Tesla," said the Frenchman. The necessary technology had not been available earlier, "but one must also recognize how right he was" (Girardeau 1953). The prototype was officially credited to Robert A. Watson-Watt of England in 1935, who was the first to effectively visualize radio signals with a cathode ray tube.

On July 4, 1917, three months after America entered the war and while others celebrated Independence Day, Tesla's dream came literally crashing to the ground. Wardenclyffe Tower was blasted down with dynamite. Rumors had spread that spies were hiding there to radio information about shipping movements to German U-boats, an idea deeply offensive to Tesla. The salvage brought a profit of $1,750 to the new owner, who wished to develop the property commercially. A local junkman sadly recalled seeing the inventor's papers blowing down the street.

Edison poses with Secretary of the Navy Josephus Daniels. (Courtesy Smithsonian Institution)

Tesla tried to defend his tower and his reputation: On this occasion I would contradict the widely circulated report that the structure was demolished by the Government, which owing to war conditions, might have created prejudice in the minds of those who may not know that the papers, which thirty years ago conferred upon me the honor of American citizenship, are always kept in a safe. . . . On the contrary, it was in the interest of the Government to preserve it, particularly as it would have made possible—to mention just one valuable result—the location of a submarine in any part of the world (Tesla 1919e).

Now looked upon as a scientific outsider, Tesla depended on the popular press to continue to advance his concepts. The *Electrical Experimenter*, founded by science editor Hugo Gernsback, carried imaginative

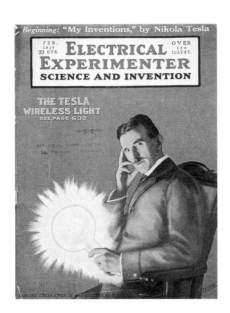

Above: The Electrical Experimenter, *February 1919, contained the first in a series of autobiographical articles by Tesla entitled, "My Inventions."*

Right: Nikola Tesla's conceptual aircraft design requiring no propeller or wings. Drawn by artist Frank Paul, it appeared in the Electrical Experimenter, *October 1919.*

drawings of Tesla's futuristic concepts, often illustrated by Frank Paul.

In 1919 Tesla introduced a completely unique idea to an unsuspecting world—the guided ballistic missile.

> I . . . am now planning aerial machines devoid of sustaining planes, ailerons, propellers and other external attachments, which will be capable of immense speeds and are very likely to furnish powerful arguments for peace in the near future. . . . By installing proper plants it will be practicable to project a missile of this kind into the air and drop it almost on the very spot designated, which may be thousands of miles away (Tesla 1919f).

Tesla had been working with remote-control devices since the turn of the century. While at Wardenclyffe, he demonstrated his robot boat to a delegation of Japanese, who were anticipating a naval war with the Russians. From a high cliff above the beach near the Shoreham Hotel, he had directed his tiny vessel out into Long Island Sound, closed a switch, and caused the boat to explode before the eyes of his amazed spectators. Oddly, when the Japanese offered to buy the device, Tesla refused to sell it to them (Steifel 1994).

Otis Pond, who was working with him during this period, recalled Tesla's worries about the instruments of war he was inventing. Tesla had just launched several model wireless torpedoes in the Sound, and caused them to circle a ship and return to shore. "Otis," he said, "sometimes I feel that I have not the right to do these things" (Duncan 1972).

But as with radar and so many of his ideas, Tesla's claims of destructive machines directed by radio waves were thought more the stuff of science fiction than a real possibility.

Critical to Tesla's concept of guided weapons was his system of "individualization," specified in patent number 723,188 granted in 1903, titled "Method of Signaling." Says author Leland Anderson,

> It became apparent that some means must be provided for secure control of remote devices in order to prevent interfering signals caused by natural effects, or the deliberate intervention from harmful sources. He would later refer to this as the art of individualization, a technique for producing a control signal that resulted from the conjoint action of two (or more) wireless AC signals (Anderson 1998, 131).

Most radio-controlled guidance systems today use Tesla's original concept

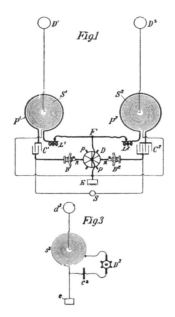

Diagram of sending apparatus and circuit connections for a secure method of signaling, from Tesla's U.S. patent number 723,188.

of conjoint action either by coincidence in time, frequency, or a combination of both. "Thus," says Anderson, "we find that Tesla was the father of both the guided weapon and secure remote-control technology on which the former is critically dependent in effective deployment."

Various patent interference cases and government secrecy over the years have added to the difficulty of pointing to a single inventor of the guided weapon. But one of the great radio pioneers, Edwin H. Armstrong, came down heavily on the side of Tesla. He wrote, "there was much research underway toward [developing] the Tesla concept of the guided weapon in various laboratories. . . . So far as I know, the credit for the concept rests entirely with him" (Armstrong 1953).

Though rejected in the United States, Tesla's ideas for electronic warfare—specifically, beam weapons—were looked upon with interest in both Germany and Russia. Tesla wrote,

> As throwing light on this point, I may mention that only recently an odd looking gentleman called on me with the object of enlisting my services in the construction of world transmitters in some distant land. "We have no money," he said, "but carloads of solid gold and we will give you a liberal amount." I told him that I wanted to see first what will be done with my inventions in America, and this ended the interview. But I am satisfied that some dark forces are at work (Tesla 1919f).

On another occasion he wrote,

> Lenin made me twice in succession very tempting offers to come to Russia but I could not tear myself away from my laboratory work (Tesla 1934a).

Following the signing of the peace treaty at Versailles in 1919, Tesla predicted,

> A few years hence it will be possible for nations to fight without armies, ships, or guns, by weapons far more terrible, to the destructive action and range of which there is virtually no limit. Any city, at a distance whatsoever from the enemy, can be destroyed by him and no power on earth can stop him from doing so. If we want to avert an impending calamity and a state of things which may transform this globe into an inferno, we should push the development of flying machines and wireless transmission of energy without an instant's delay and with all the power and resources of the nation (Tesla 1919f).

CHAPTER FOURTEEN

Poet and Visionary

Tesla's system of transmission of power to aircraft by radio.
Illustrated by Frank Paul for Radio News, *December 1925.*

NIKOLA TESLA . . . WAS SO FAR AHEAD OF HIS TIME THAT THE BEST OF US THEN TOOK HIM FOR A DREAMER. —JOHN STONE STONE

*I*n 1922, at sixty-five years of age, Tesla was tall, erect, and ascetic-looking. He continued to dress impeccably, buying his frock coats from Ketzel Tailors, at 2 East 44th Street, and his shoes from French, Shriner, and Urner at 250 Madison Avenue. Yet friends observed that his clothing, like his scientific theories, now appeared old-fashioned.

Police showed up at his office one afternoon to impound his office furniture. In a cool, debonair manner he managed to talk them out of it. There came a time when he had no money to pay his secretaries. He offered to cut his gold Edison Medal and give half to each. Miss Skerritt and Miss Arbus, loyal to the very end, did not accept.

No longer able to count on the money, credit, or patronage of John Jacob Astor, Tesla abandoned the Waldorf-Astoria, his home for more than twenty years, and took up residence in another luxury suite at the Hotel St. Regis. He began to visit the local parks more often, rescuing injured pigeons and taking them back to his hotel room. His favorites were still the birds of Bryant Park behind the Public Library. He built nests for them on his hotel window ledge, and even

Tesla's favorite "white dove"

created a tiny pigeon shower in his room. If he was unable to resuscitate an injured pigeon or to splint a broken leg, he would take the bird to a veterinarian. One white pigeon in particular was always able to find him, no matter how high the room or which towering hotel offered Tesla refuge in the vast city. Tesla claimed to enjoy a total communication with that remarkable bird (O'Neill 1944, 317–18).

Paradoxically, his increasing intimacy with pigeons coincided with a deepening of his lifelong obsessive fear of germs and microbes. He began to wash his hands more frequently and had all of his food boiled to kill bacteria. But in spite of his growing eccentricity, fruitful ideas continued to spring from his imagination. One was reported by the *Albany Telegram* on February 25, 1923: "A Giant Eye to See Round the World":

Think of it, a great mechanical eye, created of finest tempered steel, endowed with electric power and seeing to all parts of the earth! Science, in the person of Nikola Tesla announces it as a realized achievement. He lives on one of the top floors of the St. Regis, one of New York's most

Portrait photograph of Nikola Tesla in 1920 at age sixty-four

As early as 1899 in *Pearson's Magazine,* Tesla described an idea for visual telegraphy:

> One person has only to look into the receiver of an ordinary telephone in one city, and, while talking to a friend a thousand miles away, he can watch the expression on the other's face, criticize the cut of his new suit of clothing, or advise him what to do for that tired look about the eyes.

The first U.S. communications satellite was NASA's *Echo I,* a passive reflector of radio signals, followed in 1963 by the first instrumented synchronous-orbit communications satellite launched by the United States. Something of this sort had been in Tesla's mind even as a teenager, when he envisioned building a ring around the equator to revolve in synchrony with earth.

His love of pigeons resulted in Tesla's eviction from the Hotel St. Regis when the management cited concerns about sanitation. Of course, there was also the issue of back rent. Forced to move from hotel to hotel, he would often leave trunks of documents behind as security for his debts. These trunks were highly sought after following Tesla's death.

For relaxation and amusement, the inventor would often attend the movies at one of the many theaters on Times Square. He particularly enjoyed cowboy pictures, claiming that he had some of his best ideas while watching them.

Members of his large family in Yugoslavia continued to write from time to time, describing their financial needs, but he was unable to reply. Visited by his nephew Sava Kosanović in 1926, Tesla told him, "The rich financiers ask me to work with them, but I do not want to. I do not want to work with others' capital or money and be dependent" (Kosanović 1926). Kosanović would eventually play an important role in Tesla's legacy. The inventor, approaching seventy years of age, sometimes wrote to another nephew and successful inventor in Detroit, Nikola

exclusive hotels. There he has his workrooms, mysterious places never visited by outsiders. There the eye machine rests, waiting for the day, soon to come, when Tesla asserts he will vivify it and turn it over to his fellow-men for operation.

"My mechanical eye will be one of a group of associated machines," Tesla said. "The eye will teach Man to understand Man."

Tesla did not invent either television or space communications satellites, but his description of both predated their invention by many years. In the *New York Times* in 1915 he claimed,

> Some day there will be, say, six great wireless telephone stations in the world system connecting all the inhabitants of this earth to one another, not only by voice but by sight.

Tesla was ahead of his contemporaries when it came to invention, but his attitudes toward women were definitely not advanced. When asked why he had never taken a wife, he gave the following explanation:

> I had always thought of woman as possessing those delicate qualities of mind and soul that made her in these respects far superior to man. . . . Now the soft-voiced gentle woman of my reverent worship has all but vanished. In her place has come the woman who thinks that her chief success in life lies in making herself as much as possible like man—in dress, voice, and actions. . . . The world has experienced many tragedies, but to my mind the greatest tragedy of all is the present economic condition wherein women strive against men, and in many cases actually succeed in usurping their places in the professions and in industry. This growing tendency of women to overshadow the masculine is a sign of a deteriorating civilization. Perhaps the male in human society is useless. If women are beginning to feel this way about it—and there is striking evidence at hand that they do—then we are entering upon the cruelest period of the world's history. Our civilization will sink to a state like that which is found among the bees, ants, and other insects—a state wherein the male is ruthlessly killed off. In this matriarchal empire which will be established the female rules. As the female predominates, the males are at her mercy. The male is considered important only as a factor in the general scheme of the continuity of life (Tesla 1924).

With an attitude like this it is no surprise that Tesla never married.

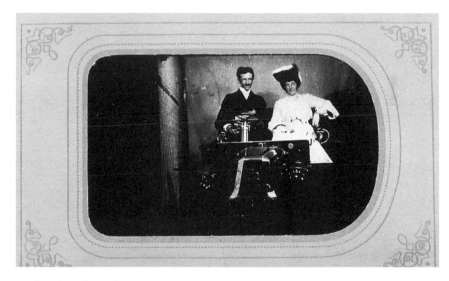

Tesla with unidentified woman

Trbojevich, to ask for needed funds. Trbojevich invited him to come and share his family's home: he had just moved into a large house on Edison Street, which prompted Tesla to decline.

His secluded life in the late 1920s and '30s led to the usual speculation about reclusive geniuses who dared to think improbable thoughts while strolling in public places. For several years, he kept suites at two luxury hotels—the Hotel Marguery on Park Avenue and the Hotel Pennsylvania near Pennsylvania Station—both apparently well out of his budget range. There were continuing rumors that he was homosexual, based on his solitary life and the unusual ideas he held about women. Predictably, there was also talk about secret labs and experiments.

At times Tesla's attitude toward women could be cruel. At least one secretary was fired for being overweight and clumsy. Another was sent home in disgrace for wearing a dress of which he did not approve. Some of his acquaintances rationalized that by eliminating the human female from prominence in his own life, his natural feelings of love and romance were sublimated into the dovecote. While other inventors seemed to worship gold, this gnostic St.

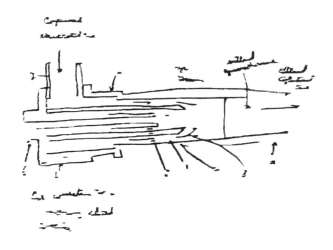

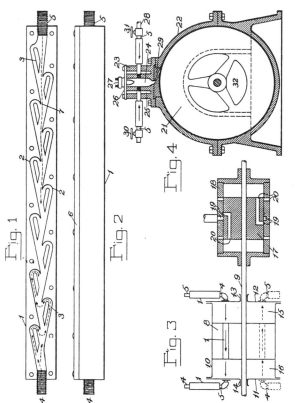

N. TESLA.
VALVULAR CONDUIT.
APPLICATION FILED FEB. 21, 1916. RENEWED JULY 8, 1919.

1,329,559. Patented Feb. 3, 1920.

Above: Tesla's drawing of his open-ended vacuum tube

Left: Patent drawing of Tesla's valvular conduit. The interior contains baffles that offer no resistance to fluid in one direction, but prevent it from flowing back. This one-way fluidic valve became a critical element in Tesla's design for an open-ended vacuum tube—with which such things as his ionized beam weapon (modern ones, too) become at least conceivable.

Francis remained devoted to the cheerful feathered outcasts of great cities.

Despite his eccentricities and vagaries, his inventive mind never flagged. Early in the 1920s Tesla applied for a set of patents with a broad range of applications. One, titled "Improvements in Methods of and Apparatus for the Production of High Vacua," contained a perfected design for a unique open-ended vacuum tube with a continuous blast of air at the tip to maintain the vacuum, and a special kind of valvular conduit "for the obtainment of vacua exceeding many times the highest heretofore realized. I think that as much as one-billionth of a micron can be attained" (Tesla 1937a).

Of his new tube Tesla said,

It is of ideal simplicity, not subject to wear and can be operated at any potential, however high, that can be produced. It will carry heavy currents, transform any amount of energy within practical limits, and it permits easy control and regulation of the same. I expect that this invention, when it becomes known, will be universally adopted in preference to other forms of tubes, and it will be the means of obtaining results undreamed of before.

This open-ended vacuum tube and its unique system of evacuation, known today as differential pumping, are believed to be the fundamental technology employed in what would later be called Tesla's "death beam." He never processed these patents to completion.

The arrival of Prohibition was a decided imposition on the inventor, who enjoyed a daily glass of warming whiskey for "medicinal" purposes. When Prohibition went into effect, he claimed it would shorten his life by several decades. His loyal associate, George Scherff, still dropped in to help with his accounts and provided him small loans when necessary. Scherff's wife complained bitterly that her husband had loaned Mr. Tesla more than forty thousand dollars, and according to Tesla's secretary, Dorothy Skerritt, "Tesla seemed to have Mr. Scherff hypnotized" (Skerritt 1955).

During the 1920s, Tesla began to develop a deep friendship with the German poet George Sylvester Viereck, the precocious son of an illegitimate offspring of the German House of Hohenzollern. Though nearly a recluse, Tesla occasionally attended dinner parties held by Viereck and his wife. Chicago lawyer and author Elmer Gertz attended one and gives a remarkable description. In attendance were the artist Leon Dabo, "who knew just about everyone . . . including Whistler"; a publisher; a columnist; another poet, Edgar Lee Masters; and the Vierecks. While they were talking, recalls Gertz,

> An apparition [Tesla] seemed to come into the room. . . . He walked so softly and he struck us as an almost unearthly creature. He spoke with a very low voice that seemed to suggest profundities even when ordinary things were being said. I remember . . . that he mentioned that he had met Sarah Bernhardt and she had given him a handkerchief, under what circumstances I do not recall, but he so treasured it he never washed it, never let it out of his possession, it was one of his priceless possessions. . . . He knew the entire body of Goethe's poetry by heart, all of Viereck's. . . . And he talked of birds, pigeons, and ESP, all sorts of what seemed to me at the time unreal things, more in the nature of psychic rather than scientific.

German poet George Sylvester Viereck in 1922 (Courtesy Library of Congress)

> He spoke at considerable length, a monologue . . . because no one wanted to interrupt him, what he said was so fascinating (interview with the authors, 1993).

Meanwhile, a new scientific star was beginning to rise. Like Tesla in an earlier time, Albert Einstein and his theory of relativity had captured the imagination of scientists and the public. Tesla was annoyed by the direction modern science was taking. He felt that the submicroscopic world of quanta clashed absurdly with the real and classical laws of Newton. Where was reality? "Today's scientists," said Tesla, "have substituted mathematics for experiments. They wander off through equation after equation and eventually build a structure which has no relation to reality" (Tesla 1934b).

In Tesla's day, mystical thought was not far removed from science. The medium of electricity was thought to possess mystical properties. Sir William Crookes, head of the Royal Society for Psychic Research, used a Tesla coil to help manifest poltergeists at séances. Tesla flatly rejected mystics but he often spoke like one:

> Have you ever abandoned yourself to the raptures of the contemplation of a world you yourself create? You want a palace and there it stands, built by architects finer than Michelangelo. All this world, real or imaginary, it matters little, you want to be able to see through some such thing as a wire, for if you succeed in transmitting sight you will see it all" (Tesla 1896c).

As a result of his acquaintance with Swami Vivikenanda he began to incorporate the terminology of Eastern philosophies into his writings:

> There manifests itself in the fully developed being, Man, a desire…to imitate nature, to create, to work himself the wonders he perceives.... Long ago he recognized that a perceptible matter comes from a primary substance, of tenuity beyond conception, filling all space—the Akasa or luminiferous ether—which is acted upon by the life-giving Prana or creative force, calling into existence, in never ending cycles all things and phenomena" (Tesla 1930).

Tesla's conviction that the universe possessed a deeper wave-like nature is held by many physicists today.

Illustration from the Kansas City Journal-Post, *September 10, 1933*

On the subject of nuclear energy, Tesla was in error. "I consider myself the original discoverer of this truth," he said, "which can be expressed by the statement: There is no energy in matter other than that received from the environment." To end the confusion created by the "relativists," he promised he would soon make public his "dynamic theory of gravity," which would explain these observations and "put an end to idle speculation and false conceptions, as that of curved space." A paper he wrote elucidating this theory never appeared and it was speculated that Tesla was losing his grasp.

As the particle revolution in science accelerated, Tesla slipped more and more into obscurity. He began to dwell on his own immortality, a concern that figured in his only poem, titled "Fragments of Olympian Gossip."

> While listening on my cosmic phone
> I caught words from the Olympus blown.
> A newcomer was shown around;
> That much I could guess, aided by sound.
> "There's Archimedes with his lever
> Still busy on problems as ever.
> Below, on Earth, they work at full blast
> And news are coming in thick and fast.
> The latest tells of a cosmic gun.
> To be pelted is very poor fun.
> We are wary with so much at stake,
> Those beggars are a pest—no mistake.
> Too bad, Sir Isaac, they dimmed your renown

And turned your great science upside down.
Now a long haired crank, Einstein by name,
Puts on your high teaching all the blame.
Says: matter and force are transmutable
And wrong the laws you thought immutable."
"I am much too ignorant, my son,
For grasping schemes so finely spun.
My followers are of stronger mind
And I am content to stay behind,
Perhaps I failed, but I did my best,
These masters of mine may do the rest.
Come, Kelvin, I have finished my cup.
When is your friend Tesla coming up?"
"Oh, quoth Kelvin, he is always late,
It would be useless to remonstrate."
Then silence—shuffle of soft slippered feet—
I knock and—the bedlam of the street.

NIKOLA TESLA, Novice

(Tesla 1934c)

Despite his Olympian fancies, however, Tesla's business was still not finished with the U.S. Patent Office. In 1928, at the age of seventy-two, he received his last patent, number 6,555,114, "Apparatus for Aerial Transportation." Like those that had come before, this concept was unique—a brilliantly designed flying machine that resembled both a helicopter and an airplane. According to Tesla, the device would weigh eight hundred pounds. Driven by one of his gasoline turbines, it would rise from a garage, a roof, or a window as desired, and would sell at one thousand dollars for both military and consumer uses.

Once in the air, the helicopter blade pitched forward to become a propeller and the pilot's seat swiveled to remain upright while the wings were moved horizontally. It was a novel departure, the progenitor of today's tiltrotor or VSTOL (vertical short takeoff and landing) plane. It may be the only one of his inventions for which, lacking money and a laboratory, he was unable to build a prototype.

And, as with all his inventions, Tesla was certain

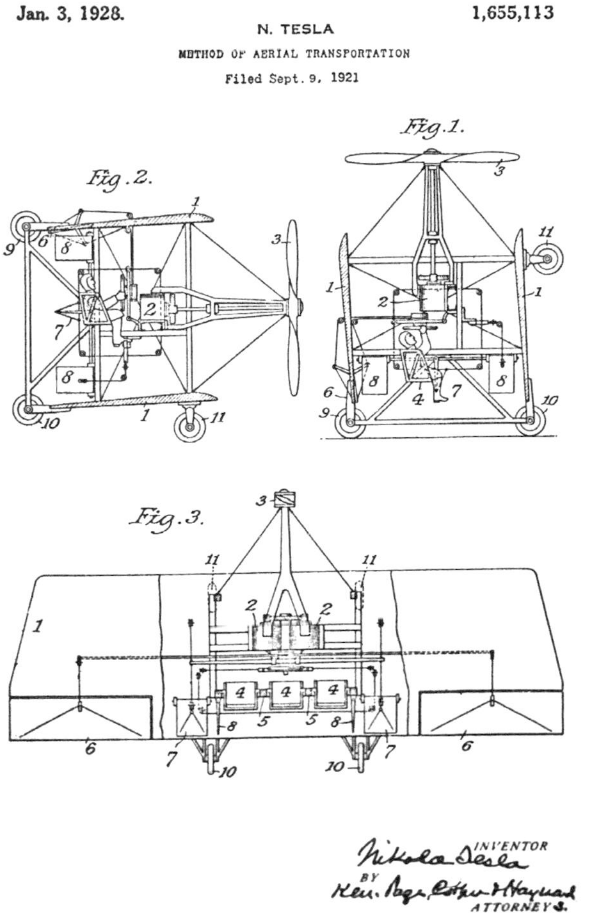

Drawing from U.S. patent number 6,555,114, Tesla's "flying flivver."

of his flying machine's success. "You should not be at all surprised," Tesla wrote, "if some day you see me fly from New York to Colorado Springs in a contrivance which will resemble a gas stove and weigh almost as much" (Tesla 1913).

He even considered flying home to Yugoslavia.

CHAPTER FIFTEEN

A Weapon to End War

Tesla converses with an unidentified newspaper reporter after one of his annual "birthday party" press conferences.

IF MR. TESLA REALLY FULFILLS HIS PROMISE, THE RESULT ACHIEVED

WOULD BE TRULY STAGGERING . . . THE AUTHORITIES IN CHARGE OF

BUILDING THE NATIONAL DEFENSE SHOULD AT ONCE LOOK INTO THE

MATTER. —WILLIAM L. LAURENCE

*I*n 1931 Kenneth Swezey, a young science writer who had befriended Tesla, organized a seventy-fifth birthday party for the inventor. Letters of congratulation came from scientists and dignitaries around the world: Sir Oliver Lodge, Ernst Frederik Werner Alexanderson, Lee De Forest, John Hays Hammond, Jr., Robert Andrews Millikan, Secretary of Commerce Robert Patterson Lamond, Henry Herman Westinghouse. Even Albert Einstein sent greetings:

> Very glad indeed to learn that you celebrated your 75th birthday and that as a successful pioneer in the field of high frequency current you were able to experience the marvelous technical development in that field. I congratulate you for your great success in your lifetime task (Einstein 1931).

The "Blue Portrait" of Tesla, painted fifteen years earlier by the Princess Vilma Lwoff-Parlaghy of Hungary, appeared on the cover of *Time* magazine. Delighted by the attention, Tesla announced to reporters at a press conference that he was on the verge of discovering an entirely new source of energy. Asked to explain the nature of the power, Tesla replied, "The idea first came upon me as a tremendous shock....I can only say at this time that it will come from an entirely new and unsuspected source."

"When do you expect to make the official announcement of your new discoveries?" he was asked. He replied,

These discoveries did not come to me

overnight, but as the result of intense study and experimentation for nearly 36 years. I am naturally anxious to give the facts to the world as soon as possible, but I also wish to present them in finished form. That may take a few months or a few years (Tesla 1931a).

It was difficult to discern how the inventor could

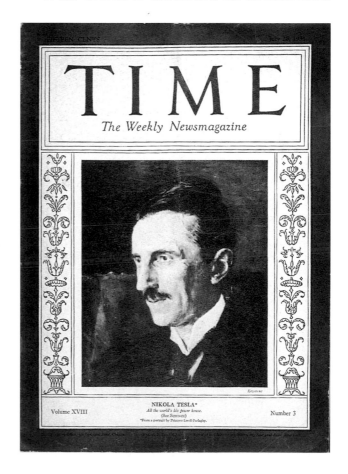

Time *magazine cover commemorating Tesla's seventy-fifth birthday, July 20, 1931. (Courtesy Time Life Syndication)*

Four candid photos taken of Tesla at a press conference at the Hotel New Yorker July 10, 1935, his seventy-ninth birthday.

accomplish this task. He now functioned without office or laboratory, working from his apartment in the Hotel Governor Clinton. He had no visible source of income; the wealthy patrons he had depended on were either dead or questioning his mental health. Yet every year, on his birthday, he continued to make extraordinary announcements about his most recent discoveries and inventions.

In 1932 he announced a new motor that would operate on cosmic rays. "I have harnessed the cosmic rays and caused them to operate a motive device," he stated. "I have hope of building my motor on a large scale" (O'Neill 1932). Asked if the introduction of his principle would upset the present economic system, Tesla replied, "It is badly upset already" (Tesla 1933).

During this period, there was a rumor that Tesla, along with another radio pioneer, Lee De Forest, had tested this cosmic ray motor in a 1933 Pierce Arrow

in a rural part of New Jersey. The story is probably apocryphal, but fantastic tales about Tesla's activities in this period persist. (One concerns a project involving Einstein and Tesla in the creation of an antigravity device; another, a means of making ships and planes invisible.) Tesla knew that a little hyperbole in the press could have a positive effect, so it is possible that he had something to do with the rumors. But rather than building his credibility, these fantastic stories and tales of uncovering the veritable secrets of nature only damaged it. Even when his ideas had substance, he had cried "wolf" too often and his audience had become skeptical.

War clouds were again darkening Europe. In 1934, during a state visit to Marseilles, France, Alexander, the Serbian king of Yugoslavia, was assassinated in a plot hatched by Croatian nationalists. Concerned about a violent breakup of the Kingdom of Yugoslavia, Tesla wrote a passionate letter to the *New York Times* on October 21, 1934, expressing a sentiment that is still appropriate today:

Much has been said about Yugoslavia and its people, but many Americans may be under a wrong impression, for political enemies and agitators have spread the idea that its inhabitants belong to different nations animated by mutual hate and held together against their will by a tyrannical power. The fact is that all Yugoslavs—Serbians, Slovenians, Bosnians, Herzegovinians, Dalmatians, Montenegrins, Croatians and Slovenes—are of the same race, speak the same language and have common national ideals and traditions.

The Balkan Peninsula is situated directly between Europe and Asia Minor. This area's long and turbulent history has caused confusion about Tesla's nationality. Both Serbs and Croats take pride in Tesla. Ethnically a Serb, he is so important to the Serbian people that his image appears on their currency. But he was born in the area that today is called Croatia, though its borders have changed many times over the years.

Croats were for centuries a part of the Austrian Empire, while Serbs formed the independent kingdom of Serbia. In the fourteenth century the Serbs were overrun by the Ottoman Turks. As a consequence many Serbs fled to Bosnia and across the border to Austria to escape Turkish oppression. A son of a Serbian Orthodox priest, Tesla was born in the border region of Lika, in a small village called Smiljan, a subject of the Austro-Hungarian Empire. There Serbs lived together with Croats in relative harmony.

Toward the end of the nineteenth century Serbs in Croatia and Bosnia began to embrace the idea of uniting Slavic peoples into a common state. The word "Yugoslavia" means "the land of Southern Slavs." Many Croats feared they would be incorporated into a "Greater Serbia." Nationalist fervor boiled over in 1914 when Archduke Ferdinand of Austria was assassinated in Sarajevo by a young Serbian named Gavrilo Princip. The First World War began shortly thereafter, and the Serbs and the Croats were drawn into it along with the major world powers.

Following Austria-Hungary's defeat in World War I, Croatia and other Balkan states agreed to join with Serbia to create a new state called the

Tesla's birthplace and church destroyed by Croatian Ustashe during World War II.

Kingdom of Serbs, Croats, and Slovenes, which was changed to the Kingdom of Yugoslavia in 1929.

Tesla's homeland was then officially called Yugoslavia. The inventor adhered to the Yugoslav ideal, believing that unity among Slavs could bring peace and stability to the region. But peace was short-lived. On April 6, 1941, Hitler attacked Yugoslavia and basically destroyed it. In Croatia and Bosnia-Herzegovina, Germany established a fascist "Independent State of Croatia" and set up a puppet government. The new state's borders included Tesla's birthplace in Lika.

The Croatian Nazi movement, the *Ustashe*, systematically persecuted the Serbs in this territory. During this time the house where Tesla was born and his father's church next to it were destroyed. Soon after World War II, Communists gained control of Yugoslavia. The territory of Lika remained within the Republic of Croatia, one of the constitutional republics of the new Socialist Federal

Republic of Yugoslavia. During the period in which Josip Broz Tito was in power, Yugoslavia was relatively prosperous. Following his death, however, economic problems aggravated ethnic and religious differences and Yugoslavia began to disintegrate. In 1992 bloody civil war pitting Serbs against Croats and Moslems broke out in Croatia and Bosnia.

The long-standing conflict in the Balkans was painfully familiar to Tesla. His early experience with complex national, religious, and political clashes led him to seek a means to eliminate warfare from modern civilization. He concluded:

When all darkness is dissipated by the light of science, when all nations shall be merged into one, and patriotism shall be identical with religion, when there shall be one language, one country, one end, the dream will have become reality (Tesla 1900a).

Postcard illustration of the Hotel New Yorker, New York City.
(Collection of The New-York Historical Society)

TESLA AT 78 BARES NEW DEATH-BEAM

Invention Powerful Enough to Destroy 10,000 Planes 250 Miles Away, He Asserts.

DEFENSIVE WEAPON ONLY

Scientist, in Interview, Tells of Apparatus That He Says Will Kill Without Trace.

Nikola Tesla, father of modern methods of generation and distribution of electrical energy, who was 78 years old yesterday, announced a new invention, or inventions, which he said he considered the

Times' Wide World Photo.
NOTED INVENTOR 78.
Nikola Tesla.

Tesla announced his new beam weapon in numerous newspaper interviews on his seventy-eighth birthday. This article is from the New York Times, July 11, 1934.

In 1934 Tesla moved to his final residence, room 3327 (still divisible by three) of the recently completed Hotel New Yorker. There he lived alone with his ideas and his pigeons for the next decade. He posted a typewritten note on the door: "Please Do Not Disturb The Occupant Of This Room." In Tesla's mind, it was time to reveal his greatest invention: a perfect and impossible idea, a weapon to prevent World War II.

On July 11, 1934, the headline on the front page of the *New York Times* screamed, "TESLA AT 78 BARES NEW DEATH-BEAM." The invention, the article reported,

> will send concentrated beams of particles through the free air, of such tremendous energy that they will bring down a fleet of 10,000 enemy airplanes at a distance of 250 miles from a defending nation's border and will cause armies of millions to drop dead in their tracks.

When put in operation, Dr. Tesla said, this latest invention of his would make war impossible. This death-beam, he asserted, would surround each country like an invisible Chinese wall, only a million times more impenetrable. It would make every nation impregnable against attack by airplanes or by large invading armies.

The idea generated considerable interest. Tesla went immediately to J. P. Morgan, Jr., in search of financing to build a prototype of his invention. He told Morgan,

> The flying machine has completely demoralized the world, so much that in some cities, as London and Paris, people are in mortal fear for aerial bombing. The new means I have perfected afford absolute protection against this and other forms of attack. . . . One of the most pressing problems seems to be the protection of London and I am writing to some influen-

tial friends in England hoping that my plan will be adopted without delay. The Russians are very anxious to render their borders safe against Japanese invasion and I have made them a proposal which is being seriously considered (Tesla 1934a).

Tesla reminded the younger Morgan that not only war, but the future of capitalism was at stake. The financier apparently did not feel sufficiently threatened to invest.

Later, Tesla also attempted to deal directly with Prime Minister Neville Chamberlain of Great Britain. For $3,000,000 he offered to provide the British War Office with an electric beam weapon that would sweep the sky and provide complete protection of the British Isles by sea or air—all this to be accomplished within three months. But Chamberlain resigned upon discovering that he had been outmaneuvered by Hitler at Munich, and to Tesla's great disappointment, interest in his weapon collapsed (O'Neil n.d.).

Reports began to circulate that Tesla intended to sell his beam weapon to the League of Nations in Geneva. This was cause for concern at the U.S. State Department.

> If such a report is founded on scientific fact and if Tesla should give the secret to Geneva, it would be in the hands of half a dozen governments in Europe and they would be using the beam instead of guns to fight one another. If the United States Government should obtain control of it, no other government would obtain it and the American Government could act as a guardian (Long 1934).

During this period, Tesla claimed that attempts were made to break into his hotel room and steal his papers. But the thieves were disappointed, he said, because he kept all of his important ideas inside his head.

Just prior to World War II a number of other inventors and scientists were also interested in the

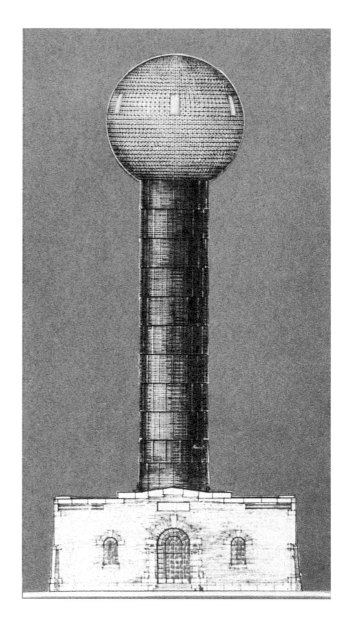

Architectural drawing by Titus deBobula shows Tesla's high potential terminal and powerhouse. This illustration was included with his beam weapon proposal.

"death beam." Marconi was reported to be working on a war ray. He claimed that when perfected, his ray would be able to stop airplanes and other motors many miles before invading forces could reach their goals. Tesla quickly pointed out the difference between the two systems:

> I want to state explicitly that this invention of mine does not contemplate the use of any so-

Tesla's great ambition was to discover a virtually inexhaustible source of energy and an inexpensive way to send it around the earth. With this larger idea in mind he had conceived AC power systems, then radio, and finally a directed beam of charged particles.

In the mid-1930s he laid out this preliminary design for accelerating microscopic flecks of mercury or tungsten to incredible velocities. He preferred that his beam be composed of a long train of single particles in order to minimize any scattering due to collisions within the beam. Electrostatic repulsion—of like charges—would impart the necessary energy: from the center of a highly charged sphere, grain-sized projectiles would be squeezed toward an opening and fly outward with a slingshot force of several million volts.

What sets Tesla's proposal apart from the usual run of fantasy "death rays"—besides the obvious fact that he could actually construct megavoltage apparatus—is a unique vacuum chamber open without obstruction to the atmosphere. A vacuum must be held in the interior to sustain high voltages, yet a particle stream would puncture any kind of container shell as it escaped. To meet these tricky conditions, Tesla devised a unique one-way barrier by directing a high-velocity air stream past the tip of his gun to maintain "high vacua." The necessary pumping action was accomplished with a large Tesla turbine.

Some details of the design remain problematic, if not altogether unworkable. There is, for example, the problem of how to get the particles into the gun. But in supplying an electromagnetic "propellant" for his cannon and the revolutionary open-end vacuum, Tesla substantively anticipated researches into various modern "Star Wars" weaponry. His attempt at Wardenclyffe to prepare the beam path with an ultraviolet "leader" also prefigures certain ion beam designs. As happened frequently during the inventor's career, technological means were not up to the challenges of his imagination (Tesla n.d.).

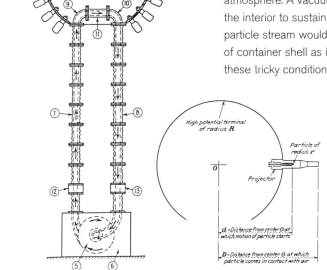

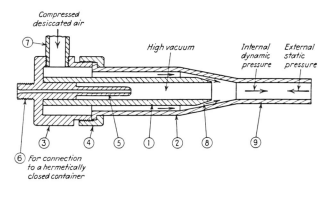

called "death rays." Rays are not applicable because they cannot be produced in requisite quantities and diminish rapidly in intensity with distance. All the energy of New York City (approximately two million horsepower) transformed into rays and projected twenty miles, could not kill a human being (Tesla and Viereck 1935).

So appealing was the prospect of the beam weapon that when radar was first presented to Her Britannic Majesty's General Staff, its members were disappointed to learn that it could only indicate location. They had hoped it would disable the engines of planes (de Arcangelis 1985, 214). It was recently discovered in Albert Einstein's FBI records that even he was working on a beam weapon device in the 1930s.

By 1937 war had again become inevitable. Tesla was made aware of the Nazis' intentions through Viereck and his own family in Yugoslavia. Frustrated in his attempts to generate interest and financing for his "peace beam," he sent an elaborate technical paper, including diagrams, to a number of Allied nations, including the United States, Canada, England, France, the Soviet Union, and Yugoslavia. Titled "New Art of Projecting Concentrated Non-Dispersive Energy Through Natural Media," the paper provided the first technical description of what is today called a charged-particle beam weapon.

Joseph Butler, a U.S. Air Force expert on beam weapons, has said of Tesla's idea, "Definitely, he had the concept of a charged particle beam weapon back in the 1930s. The concept was right on the mark . . . particles projected out long distances to do damage to some enemy airplanes, in his particular case." But Butler added, "I haven't a clue how he meant to actually do it" (interview with the authors, 1998).

Of all the countries to receive Tesla's proposal, the greatest interest came from the Soviet Union. In 1937 Tesla presented a plan to the Amtorg Trading Corporation, an alleged Soviet arms front in New York City. Two years later, in 1939, one stage of the plan was tested in the USSR and Tesla received a check for $25,000, not a small sum in those days. During this period he also received some payments through Yugoslavian Ambassador Konstantin Fotić for information relating to a system for national defense. A Tesla Institute was created in Belgrade, which provided him with a yearly honorarium of $7,200.

One evening in 1937 the eighty-one-year-old inventor left the Hotel New Yorker around midnight and headed toward the Public Library to feed his pigeons. Suddenly, while crossing the street, he was hit by a taxicab and knocked to the ground. For a while he lay motionless on the pavement. Then, refusing assistance, he made his way to his feet and

Tesla in his hotel room in the late 1930s. After his accident, he walked with a cane.

slowly returned to his hotel room. On arriving, his first act was to telephone Western Union to try to hire a messenger to finish his rounds feeding the pigeons. He collapsed on his bed. "It merely caused the customary bruises and upset the digestion a bit," he later commented. Other sources reported that the inventor had suffered three broken ribs. ⤴

CHAPTER SIXTEEN

Enigmatic to the End

Tesla meets King Peter II of Yugoslavia on July 15, 1942.
Tesla's nephew, Sava Kosanović, is third from the left.

HIS ONLY VICE IS HIS GENEROSITY. —HUGO GERNSBACK

During a six-month convalescence from his auto accident, Tesla was often feverish and irrational. Forgetting that Mark Twain had been dead for many years, he sealed currency in an envelope and instructed a messenger to deliver it to the humorist's old address. When told that Twain no longer lived there or anywhere else on earth, Tesla grew angry and insisted that his old friend was in need. The messenger, exhausted after further search, eventually opened the envelope to find five twenty-dollar bills (O'Neill 1944, 274).

Pigeons continued to play an important part in Tesla's day-to-day existence. Charles Hausler, who had worked regularly for Tesla from 1928 until shortly before the latter's death, and who raised racing pigeons, described his experiences with the inventor and his birds:

> My job was only to feed the pigeons, hungry and cold, at the New York Public Library . . . at 12 o'clock each day and then walk about the four sides of the building where young or injured birds would seek shelter on the window sills and behind the large statues, where they were safe from stray cats and dogs. . . . I would then take them to the Governor Clinton Hotel and later to the New Yorker Hotel. He would nurse the sick and injured back to health, and I would release them at

the Library for him. In his room he had many fine cages to house the pigeons, made by a fine carpenter. As Mr. Tesla was in all his doings, it had to be done right (Hausler 1979).

Former Westinghouse colleagues, becoming concerned about Tesla's financial condition and fearing negative publicity for the company, retained him as a consulting engineer at $125 per month, a stipend that he received for the rest of his life. Westinghouse historian Charles Ruch reports a puzzling incident described to him by E. H. Sniffen, a Westinghouse assistant vice president. One day, while Sniffen and Tesla were walking down a street in New York, the

Tesla with Victor Beam (center), patent counsel, Westinghouse Electric & Manufacturing Company. An alternator that had escaped destruction in Tesla's laboratory fire in 1895 was brought to Beam's office. The Westinghouse Company had borrowed the alternator, but the fire disaster so absorbed Tesla's efforts in reestablishing his laboratory that the machine was forgotten.

Above: Tesla, "Illustrious dean of inventors," being interviewed by reporters, January 10, 1935.

Left: July 11, 1937. Tesla receives the Order of the White Lion from the Czechoslovak government.

In 1937 Tesla announced that he had devised a means to communicate with other planets. For this he hoped to receive the Pierre Guzman Prize of 100,000 francs for being the first person to communicate with other worlds. He said, "I am just as sure that prize will be awarded to me as if I already had it in my pocket."

Throughout his life, the inventor never wavered in his belief that there was intelligent life on other planets—or that he had received an extraterrestrial communication while at Colorado Springs.

"At the present stage of progress,"

Photo montage of the planets. (Courtesy NASA)

Tesla said in 1901, "there would be no insurmountable obstacle in constructing a machine capable of conveying a message to Mars, nor would there be any great difficulty in recording signals

transmitted to us by the inhabitants of that planet" (Tesla 1901b).

Asked to describe his means for communication with other worlds, Tesla said, "it employs more than three dozen of my inventions, it is a complex apparatus, an agglomeration of parts." But he would not say what or where the parts were (Tesla 1937b).

Tesla was ridiculed for his otherworldly ideas, but today governments and universities spend millions trying to receive an extraterrestrial communication, without a shred of evidence that life exists on other planets.

---

inventor stopped to buy a few newspapers and magazines. He pulled out an enormous roll of bills and blithely gave the news dealer a hundred dollars. "So we can see," said Ruch, "why Tesla might eventually get in trouble" (interview with the authors, 1994).

Taking his consulting role with Westinghouse quite seriously, he sent a proposal to Pittsburgh to develop his system of "Telegeodynamics," in which vibrations from an artificial earthquake would be directed into the earth for purposes of detecting the presence of mineral deposits. A Westinghouse representative dropped in on Tesla at the Hotel New Yorker and reported: "He appeared to be thoroughly clear-headed, in fact said that since his accident his mind seemed to be clearer than ever" (Sniffen 1939). Odd as it sounded at the time, this technique of measuring reflected acoustic waves is used in geo physical work today.

The annual birthday press conferences were still well attended, largely because of the fine wine and

gourmet meals served up for the hungry reporters, even during the Great Depression. The *pièce de résistance* in 1937 was *Canard en casserole à la Tesla*, a dish the inventor had planned himself, though he ate none of it. Instead he sipped milk heated to precisely the right temperature in a silver chafing dish. At that same birthday party Tesla predicted that interplanetary communication would become a reality in the immediate future.

Two years earlier, on his seventy-ninth, Tesla had claimed that with a pocket-sized device and five pounds of air pressure, he could destroy the Empire State Building. According to the *New York World-Telegram* of July 11, 1935,

Twenty-odd newspapermen came away from his Hotel New Yorker birthday party yesterday, which lasted six hours, feeling hesitantly that something was wrong either with the old man's mind or else with their own, for Dr. Tesla was serene in an old-fashioned Prince

Tesla entertains Fritzie Zivić, one of the fighting Zivić brothers of Pittsburgh, at a luncheon in the inventor's suite in the Hotel New Yorker, January 17, 1941. Tesla sponsored Fritzie and attended his bouts at Madison Square Garden.

Albert and courtly in a way that seems to have gone out of this world.

Another interesting diversion for the great pacifist was a passionate love of boxing—especially when the boxers were from his native Yugoslavia. He occasionally dined with a broken-nosed welterweight, Fritzie Zivić, and his five prize-fighting brothers from Pittsburgh. Tesla glowed one night when Fritzie stopped mid-fight, gestured to the famous inventor in the audience and shouted, "Hello, Mr. Tesla." In his later years Tesla even sponsored several Yugoslav boxers.

Hausler, the pigeon caretaker, described another strange detail of Tesla's enigmatic existence:

There is one thing that stands out. In one of my visits, he had a large box in his room near the pigeon cages, and he told me to be very careful not to disturb the box as it contained something that could destroy an airplane in the sky and he had hopes of presenting it to the world. . . . I often wonder why I did not go to the government and tell them about this container; instead it most likely was disposed of in the room or storage cellar of the hotel after his death (Hausler 1979).

The mysterious box, some said, was Tesla's private joke—used to scare meddlers away from his papers and his pigeons. Others believe it contained the open-ended vacuum tube. In any case, the box succeeded in generating the drama Tesla intended to create.

When his old friend Robert Johnson fell ill suddenly, he wrote to Tesla:

> At 83 I have just published my book, *Your Hall of Fame*....I shall not live to see your bust placed there...but there it will be, never doubt, my great and good friend....My heart is still yours, for of all the years of friendship every day is dear (R. Johnson n.d.).

Johnson died on October 14, 1937.

In 1939 the Nazis invaded Poland without warning and the hell of World War II broke loose. Within a year storm troopers were goose-stepping down the Champs Élysées in Paris. Eventually, radio-guided V-2 rockets buzzed through the sky over London, wreaking terror on the population. This was the war Tesla had long anticipated, and his antiwar machine was, it seemed, a hopeless failure.

With the Nazi invasion of Yugoslavia imminent, Tesla sent an urgent telegram to his nephew Sava Kosanović, now a rising government official of the Yugoslav monarchy. In it he proposed a system to defend the borders of his homeland:

> There should be needed nine stations: four for Serbia, three for Croatia, and two for Slovenia. Each should be 200 kW, and they give protection to our dearest homeland against all the attacks (Tesla 1941).

But all hopes were quickly dashed. On Palm Sunday of 1941, Luftwaffe bombers roared over the capital city of Belgrade, killing twenty-five thousand defenseless civilians. German troops quickly marched in and the young king of Yugoslavia fled to England for safety.

By now Tesla was out of touch with the political twists and turns taking place in Yugoslavia. Slavic factions in the United States began to exploit him for political reasons. A battle ensued between Serbs and Croats to appropriate Tesla's prestige, and it contin-

ues to this day. Sava Kosanović wrote to Tesla, "Traitors are everywhere, there are some among the Serbs; one should not generalize" (Kosanović 1941).

Employed by the Yugoslav Information Center on Fifth Avenue, Kosanović crafted statements for his uncle's signature. One was sent to the peoples of Yugoslavia and to the Soviet Academy of Sciences, encouraging them in the "revolutionary struggle" now backed by the USSR. Tesla was a monarchist and unaware that he was being used for communist propaganda.

In 1942 the young King Peter of Yugoslavia traveled to the United States to meet with President Roosevelt. In New York he met with Tesla at the Hotel New Yorker. Tesla told him,

> It is my greatest honor, I am glad you are in your youth, and I am content that you will be a great ruler. I believe I will live until you come back to a free Yugoslavia. . . . [I] am proud to be a Serbian and a Yugoslav. Our people cannot perish. Preserve the unity of all Yugoslavs (King Peter, 1942).

When Peter was dethroned in 1945, Marshal Tito became Prime Minister of Yugoslavia. Sava Kosanović quickly switched loyalty from the Yugoslav monarchy to Tito's communist regime. But all this transpired after Tesla's death.

In the fall of 1942 Tesla telephoned the offices of the Yugoslav Monarchy in Exile, then headquartered at the embassy on Fifth Avenue in New York. Kosanović was ill at the time and Charlotte Muzar, a young secretary, took the call. Tesla told her that he urgently needed $50 in cash. She went at once to his hotel, knocked, and was told to enter. She recalled,

> When I came in I wanted to see everything all at once because here was this great man and I had a chance to see him and how he lives. He was in bed, facing the door. He was sitting up in pajamas, very fragile . . . and I didn't know if this man was going to live through to the

Above: Charlotte Muzar, assistant to Sava Kosanović

Left: The master of lightning in old age in his room at the Hotel New Yorker.

next day because he looked very, very ill and very frail to me (interview with the authors, 1993).

Tesla's friend Kenneth Swezey also visited and was equally alarmed by his condition, particularly when he saw that Tesla was subsisting on warm milk and Nabisco crackers. He noted that the empty enameled cracker cans were stacked on shelves and used to hold various things. Word began to spread that the great inventor was near death.

Late in December of 1942, with the war at its height, two young men identifying themselves as U.S. government agents suddenly entered Tesla's life. One was a member of the OSS (predecessor to the CIA) named Ralph Bergstresser. The other, Bloyce Fitzgerald, was an expert on ballistics technology working with the Massachusetts Institute of Technology. According to Bergstresser, Tesla agreed to share his most sensitive documents with them and allowed them to carry stacks of material away for microfilming. Based on their review, the two men were able to arrange a meeting at the White House on January 8, 1943, with Roosevelt's science advisor and other high-ranking officials. Tesla was too ill to attend (interview with the authors, 1993).

Meanwhile a prominent Yugoslav writer, Louis Adamic *(The Immigrant's Return)*, wrote a letter to Eleanor Roosevelt on December 29 describing the inventor's circumstances:

> Today he is . . . worse than penniless. He is extremely frail, weighing less than 90 pounds. His health is poor; he has grown somewhat bitter against his country, the United States. . . . He suffers, too, to the point of bit-

Nikola Tesla Dies At 85 Alone in His Hotel Suite

Celebrated Inventor, Born in Yugoslavia, An Electrical Wizard

Nikola Tesla, 85, inventor of the Tesla coil, the induction motor and hundreds of other electrical devices, died last night in his suite at the Hotel New Yorker. According to hotel officials, he had been in failing helath for two

Obituary in the New York World Telegram, *January 8, 1943.*

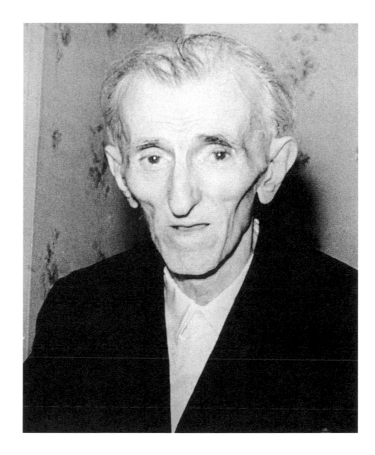

Probably the last photograph taken of Tesla.

terness, because he feels that everyone in America, including beneficiaries of fortunes created by his inventions, has forgotten him. . . . The fact now is that he is up against it. . . . This letter is not an appeal to help him financially. . . . This is merely to suggest that the President write him a letter which will indicate that America has not forgotten [him]. Perhaps this coming New Year is a good occasion for such a letter (Adamic 1942).

New Year's Eve came and went, and there was no letter. Tesla's loyal associate, George Scherff, visited him on January 4 to help him prepare for an experiment. The final project, its nature unknown, was terminated when Tesla complained of sharp pains in his chest. He refused medical aid. Scherff left the hotel, bidding him goodbye for the last time.

On the night of January 7, 1943, the eve of the Orthodox Christmas, snow fell on New York City. In a darkened room on the thirty-third floor of the Hotel New Yorker, Tesla lay listening to the clamor of traffic below. His great legacy, the technological world he had helped create, would continue without him. There would be no more riveting announcements, or shrieks of "Eureka," or terrifying bolts of lightning leaping in his laboratory. The pigeons on the window ledge stirred their feet and ruffled their feathers. Hard times lay ahead for the pigeons; he had nothing to leave them.

Nikola Tesla, aged eighty-six, died in his sleep. The coroner's report read: "No suspicious circumstances."

CHAPTER SEVENTEEN

The Paper Trail

Tesla's suite at the Hotel New Yorker following his funeral on January 12, 1943. Left to right: an unknown messenger; Professor Boris Furlan, a Slovene active during the war in the United States; Sava Kosanović, Tesla's nephew and member of the Yugoslav Royal Government in exile.

The morning after Tesla's death Sava Kosanović hurried to his uncle's room at the Hotel New Yorker. He was now an important Yugoslav government official—director of the Eastern and Central European Planning Board for the Balkans. By the time he arrived, Tesla's body had already been removed. Kosanović suspected that someone had already searched Tesla's room. Technical papers were missing as well as a black notebook he knew Tesla kept, some pages of which were marked "Government" (FBI 1943a). He called in a locksmith to open the safe. Kosanović's assistant, Charlotte Muzar, recalls:

> When I got there, the locksmith was just leaving. Mr. Kosanović had asked him to come and open the safe thinking there might be a testament, a will in the safe.... There was a lot of talk then about secret weapons and negotiations with the USSR and he was supposed to have a meeting with Mrs. Roosevelt about some kind of a war weapon that he had developed (interview with the authors, 1993).

No will was ever found. The box described by the pigeon feeder, Hausler, was also missing. "I've had a number of people call me and ask me if I saw in the hotel room a certain kind of box," said Muzar. "They were looking for some kind of secret contraption that Tesla had invented.... I never saw anything like that."

What Muzar did see was a door to an adjoining room that she had not noticed on her earlier visit:

> I just remember how flabbergasted I was this

time to see the door open in the room next to where Tesla was, to see all of this paperwork.... There were boxes and barrels of papers and file cabinets and everything in this room. . . . It's possible that he had some sort of death ray or some sort of secret weapon. Maybe some of it was used, we don't know. Because these people don't advertise where they get their ideas and their weapons.

P. E. Foxworth, assistant director of the New

Articles in Tesla's hotel room after his death. Note cabinets and one of the inventor's safes. Three packages of Nabisco crackers can be seen on one of the upper shelves of the cabinet at left.

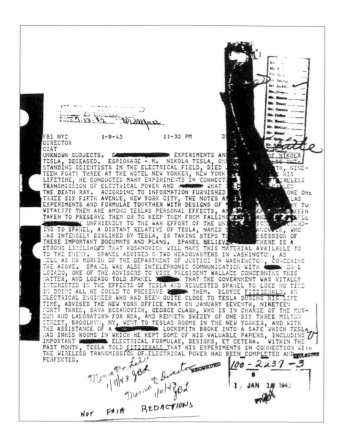

York FBI office, was called in to investigate. His report verified Kosanović's concerns:

> Experiments and research of Nikola Tesla, deceased. Espionage—Nikola Tesla, one of the world's outstanding scientists in the electrical field, died January 7th, 1943, at the Hotel New Yorker, New York City. During his lifetime he conducted many experiments in connection with the wireless transmission of electrical power and...what is commonly called the death ray. According to information furnished by [name deleted], New York City, the notes and records of Tesla's experiments and formulae together with designs of machinery...are among Tesla's personal effects and no steps have been taken to preserve them or to keep them from falling into the hands of people...unfriendly to the war effort of the [Allies] (Foxworth 1943).

According to Foxworth, the government was "vitally interested" in preserving the papers.

On January 9, representatives of the Office of Alien Property went to the Hotel New Yorker. They seized all of Tesla's belongings and transmitted them under seal to the Manhattan Storage and Warehouse Company. Two truckloads of papers, furniture, and artifacts were added to some thirty barrels and bundles that had been in storage since the 1930s, and the entire collection was placed under OAP seal.

Tesla's body had been removed to the Frank E. Campbell Funeral Home at Madison Avenue and 81st Street, where it lay in state while local Serb and Croat factions quarreled over arrangements for the funeral. Tesla's long-time friend Hugo Gernsback arranged for a death mask to be made.

More than two thousand people crowded into the Cathedral of St. John the Divine for the funeral on January 12, 1943. Bishop William T. Manning con-

*Tesla's casket in St. John the Divine Cathedral with U.S. and Yugoslav flags draped over it,
January 12, 1943.*

ducted the service, having decreed in advance that no
political speeches were to be given. Serbs and Croats
sat on opposite sides of the aisle. President and Mrs.
Roosevelt sent a belated message expressing their gratitude for Tesla's contributions to science and industry
and to the United States of America.

That same day FBI agent Foxworth was flying on
an urgent mission to meet with President Roosevelt at
the Casablanca Conference. Over the Atlantic, the
military transport carrying him and thirty-five others
exploded in midair. The cause of the explosion was
never determined, but Agent Foxworth's untimely
death, most likely unrelated, heightened concerns
about the possibility of a secret weapon. A broad

search was initiated by the FBI throughout New York
City to find any papers or artifacts relating to Tesla.
Even the inventor's tailor and shoemaker were inter-
viewed. Trunks of documents were located and added
to the collection at the Manhattan Storage and
Warehouse Company.

Dr. John G. Trump, an electrical engineer with the
National Defense Research Committee of the Office of
Scientific Research and Development, was called in to
analyze the Tesla papers in OAP custody. Following a
three-day investigation, Dr. Trump concluded:

> As a result of this examination, it is my con-
> sidered opinion that there exist among Dr.
> Tesla's papers and possessions no scientific

The death mask of Nikola Tesla in the offices of Gernsback Publications, New York City, in celebration of the Tesla centennial, June 25, 1956. The mask was heavily electroplated with copper, a process that took ten days, and was mounted on a marble-composition pedestal. Three medallions, executed in bas-relief on the base, commemorate Tesla's greatest inventions: the Tesla oscillation transformer, the first AC induction motor, and the tower for wireless power transmission.

notes, descriptions of hitherto unrevealed methods or devices, or actual apparatus which could be of significant value to this country or which would constitute a hazard in unfriendly hands. I can therefore see no technical or military reason why custody of the property should be retained (Trump 1943).

Trump mentioned several items of scientific apparatus among the effects. One in particular, thought to be "the secret weapon," was found in a depository at the Governor Clinton Hotel. The inves-

tigator slowly untied a cord and peeled back brown paper wrapping to reveal a neat wooden box. Taking a deep breath, he gently raised the hasp—and exhaled. Tesla's last jest was a piece of common laboratory equipment, a box used for resistance measurements. Trump noted,

> His thoughts and efforts during at least the past 15 years were primarily of a speculative, philosophical, and somewhat promotional character—often concerned with the production and wireless transmission of power—but did not include new, sound, workable principles or methods for realizing such results.

Microfilms of the entire collection were made, just in case, by U.S. Navy technicians. In view of the technological advances in beam weaponry since Tesla's death, it is possible that Trump may have overlooked important details in his cursory examination of the papers.

Six months later the contentious issue of who was the real inventor of radio was legally put to rest. Overturning decades of lower court decisions, the U.S. Supreme Court ruled that the "Marconi patents" for radio incorporated the earlier work of Tesla, primarily, and two other radio pioneers, Sir Oliver Lodge and John Stone. News from the battlefronts of World War II pushed the announcement to the back pages of newspapers, where it went unnoticed by the editors of reference books, university professors, and directors of museums. And to this day school children are still taught, erroneously, that Marconi is the "father" of radio. The error is still perpetuated by the Smithsonian Institution.

Tesla's problems with the Smithsonian Institution go back some distance. While undergoing extreme financial worries at Wardenclyffe on Long Island, he was repeatedly dunned by the Smithsonian to pay for his magazine subscription. Pleading financial misfortunes which prevented his sending a check immediately, Tesla wrote, "I hope, therefore, that you will interpret the term 'immediate attention' in a liberal, I might say geological sense." Perhaps the Smithsonian didn't enjoy the humor (Tesla 1906b).

Tesla's remains were taken to Ferncliffe Cemetery at Ardsley-on-the-Hudson and later cremated. This was an unusual procedure, in violation of his Serbian Orthodox tradition. The decision was probably made because of wartime conditions. More disconcerting was the fact that no one knew what to do with the ashes, which reposed on a shelf for the next fifteen years.

The situation finally changed in 1952, when Tesla's entire estate, comprising more than fifty years of research work and records of five thousand experiments, was released to Sava Kosanović and returned to Belgrade, Yugoslavia, for a museum planned in Tesla's honor. When the inventor's safe was opened, it was immediately apparent that someone had gone through its contents. The gold Edison Medal was missing. Kosanović was told by a worker at the Manhattan Storage Company that men presenting themselves as federal agents had come and photographed documents.

For many years, under Tito's Communist regime, it was all but impossible for Western journalists and scholars to gain access to the Tesla collection; even then they were allowed to see only selected papers. This was not the case for Soviet scientists who came in delegations during the 1950s. Their findings seemed to have a direct influence on Peter Kapitsa, who served as the technical advisor to Soviet Premier Nikita Khrushchev in the 1950s, and who initiated early Soviet work on directed energy weapons (Department of Defense 1981).

As to the photocopies of documents made by Bloyce Fitzgerald and his OSS colleague, they wound up at the Air Technical Services Command, Special Weapons Section, at Wright Field near Dayton, Ohio. A highly secret operation code-named "Project Nick" was heavily funded and placed under the com-

The Liberty Ship SS Nikola Tesla *was christened on September 25, 1943.*

mand of Brigadier General L. C. Craigie. Within six months, results suggested that Tesla's particle beam weapon was practicable. Now an Army private, Bloyce Fitzgerald headed the research team. "According to Fitzgerald," reads an FBI document, "perfection of Tesla's death ray is the only possible defense against offensive use by another nation of the Atomic Bomb" (Conroy 1945).

Within a year, the program was disbanded. Project reports disappeared, along with all copies of Tesla's scientific papers. Fitzgerald, the man in charge of an important defense program, was arrested for allegedly writing bad checks and sent to Folsom Prison for ten years. Recently released FBI documents reveal that his actual crime was "impersonating" a

At 51 Krunska Street in Belgrade, Yugoslavia, there is a stately mansion that houses the Tesla Museum. It was founded in 1952 and opened to the public in 1955. A visitor to the museum will first notice the bust of Nikola Tesla sculpted by Ivan Mestrović. The museum has only a few original exhibits, the most important of which is a two-phase AC induction motor made for Westinghouse in 1895. There are glass cases displaying Tesla's personal effects and a number of reconstructed devices. Tesla's ingenious "egg of Columbus," first shown in 1893 in Chicago, is demonstrated for visitors. There is also a replica of a plate from one of the generators at the hydroelectric power station at Niagara Falls. Naturally, there are Tesla coils on display. One of these produces 500,000 volts and lights neon tubes without wire connections. A model of Tesla's remote-controlled boat, the "teleautomaton," is also demonstrated, its intricate workings revealed through a plexiglass housing.

Museum archives contain 150,000 archival documents including manuscripts, drawings, and several hundred photographs. There are letters representing more than 6,700 correspondents. Tesla's personal library is also on display, showing the inventor's wide range of interests.

In a separate room of the museum, on a stone pedestal, there is a golden urn, shaped like a sphere, with Tesla's ashes which were brought to Belgrade from New York in 1957. At the exit hangs Tesla's death mask with the words of the American inventor Edwin H. Armstrong next to it: "The world will have to wait for a long time for a mind that would equal Tesla's."

Tesla Museum exterior

"Egg of Columbus" exhibit demonstration of rotating magnetic field

Exhibit area

Library archives

federal agent (Hoover 1947). Fitzgerald died in 1980, but the mystery of his involvement with Tesla continues.

Joseph Butler of the National Air Intelligence Center, whose official mission is to look for "technological surprise," conducted an extensive search for Tesla's papers in the late 1970s. According to Butler,

Copies of some of his papers were sent to Wright Patterson in 1945, not to my facility, not even a predecessor of my facility, but to another part of the base for analysis. And then they vanished. Nobody seems to know what happened to them. I checked the archives of my classified particle beam weapons research and there is no mention in there of any of the Tesla papers (interview with the authors, 1995).

In spite of several official reports that Tesla's technical papers were microfilmed by both the Navy and the Army, no confirmed copies exist within any agency of the U.S. government.

Whatever happened, his unpatented wireless weapons concepts apparently found their way not only into U.S. Naval and Army Air Force Intelligence, but also to various defense contractors and university research laboratories engaged in beam weapon work. In 1958 the Defense Advanced Research Projects Agency (DARPA) initiated a top-secret U.S. beam weapon project code-named "Seesaw" at Lawrence Livermore Laboratory. More than ten years and twenty-seven million dollars later, the project was abandoned "because of the projected high costs associated with implementation as well as the formidable technical problems associated with propagating a beam through very long ranges in the atmosphere" (Department of Defense 1982).

Meanwhile, Soviet research on directed energy weapons seemed to be advancing. An article in *Pravda*, October 1960, reported equipment that had been developed for producing artificial ball lightning.

Yugoslav author Louis Adamic congratulates science writer John J. O'Neill on the publication of his biography of Tesla, Prodigal Genius, *in 1944.*

It consisted of a quartz tube having a unique heat-resistant and nonconducting profile, with one end open to the atmosphere—technology strikingly similar to that described by Tesla in the 1930s. As mentioned, Soviet physicist Peter Kapitsa had explored the use of ball lightning in directed energy weapons applications.

Speculation that the Soviets were developing beam weapon technologies increased when on January 15, 1960, Khrushchev announced to the Supreme Soviet that "a new and fantastic weapon was in the hatching stage" (*New York Times* 1960).

Richard Briggs, a project director on the Seesaw program, confirmed that a secret, nonnuclear weapons race was under way during most of the Cold War era:

There was certainly concern that the Soviets would be developing directed energy weapons,

Robert Golka, an electrical engineer with access to Tesla's notes in the Tesla Museum in Belgrade, attempted to recreate Tesla's Colorado Springs experiments for the U.S. Air Force in the 1970s in the same hangar that housed the Enola Gay.

just as they were concerned that we might successfully develop a directed energy weapon. You have to realize that the thing in military technology that causes grave concern is a technological breakthrough. Directed energy weapons, if successfully developed, would totally change the nature of engagement, offense and defense (interview with the authors, 1998).

The term "directed energy weapon," or DEW, was not declassified until the 1980s.

In 1980 the Soviets' "fantastic" weapon appeared. U.S. spy satellite images revealed that an enormous beam weapon facility was under construction at Saryshagan near the Sino-Soviet border in southern Russia. The head of U.S. Air Force Intelligence, Major General George J. Keegan, Jr., was frustrated by the arguments of U.S. scientists that the Soviets were incapable of building such a device. He resigned and took the story public. According to Keegan, successful tests of the weapon had already taken place and the United States was "completely unprepared" for the consequences. An article in *Aviation Week & Space Technology*, July 28, 1980, warned that "the beam weapon threat from the USSR seemed capable of neutralizing the entire United States ballistic missile force and checkmating this country's strategic doctrine."

The American response to this "technological surprise" was the Star Wars program announced by President Ronald Reagan on March 23, 1983. Reagan's 1940 film *Murder in the Air* depicted a ray weapon used to destroy aircraft. Now the threat was real, and teams of government scientists were urged to "turn their great talents now to the cause of mankind and world peace, to give us the means of rendering these nuclear weapons impotent and obsolete" (Reagan 1983).

At the same time, there was renewed U.S. interest in the technical papers of Nikola Tesla, as evidenced by a secret document declassified in the 1990s:

> The Soviet Union has allegedly had access to some of Tesla's papers, possibly in Belgrade and/or elsewhere, which influenced their early research into directed energy weapons. . . . Access to Tesla's papers on lightning, beam weapons and/or "death rays" would give more insight into the Soviet beam weapons program (FBI 1983).

It is likely that some of Tesla's documents were finally located, or were never lost at all, as many of his key concepts have appeared in directed energy weapons research—in particular his open-ended vacuum tube.

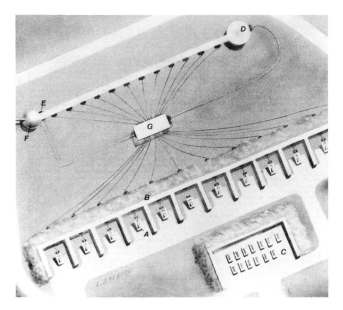

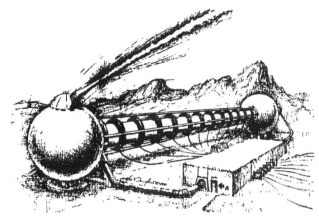

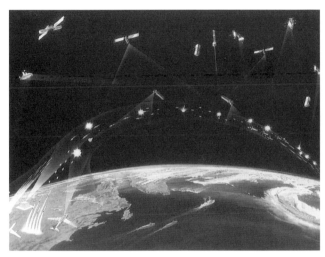

Above: U.S. satellite reconnaissance photo of suspected Soviet beam weapon installation near Semipalatinsk. Published July 28, 1980. (Courtesy Aviation Week & Space Technology*)*

Top right: Artist's conception of Soviet beam weapon in operation.

Right: Artist's conception of U.S. Strategic Defense Initiative. (Ballistic Missile Defense Organization)

Today no one seems to know the exact origin of the Star Wars program, with its plan to build an electronic defense shield in space. But the idea has inspired military imaginations since Tesla first announced it in the 1930s. Today, a number of his enthusiasts contend that he is the "father" of the Strategic Defense Initiative. This may be a dubious honor. According to Richard Briggs, "No one at this point has developed, successfully, and deployed directed energy weapons of any kind." But Briggs does allow that "if you take the view of decades off in the future, of course things like this will happen. It doesn't defy physics" (interview with the authors, 1998).

The use of beam weapons in space poses a different set of technical problems than beams propagated through the atmosphere. Development in both areas has been slow, primarily due to technological hurdles and wavering commitment in the United States, Russia, and other nations.

Over the years, numerous researchers have sought to discover the missing papers of Nikola Tesla. Since the end of the Cold War era, many new documents and clues have appeared which suggest that Tesla's papers and ideas were used in U.S. Department of Defense experiments. The outcome of these experiments is what remains a mystery. ⤛

CHAPTER EIGHTEEN

The Cosmic Signature

The aurora borealis, a swirling mass of electronic energy, creates a luminous discharge in the upper atmosphere. (Courtesy NASA)

A strange prediction appeared in the *New York Times* on July 11, 1937:

Some evening not far off, as a new moon sails across the early evening sky, a spot of light may flash in the dark area between the two horns of light that terminate its crescent. That spot of light will be the cosmic signature of Nikola Tesla, from whose fertile mind have blossomed many inventions.

Above the surface of the earth, some seventy to eighty kilometers in height, is a region of the atmosphere called the ionosphere. Here particles of cosmic matter from the sun are trapped between the vacuum of space and the earth's atmosphere. Those electrically charged particles create, in essence, a huge electrodynamic circuit about the earth that carries up to a million megawatts of power, equivalent to a thousand large power plants. The swirling energy or plasma inside the ionosphere can be seen at night near the magnetic poles of the earth in the magnificent display of light known as the aurora borealis.

Technically, the ionosphere was not discovered until 1926, by the British physicist E. V. Appleton. Yet in 1900 Nikola Tesla filed a patent for the wireless transmission of power through this little-known region.

Only in the 1980s did Bernard Eastlund, a physicist working for the Atlantic Richfield Oil Company (ARCO), revisit the idea. On the north slope of

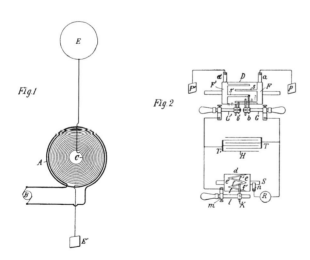

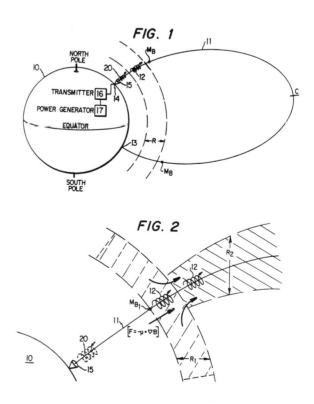

Above: Drawing from Tesla's U.S. patent number 787,412, "Art of Transmitting Electrical Energy Through the Natural Mediums."

Right: Drawing from U.S. patent number 4,686,605, granted August 11, 1987, to Bernard Eastlund, depicting a method and apparatus for altering a selected region above the earth's surface.

The earth-ionosphere cavity is the spherical shell about sixty to ninety miles thick extending from the earth's surface to the underside of the ionosphere. As a result of his experiments at Colorado Springs, Tesla believed radio waves at frequencies that resonated with the planet-sized dimensions of this cavity might be efficiently employed to keep energy on tap around the globe. That is, large broadcast facilities would generate power at frequencies that vibrate most naturally within the cavity, losing a minimum of intensity to absorption or destructive interference.

Decades later, in the 1950s, W. O. Schumann discovered regular peaks always present in the general electromagnetic noise around the planet. Peaks occurred in the ultra-low (ULF) and extremely-low (ELF) frequency range, lying between approximately 6 and 50 hertz. Energy distributed across a wide frequency spectrum is constantly added to the atmosphere, by lightning chiefly, but the resonant frequencies (the "Schumann resonances") are detectable at much higher levels than the rest.

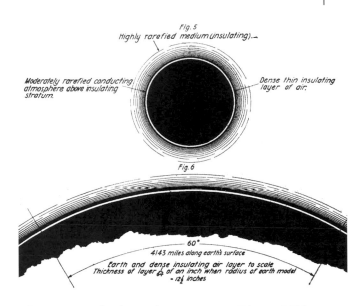

Illustration from the Electrical Experimenter, *February 1919.*

Tesla had conjectured just such an origin for persistent low-frequency readings he obtained at Colorado Springs. He recognized that he was receiving evidence of lightning storms at a great distance, and was aware of the presence of characteristic frequencies; his measurements are in agreement with peaks in the Schumann series. As for broadcasting power, the amounts that would have to be stored in the Schumann cavity (also referred to as the Tesla-Schumann cavity) are probably beyond practicality. Scientists continue to monitor these natural signals, though, to find what relation their changing strengths might bear to earth's overall storm activity or indeed to other phenomena, such as earthquakes and solar flares.

Alaska are huge deposits of natural gas, but these reserves remain idle because of their remote location and the expense involved in constructing a pipeline. Eastlund proposed an ARCO pipeline in the sky. Natural gas reserves would be used to power microwave transmitters. The microwaves would be beamed into the ionosphere above Alaska, transmitted great distances through the earth's celestial circuit, then beamed back down via satellite and converted back into electrical power. Was this the mechanism Tesla intended to use for wireless power transmission?

Before his patent was granted, Eastlund was surprised to learn that someone had been there before him. The patent examiner insisted that Tesla be referenced because he had originated so many of the concepts. A patent was granted to Eastlund in 1987: "Method and Apparatus for Altering a Region in the Earth's Atmosphere, Ionosphere, and/or Magnetosphere."

The patent specification reads like Tesla's *curriculum vitae:*

The invention has a phenomenal variety of possible ramifications and potential future developments...missile or aircraft destruction, deflection, or confusion could result.... Weather modification is possible by, for

HAARP antenna array in Gakona, Alaska (Courtesy U.S. Department of the Air Force)

example, altering upper atmosphere wind patterns or altering solar absorption patterns by constructing one or more plumes of atmospheric particles which will act as a lens or focusing device (Eastlund 1987).

Such astonishing possibilities did not escape the notice of the U.S. military. The patent remained sealed for a year under a government secrecy order. In the 1990s it evolved into the High Altitude Auroral Research Project (HAARP) in Gakona, Alaska. The project consists of a huge antenna array covering many acres that is designed to transmit microwave energy into the ionosphere. The project is sponsored by the Air Force's Phillips Laboratory, the Office of Naval Research, and the National Science Foundation. It is under the direction of physicist Dennis Papadopoulos, a great admirer of Tesla. Said Papadopoulos,

> Look around you, you see his imprint everywhere. Tesla was a genius because way before anybody knew or even understood the earth and what we call today the ionosphere, he conceived it and tried to use it to produce a

variety of new concepts (interview with the authors, 1998).

In the early 1900s Tesla proposed the use of low-frequency waves for underwater and underground communications. He realized that the lower the wave frequency, the deeper it would penetrate into the earth and the sea.

The initial goal of HAARP was to create a system for extra-low-frequency submarine communications by literally turning a region of the ionosphere into a gigantic antenna. There are regions in the auroral zones and at the equator called electro-jets where currents flow constantly. Interfering with these currents and reversing their direction creates an alternating current in the heavens, which in turn produces a powerful radio signal. "We had problems persuading people about this concept in the '70s," said Papadopoulos. "And Tesla, without knowledge of satellites or solar UV radiation—all those things—he could really see the correct mode of propagation. Stunning."

This technology also brings new remote sensing capabilities for over-the-horizon radar, as well as

Humankind has long dreamed of controlling the weather for purposes good and bad. With the introduction of the airplane, farmers began seeding the clouds with silver iodide (as condensation nuclei) to form particles of ice or rain. Tesla was the first to suggest that weather could be modified by electrical means, believing that lightning was part of a natural mechanism that triggered atmospheric changes.

In 1908 he attempted to patent a device to precipitate water from the sky. But, he said, "The Patent Office Examiner was from Missouri, he would not believe that it could be done, and my patent was never granted" (Tesla 1917).

Military strategists are keenly aware that weather conditions can change the course of battle. But only in the 1950s and 60s did the technology exist for serious experiments. The Soviets had access to Tesla's papers in the Tesla Museum in Belgrade and

Lightning strikes again (Courtesy National Archives)

were probably influenced by his ideas to use radio waves for weather modification. There is reason to believe that the so-called "woodpecker" signal, a low-frequency transmission emanating from Latvia in the late 1970s, was a Soviet global weather experiment. (Imagine spring year-round in Siberia.)

During the same period, U.S. Navy researchers contemplated creating localized weather effects by heating

the ionosphere with particle beam weapons—an idea first described by Tesla. According to a U.S. Department of Defense publication, "A large negative electric charge disposed into the atmosphere would theoretically release a large X-ray flash, producing many pairs of positive and negative ions, thus creating channels of high electrical conductivity. These greatly increase electrical fields and enhance precipitation and thundercloud electrification" (Beane 1981).

In 1974 the UN General Assembly adopted a resolution prohibiting actions that influence the environment or the climate. Although most scientists believe that the prospects of weather modification are slim, the need for such a treaty speaks for itself. Tesla said of weather modification, "If I do not live to carry it out, somebody else will" (Tesla 1917).

detection of mineral deposits and military sites beneath the earth—both ideas first advanced by Tesla. HAARP can also be used to disrupt global communications, since the presence of charged particles in the ionosphere controls the performance of many military and civilian systems using the electromagnetic waves.

With the twenty-first century comes a new era of ionospheric physics in which it has become possible to alter the state of the upper atmosphere. HAARP is an advanced form of what is called an ionospheric heater, sending microwave radio signals into the electrically charged zones above the earth where they operate like a microwave oven.

Papadopoulos elaborated:

See a microwave oven, and think of Tesla. The radiation frequency concept of the microwave oven was his. HAARP works the same way. We send microwaves up to interact with matter as Tesla conceived they interact. We have really a frequency transformer similar to what Tesla was thinking about with his Tesla coil. As soon as it finds charged particles, it starts shaking them up and down. They collide with a lot of neutral particles and it makes them hotter.

The ability to superheat portions of the ionosphere provokes concerns both real and imagined.

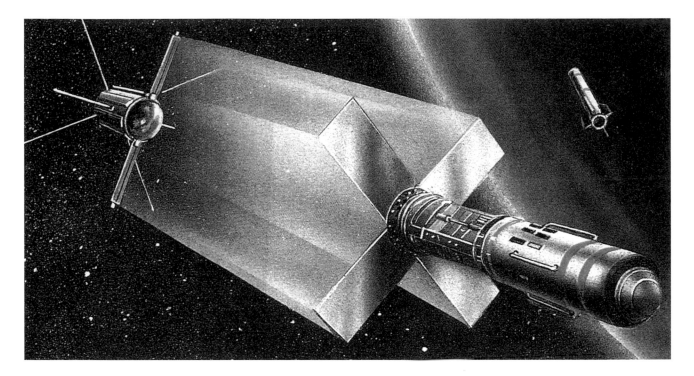

Conception of wireless energy transmission in space by Nabuyuki Kaya.

Most pressing among these are the possible effects on the global environment. The ionosphere, atmosphere, and magnetosphere form a protective layer above the earth against solar wind and radiation. Changes in this layer influence both weather and communications. If this protective layer above the earth were damaged the results could be catastrophic. Tesla once expressed the concern, "So energetic are these actions that I have often experienced a fear that the atmosphere might be ignited, a terrible possibility" (Tesla 1899c).

For those who fear that HAARP is some infernal weather machine, Papadopoulos says it is impossible with such a facility. The power HAARP can transmit is "one-billionth of the energy of a tornado," he declares. "It's like trying to stop a tank with a fly. There's just no way... it's pure nonsense that a radio facility even a million times stronger than HAARP would be able to change the weather." As to the rather terrifying speculation that HAARP could set the upper atmosphere on fire, Papadopoulos added, "Lightning, which is one-tenth of the world's produc-

tion of electricity, doesn't ignite the atmosphere. How can you ignite it with anything else?"

And what has become of Tesla's dream to transmit wireless power "by conduction" through the upper atmosphere? According to Papadopoulos,

He was dreaming, but he was doing very few calculations on paper, because on paper he could have realized that because the dimensions of the waveguide are so enormous, you can transmit power, but not very much power. You can transfer power to hear the radio, or for television, or for a telephone. But once you want to start turning on lights in which you really need high currents, the power gets diluted because the space is very large.

Wireless transmission of energy continues to intrigue scientific investigators. Following the oil crisis of the 1970s NASA scientists studied the possibility of putting satellites with enormous arrays of solar cells into geosynchronous orbit to transmit microwave energy from the sun to earth. The plan

The supreme honor for a scientist is to become part of the scientific vocabulary itself. Deciding on units to be used in scientific measurement, and refining their precision, is the work of the General Conference on Weights and Measures (CGPM) in Geneva. The International System of Units (SI) is for scientists the ultimate set of "yardsticks." Since 1956, the SI unit of magnetic flux density is the tesla (symbol: T).

What exactly the tesla measures may be thought of as the concentration of a magnetic field, the number of field lines per square meter. Overall strength is denominated in webers, after another pioneer, so that one tesla equals one weber per square meter.

How handy is the tesla? It is large, equal to 10,000 gauss—a unit used in the "cgs" system of measure. The T unit fits more naturally into a larger scale, for fields used in MRI equipment, or for describing the world's strongest magnets, supercooled behemoths that energize and aim particle beams within "atom-smashing" accelerators—an application that Tesla himself would have appreciated. Such magnets achieve densities in the range .5T to 6T. An average reading of the earth's own flux density, to make a comparison, would register about one fifty-thousandth of a tesla.

proved feasible, but too costly under prevailing economic conditions; this would change when the price of oil had reached about $70 a barrel. It seems far-fetched, but some day our survival could depend on such technology.

For our existance we are dependant on a rapidly increasing supply of energy. Where will we go when there are no more forests to cut down, when the coal fields are exhausted, when no more oil can be pumped from the ground? Like Tesla we will probably turn our eyes to the heavens. To him, the cosmos was nothing more than a gigantic electrical system:

Is not the universe with its infinite and impenetrable boundary a perfect vacuum tube of dimensions and power inconceivable? Are not its fiery suns/cathodes/electrodes at temperatures far beyond any we can apply in the puny and crude contrivances of our making? Is it not a fact that the suns and stars are under immense electrical pressures transcending any that man can ever produce and is this not equally true of the vacuum in celestial space? Finally, can there be any doubt that cosmic dust and meteoric matter present an infinitude of targets acting as reflectors and transformers of energy? (Tesla 1932b)

The world would be a very different place without the ideas and inventions of Nikola Tesla. With the flick of a switch the power of the waterfall and the coal furnace is transported to our fingertips. Worldwide communications reach nearly every person on the planet. A remote-controlled device has explored the surface of Mars. And at this moment, receivers are pointed at the heavens waiting for a message from afar. One can picture the inventor nodding, then shrugging, and perhaps wondering what took us so long. In the end, Tesla was one of our greatest dreamers, and great dreams have a way of becoming reality. The inventor consoled himself by saying,

The scientific man does not aim at an immediate result. He does not expect that his advanced ideas will be readily taken up. His work is like that of a planter—for the future. His duty is to lay the foundation for those who are to come, and point the way (Tesla 1919a).

Top: Nikola Tesla monument installed at Goat Island, Niagara Falls, a gift to the United States on the occasion of its bicentennial and Tesla's 120th anniversary, July 23, 1976. The monument is a second casting of the sculpture by Fran Krsinić. The first casting is installed in front of the Faculty of Electrical Engineering Building, University of Belgrade.

Above: Urn in Tesla Museum, Belgrade, containing the inventor's ashes.

Right: Sarony photograph of Tesla taken October 13, 1933.

Sources frequently cited have been identified by the following abbreviations:

TMA   Nikola Tesla Museum Archives, Belgrade, Yugoslavia

LAA   Leland Anderson Archives, Serb National Federation, Pittsburgh

Adamic, Louis. 1942. Letter to Eleanor Roosevelt (December 29). LAA.

Anderson, Leland. 1968. Wardenclyffe—a fortified dream. *Long Island Forum* (August, September).

———. 1980. Priority in the invention of radio, Tesla v. Marconi. *Antique Wireless Association Review* (March).

———. 1986. John Stone Stone on Nikola Tesla's priority in radio and continuous wave RF. *Antique Wireless Association Review* 1.

———, ed. 1992. *Nikola Tesla on His Work with Alternating Currents.* Denver: Sun Publishing.

———, ed. 1998. *Nikola Tesla: Guided Weapons and Computer Technology.* Breckenridge, CO: Twenty First Century Books.

Armstrong, Edwin H. 1953. Letter to Leland Anderson (November 16). LAA.

Beane, William J. 1981. The Navy and directed energy weapons. *Department of Defense Proceedings* (November).

Cheney, Margaret. 1981. *Tesla: Man Out of Time.* New York: Prentice-Hall. Reprint, 1991. New York: Barnes & Noble Books.

Chester, Franklin. 1897. *The Citizen* (August 22).

Conroy, E. E. 1945. Experiments and research of Nikola Tesla (October 17). Tesla FBI FOIA file.

Crookes, William. 1897. *President's Address, Society for Psychical Research* (August 2). Archives of Society for Psychical Research, London.

de Arcangelis, Mario. *Electronic Warfare.* Dorset, UK: Blandford Press, 1985.

Department of Defense. 1981. *Soviet Military Power* 75 (October). Washington, D.C.: U.S. Government Printing Office.

———. 1982. Fact sheet: particle beam technology (February): 7.

Duncan, Don. 1972. Driftwood days. *Seattle Sunday Times* (July 1).

Eastlund, Bernard J. 1987. U.S. patent number 4,686,605.

Edison, Thomas A. 1905. *New York World* (n.d.).

———. 1915. *New York Times* (December 8).

Einstein, Albert. 1931. Letter to Nikola Tesla (June). TMA.

FBI. 1943. List of persons associated with Tesla. Tesla FBI FOIA file.

———. 1983. Memo to FBI director (August 18). Tesla FBI FOIA file.

Finn, Bernard S. 1996. Rebuttal to Wagner. *Amateur Radio Today* (August).

Foxworth, P. F. 1943. Memo to FBI NYC director (January 9). Tesla FBI FOIA file.

Girardeau, Emil. 1953. Nikola Tesla, radar pioneer. Nikola Tesla Kongress, Vienna (September). TMA.

Hausler, Charles. 1979. Letter to Leland Anderson (April 12). LAA.

Hayes, Jeffery A., ed. 1993. *Tesla Engine Builders Association Journal* 1 (October): 18. Milwaukee: Tesla Engine Builders Association.

Hoover, J. Edgar. 1947. Memo to FBI Los Angeles headquarters (February 12). Fitzgerald FBI FOIA file.

Hunt, Inez, and Leland Anderson. 1976. Lightning over little London. *Empire Magazine* in the *Denver Post* (July 11).

Johnson, Katharine. 1895. Letter to Nikola Tesla (March 14). TMA.

———. 1905. Letter to Nikola Tesla (December 28). Columbia University: Special Collections, Butler Library.

———. n.d. Letters to Nikola Tesla. TMA.

Johnson, Robert Underwood. 1923. *Remembered Yesterdays.* New York: Little Brown & Company.

———. n.d. Letter to Nikola Tesla. Library of Congress.

Josephson, Matthew. 1959. *Edison.* New York: McGraw-Hill Book Company.

Kosanović, Sava. 1926. *A Visit to Nikola Tesla.* TMA.

———. 1941. Letter to Nikola Tesla (November 20). In *Nikola Tesla: Correspondence with Relatives.* Belgrade, YU: Nikola Tesla Museum, 1993.

Litt, Leon L. 1940. Letter to Adjutant General E. S. Adams (December 29). National Archives AGO 381, Washington, D.C.

Long, Breckinridge. 1934. Letter to Secretary of State (July 12). National Archives AGO 381, Washington, D.C.

Marriott, Robert H. 1925. *Radio Broadcast* (December 2).

Morgan, J. Pierpont. 1903. Letter to Nikola Tesla (July 14). Library of Congress.

New York Herald. 1897. Columbia University: Special Collections, Butler Library.

New York Times. 1960. Khrushchev says Soviet will cut forces a third; Sees 'fantastic' weapon (January 15).

O'Neill, John J. 1932. *Brooklyn Eagle* (July 10).

———. 1944. *Prodigal Genius—The Life of Nikola Tesla.* Reprint, Albuquerque, NM: Brotherhood of Life (1994).

———. n.d. Tesla tries to prevent World War II. In "Tesla Collection," Smithsonian Institution, Dibner Library.

King Peter of Yugoslavia. 1942. Diary notes (July 8). TMA.

Petković, Dragislav L. 1927. A visit to Nikola Tesla. *Politika* (April 27).

Quinby, E. J. 1977. Letter to Margaret Cheney (November 19).

———. 1983. *Radio Electronics* (August).

Rankine, deLancy, comp. 1926. *Memorabilia of William Birch Rankine.* Niagara Falls, NY: Power City Press.

Reagan, Ronald. 1983. Presidential television address (March 23). National Archives.

Rice, Warren. 1980. Letter to Margaret Cheney (September 5).

Roentgen, Wilhelm K. 1895. Letter to Tesla. TMA.

Ruch, Charles A. 1984. George Westinghouse—engineer and doer!!! *IEEE Transactions on Industry Applications* 1A, no. 6 (November/December): 1397.

———. 1986. The magic city of 1893. *Westinghouse Retirees News.* Westinghouse Archives.

Scott, Charles F. 1943. Nikola Tesla's achievements in the electrical art. *Electrical Engineering–New York* (August).

Skerritt, Dorothy. 1955. Conversation with Leland Anderson (March 24). LAA.

Sniffen, E. H. 1939. Westinghouse memorandum (January 3). Westinghouse Archives.

Steifel, Natalie. 1994. *Community Journal of Wading River Long Island* (November/December).

Stockbridge, Frank Parker. 1911. Latest marvel of the famous inventor. *New York Herald Tribune* (October 15).

Tesla, Nikola. 1888. Address before American Institute of Electrical Engineers (May 16). In *The Inventions, Researches, and Writings of Nikola Tesla,* ed. T. C. Martin. Second edition (1992). New York: Barnes & Noble Books.

———. 1892. Experiments with alternating currents of high potential and high frequency. Lecture before Institution of Electrical Engineers, London (February). In *The Inventions, Researches, and Writings of Nikola Tesla,* ed. T. C. Martin. Second edition (1992), New York: Barnes & Noble Books.

———. 1893. On light and other high frequency phenomena. Lecture before the Franklin Institute, Philadelphia (February). In *The Inventions, Researches, and Writings of Nikola Tesla,* ed. T.

C. Martin. Second edition (1992), New York: Barnes & Noble Books.

———. 1895. Letter to Alfred Schmid (March 30). Library of Congress.

———. 1896a. On Roentgen rays. *Electrical Review* (March 11).

———. 1896b. On the Roentgen streams. *Electrical Review* (December 1).

———. 1896c. Tesla as a seer. *American Electrician* (September).

———. 1897. Address on commemoration of introduction of Niagara Falls power in Buffalo. In *Electrical Review* (April 14).

———. 1899a. Letter to Robert Underwood Johnson (October 1). LAA.

———. 1899b. Diary notes (June 6). In *Colorado Springs Notes*. Beograd: Nolit, 1978.

———. 1899c. Some experiments in Tesla's laboratory. *Electrical Review* (March 29).

———. 1899d. Letter to R. U. Johnson (November 29). Library of Congress.

———. 1900. The problem of increasing human energy. *Century Magazine* (June).

———. 1901a. Letter to Stanford White (September 13). Library of Congress.

———. 1901b. Talking with planets. *Collier's* (February 9).

———. 1903a. Letter to J. P. Morgan (April 8). Library of Congress.

———. 1903b. Letter to J. P. Morgan (July 3). Library of Congress.

———. 1904a. The transmission of electrical energy without wires. *Electrical World and Engineer* (March 5).

———. 1904b. Letter to J. P. Morgan (October 13). Library of Congress.

———. 1905. *Electrical World and Engineer* (January 7).

———. 1906a. Making your imagination work for you. *American Magazine* (April 21).

———. 1906b. Letter to Secretary of Smithsonian Institution (July 19). TMA.

———. 1913. Letter to E. C. Mears (July 7). Westinghouse Archives.

———. 1915a. Some personal recollections. *Scientific American* (June 5).

———. 1915b. Letter to Robert Underwood Johnson (November 16). Library of Congress.

———. 1915c. *New York Times* (December 8).

———. 1917. Minutes of AIEE Annual Meeting (May 18). Reprinted in *Electrical Review & Western Electrician* (May 26).

———. 1919a. My inventions: My early life. *Electrical Experimenter* (February).

———. 1919b. My inventions: My first efforts in invention. *Electrical Experimenter* (March).

———. 1919c. My inventions: My later endeavors. *Electrical Experimenter* (April).

———. 1919d. My inventions: The discovery of the Tesla coil and transformer. *Electrical Experimenter* (May).

———. 1919e. My inventions: The magnifying transmitter. *Electrical Experimenter* (June).

———. 1919f. My inventions: The art of teleautomatics. *Electrical Experimenter* (October).

———. 1919g. The true wireless. *Electrical Experimenter* (May).

———. 1924. Mr. Tesla explains why he will never marry. *Detroit Free Press* (October 10).

———. 1930. Man's greatest achievement. *New York American* (July 6).

———. 1931a. Tesla, 75, predicts new power source. *New York Times* (July 5).

———. 1931b. Our future motive power. *Everyday Science and Mechanics* (December).

———. 1932a. Chewing gum more fatal than rum. *New York World Telegram* (August 10).

———. 1932b. *The Eternal Source of Energy of the Universe; Origin and Intensity of Cosmic Rays* (October 13). Unpublished ms. TMA.

———. 1933. Tesla harnesses cosmic energy. *Philadelphia Public Ledger* (November 2).

———. 1934a. Letter to J. P. Morgan, Jr. (November 29). Library of Congress.

———. 1934b. *Modern Mechanix and Inventions* (July).

———. 1934c. Letter to G. S. Viereck (December). LAA.

———. 1937a. Press release on Tesla's eighty-first birthday (July 10). LAA.

———. 1937b. Sending messages to planets predicted by Dr. Tesla. *New York Times* (July 11).

———. 1938. Letter to Institute of Immigrant Welfare. TMA.

———. 1939. Letter to Pola Fotić (n.d.). TMA.

———. 1941. Telegram to Sava Kosanović (March 1). In *Nikola Tesla: Correspondence with Relatives.* Belgrade, YU: Nikola Tesla Museum, 1993.

———. n.d. New art of projecting concentrated non-dispersive energy through natural media, 1935–37. Unpublished ms. TMA.

Tesla, Nikola, and G. S. Viereck. 1935. A machine to end war. *Liberty Magazine* (February).

Trump, John G. 1943. Report to Office of Alien Property custodian (January 30). Tesla FBI FOIA files.

Twain, Mark. n.d. Handwritten note to Tesla. TMA.

Westinghouse. 1888. Memorandum of agreement between Westinghouse Electric Company and Tesla Electric Company (July 7). Westinghouse Archives.

Whitesell, John C. 1963. Letter to Leland Anderson (May 29). LAA.

BOOKS

Anderson, Leland I. *Ball Lightning & Tesla's Electric Fireballs.* Breckenridge, CO: Twenty First Century Books, 1997.

———. *Tesla's Teleforce & Telegeodynamics Proposals.* Breckenridge, CO: Twenty First Century Books, 1998.

Applebaum, Stanley. *The Chicago World's Fair of 1893: A Photographic Record.* New York: Dover Books, 1980.

Glenn, Jim., ed. *The Complete Patents of Nikola Tesla.* New York: Barnes & Noble Books, 1994.

Harris, Neil, Wim de Wit, James Gilbert, and Robert W. Rydell. *Grand Illusions: Chicago's World's Fair of 1893.* Chicago: Chicago Historical Society, 1993.

Hecht, Jeff. *Beam Weapons: The Next Arms Race.* New York: Plenum Press, 1984.

Hunt, Inez, and Wanetta Draper. *Lightning in His Hand.* Hawthorne, CA: Omni Publication, 1964.

Kevles, Daniel J. *The Physicists.* New York: Alfred A. Knopf, 1978.

Manning, Jeane. *The Coming Energy Revolution—The Search for Free Energy.* Garden City Park, NY: Avery Publishing Group, 1996.

Metzger, T. *Blood and Volts: Edison, Tesla, and the Electric Chair.* New York: Autonomedia, 1996.

Pocock, Rowland F. *The Early British Radio Industry.* Manchester, UK: Manchester University Press, 1988.

Prout, Henry G. *A Life Of George Westinghouse.* New York: Scribner, 1922,1971.

Ratzlaff, John T., ed. *Tesla Said.* Millbrae, CA: Tesla Book Company, 1984.

Ratzlaff, John T., and Leland I. Anderson. *Dr. Nikola Tesla Bibliography.* San Carlos, CA: Ragusan Press, 1979.

Siemens, Georg. *History of the House of Siemens: Vol. I.* New York: Arno Press, 1977.

Silverberg, Robert. *Edison and the Power Industry.* Princeton, NJ: Van Nostrand, 1967.

Storm, Margaret. *Return of the Dove.* Mokelumne Hill, CA: Health Research, 1972.

Sullivan, Walter. *We Are Not Alone: The Search for Intelligent Life on Other Worlds.* New York: McGraw-Hill, 1964.

Tate, Alfred O. *Edison's Open Door.* New York: Dutton, 1938.

Tesla, Nikola. *Nikola Tesla: Lectures, Patents, Articles.* Belgrade: Nikola Tesla Museum, 1956.

———. *My Inventions.* New York: Barnes & Noble Books, 1998. Zagreb, Croatia: Skolska Knjiga, 1977.

ARTICLES

Dumych, Daniel M. "Nikola Tesla and the Development of Electric Power at Niagara Falls." *The Tesla Journal* 6 & 7 (1989/1990): 4–10.

"Edisonian Vignettes." *IEEE Spectrum* 15, no. 9 (September 1978).

Hall, Stephen S. "Tesla: A Scientific Saint, Wizard or Carnival Sideman?" *Smithsonian* (June 1986): 120–34.

Herskovits, Zara. "To the Smithsonian Or Bust—The Scientific Legacy of Nikola Tesla." *Yale Scientific* 71, no. 4 (Fall 1997).

Wagner, John W. "Nikola Tesla, the First Radio Amateur and the Real Inventor of Radio." *Amateur Radio Today* 73 (December 1995).

Wait, James R. "Propagation of ELF Electromagnetic Waves and Project Sanguine/Seafarer." *IEEE Journal of Oceanic Engineering* 2 (April 1977): 161–72.

BIBLIOGRAPHICAL ESSAY

Microfilm correspondence of Tesla, George Scherff, Robert Underwood Johnson, Mark Twain, the J. P. Morgan family, George Westinghouse, and the Westinghouse Electric and Manufacturing Company may be found at the Library of Congress, Manuscripts Division. The Butler Library, Rare Books and Manuscripts, Columbia University, contains original correspondence and photographs, including letters of Tesla and Johnson, Scherff, and others. The New York Public Library holds additional material, and the Engineering Societies Library, New York, has a substantial collection of material on legal proceedings over Tesla's AC patents.

Leland I. Anderson's private collection of Tesla documents and letters was used extensively in preparation of this book, thanks to access provided by Mr. Anderson. The collection has been donated to the Serb National Federation in Pittsburgh, Pennsylvania, George Martich, President.

Many of the photographs and documents in this book are contained in the collections and archives of the Muzej Nikole Tesle, at 51 Krunska Street, Belgrade, Yugoslavia. The Tesla Wardenclyffe Project, P.O. Box 990, Shoreham, NY 11786, has also been a source for many of the photographs contained herein.

An unembellished portrait of the awesome J. Pierpont Morgan can be found in George Wheeler's *Pierpont Morgan & Friends: The Anatomy of a Myth* (Englewood Cliffs, NJ: Prentice-Hall, 1973). See also Frederick Lewis Allen's *The Great Pierpont Morgan* (New York: Harper & Bros., 1949) and Jean Strouse's "Annals of Finance—The Brilliant Bailout" (*New Yorker*, November 23, 1998) and *Morgan, American Financier* (New York: Random House, 1999).

The bushwhacking (*takeover* was not yet a common term) of individual entrepreneurs by corporations and Wall Street financiers during the frontier era of American industrial growth is colorfully described in Matthew Josephson's *Edison* (New York: McGraw-

Hill, 1959) and *The Robber Barons* (New York: Harcourt, Brace & World, 1934, 1962); Ronald W. Clark's *Edison* (New York: Putnam, 1977); and Robert A. Conot's *A Streak Of Luck* (New York: Seaview Books, 1979).

The Tesla Memorial Society has an extensive collection of materials and information on Tesla. Contact William Terbo at: Tesla Memorial Society Newsletter and Publications, 21 Maddaket, Southwyck Village, Scotch Plains, NJ. The Kenneth M. Swezey "Tesla Collection" at the Smithsonian Institution, Dibner Library, Washington, D.C., contains extensive biographical materials on Tesla.

Publications on Tesla's "bladeless" turbine are available from the Tesla Engine Builders Association, 5464 N. Port Washington Road, Suite 293, Milwaukee, WI 53217. Information on the Tesla coil can be obtained from Harry Goldman at the Tesla Coil Builders Association, 3 Amy Lane, Queensbury, NY.

Twenty First Century Books, P.O. Box 2001, Breckenridge, CO 80424 (www.TFCbooks.com), publishes many interesting books and works on Tesla including numerous titles by Leland I. Anderson.

Barnes & Noble Books also publishes and sells a wide selection of books on Tesla. They may be ordered online at www.barnesandnoble.com or www.bn.com.

The U.S. Freedom of Information Act has been a means of obtaining FBI, CIA, and other material related to the Tesla papers.

AC, *see* alternating current
Adams, Edward Dean, 55, 58, 65
airplanes and flying machines, 112,
    113–14, 139
alternating current, 10. *See also*
    polyphase systems
    creation of isochronous waves with
        an oscillator, 77
    "Egg of Columbus," 33, 162
    historical background, 15, 18–19,
        24, 26, 27, 56
    human health effects, 35, 41, 44, 48
    invention of motor, 11, 21
    physical properties of, 15
    switchboard, 29
American Institute of Electrical
    Engineers, 23, 38, 62, 68,
    122–23
antenna, for radio reception, 70
antigravity, 142
Appleton, E. V., 167
Arbus, Muriel, 117, 133
Armstrong, Edwin H., 131, 162
Astor, John Jacob, 58, 85, 103, 118, 133
Atlantic Richfield Oil Company,
    167–68
atomic bomb, 161
audion, 71
automobiles, 112, 115

Balkan Peninsula, 142–43
ball lightning, 94, 95
Batchelor, Charles, 17
Behrend, B. A., 122
Bell, Alexander Graham, 120
Bell Telephone, 29
Bernhardt, Sarah, 50, 137
boats, remote-controlled, 79–82, 107,
    130, 162
Boldt, George C., 107
Braun, Carl F., 68, 120
Briggs, Richard, 163
Brisbane, Arthur, 36
Brown, Harold P., 24, 27
Brown, James K., 16
Budd Company, 114
Butler, Joseph, 163

capacitors, 37, 43, 100, 105
carbon-button lamp, 38, 75
Carnegie, Andrew, 68, 98
"carrier" frequency, 70
Cataract Construction Company, 55
cathode ray tube, 76–77, 129
Central Telephone Exchange, 11
Chamberlain, Prime Minister Neville,
    145

charged-particle beam weapon, 146,
    147, 161
Chicago World's Fair, Columbian
    Exposition, 27, 28–29
clocks, 77, 99
"coherers," 70
communication
    with birds, 133
    with other planets, 94–95, 151
    secure, 81, 82, 127, 131
commutators, 21
computer design, 82
conduction, transmission of power by,
    92, 106, 171
Continental Edison Company, 17
Craigie, L. C., 161
Crawford, Marion, 47
Crookes, Sir William, 66–67, 75, 138
Crow, W. D., 100
current, *see also* alternating current;
        direct current; War of the
        Currents
    definition, 8
    resonance and, 43, 66, 70
    U.S. household, 15
Curtis, Leonard E., 85
Czito, Julius C., 53, 110
Czito, Kolman, 53, 85, 89, 90

Dabo, Leon, 137
Dahlstrand, Hals, 113
d'Arsonval, Arsène, 48
Da Vinci, Leonardo, 126
Davis, George R., 28
DC, *see* direct current
"death beam," 77, 136, 144–47,
        164–65. *See also* directed energy
        weapons
De Forest, Lee, 70, 71, 142
diathermy, 48, 104
digital logic gates, 82
direct current
    historical background, 13, 15, 19,
        20, 27, 47
    human health effects, 48
    short range of, 16, 21
directed energy weapons, 161, 163–64
disk turbine, bladeless rotary, 9, 109–15
distribution of electricity, *see also* elec-
        trical wires
    by Edison Electric Light Company,
        17, 20
    limitations of direct current, 16
    power transmission patents by Tesla,
        23
    three-phase, in the Niagara Project,
        58–59

Dodge, Flora, 50
Dvořák, Anton, 49

Eastlund, Bernard, 167
Echo I, 134
Edison, Thomas Alva
    electric torpedo by, 80
    as head of the Naval Consulting
        Board, 129
    investment in radio transmission, 68,
        109
    rumor of Nobel Prize for, 120
    Tesla and, 17–21, 63, 112
    wireless communication research, 97
    work habits, 19
    X-ray research, 75
Edison Electric Light Company, 16, 28,
    61
Edison Medal, 120, 122–23, 133, 161
Edison Waterside Power Station, 112
"Egg of Columbus," 33, 162
Einstein, Albert, 141, 142, 146
Electrical Exhibition in Madison Square
        Garden, 79, 82
electrical wires
    copper, 15, 28
    financial aspects of development, 41
    from hydroelectric plants, 57
    overhead, 13, 15, 16, 26
    underwriters', 15
electricity
    as catalyst for weather changes, 40–41
    definition and properties of, 8
    first experience of, 4
    human health effects, 35, 41, 44, 48
    hydroelectric systems, 57
    the power of resonance, 43. *See also*
        Tesla coil
electric lights, 16, 17, 19–20, 36–37
electric water fountain, 115
electrocution, 27
electromagnetic induction, 10, 21
electromagnetic radiation, 8, 21, 65–66
    extra-low-frequency, 88, 100, 169
    human health effects, 41, 44
    propagation by an electric spark, 35
    propagation of radio waves, 71
electrons, 8, 15
electrostatic repulsion, 146
El Paso Power Company, 85, 90
extra-low-frequency waves, 88, 100, 169
extrasensory perception, 67, 137
extraterrestrial communication, 94–95,
    151
Faraday, Michael, 10, 62
Federal Bureau of Investigation, 157,
    159, 161

Finn, Bernard S., 71–72
fire, destruction of laboratory by, 53, 61, 75
Fitzgerald, Bloyce, 154, 161, 163
fluorescence, 37, 75
Ford, Henry, 47, 113–14
Fotić, Konstantin, 147
Fotić, Pola, 4
Foxworth, P. E., 157–58, 159
"Fragments of Olympian Gossip," 138–39
Franklin Institute, 42, 120

General Electric Company
    investment in bladed turbines, 110
    role in the Niagara Project, 56, 58, 63
    takeover of Edison Electric Light Co., 16, 21, 28, 56, 61, 63
generators
    for the Chicago World's Fair, 29
    hydroelectric, 9, 57, 58
    residential, 16, 59
    rotary AC, 36
    three-phase AC, 57
    for the Wardenclyffe Tower, 104
geosynchronous orbit, 9, 134, 171–72
geothermal power, Tesla on, 114
Gernsback, Hugo, 129, 158
Gertz, Elmer, 137
Girardeau, Emile, 129
Golka, Robert, 92
Gould, Jay, 47
gravity, dynamic theory of, 138
guided weapons, 130, 131, 164

Hammond, John Hays, Jr., 82
Harriman, Edward H., 47
Hausler, Charles, 149, 152
Hertz, Heinrich, 35, 65, 66
High Altitude Auroral Research Project, 169, 170, 171
Houston, Edwin J., 75
hydroelectric generation, 9, 53, 54–63

incandescent lamp, "stopper," 28
"individualization," 81, 131
induction, 10, 21, 37
inductors, 43. See also Tesla coil
Institute of Electrical Engineers, 120
Institute of Radio Engineers, 72
Institution of Electrical Engineers, 40
International System of Units, 172
ionosphere, transmission of energy
    through the, 85–92, 105, 106, 167, 168–70

Jackson, Helen Hunt, 49

Jefferson, Joseph, 47
Johnson, Katharine and Robert, 48, 49–50, 53, 90, 97, 118–19, 153

Kapitsa, Peter, 95, 161, 163
Keegan, George J., Jr., 164
Kelvin, Lord, 56, 58
Kennelly, Arthur E., 75
Kosanović, Sava (nephew), 134, 153, 157, 161

laboratories of Tesla
    in Colorado Springs, 85–87, 95
    on Houston Street, 65, 78, 86
    on South Fifth Avenue, destruction by fire, 53, 61, 75
    Wardenclyffe Tower in Shoreham, 100–107, 129
Lenard, Phillipp, 76
light, visible, 8, 35, 36
lightning, man-made, 89, 94, 95, 98, 163
Lodge, Sir Oliver, 65, 160
LORAN, 89
Löwenstein, Fritz, 53, 85, 87, 127

magnetic field, tesla unit quantification, 172
magnetosphere, 168–69, 171
Mandić, Georgina (mother), 3, 4, 117
Mandić, Nikolai (uncle), 5
Mandić, Pajo (uncle), 5
Mandić, Trifun (uncle), 5
Manhattan Storage and Warehouse Company, 158, 161
Marconi, Guglielmo
    companies of, 68, 97, 109
    lawsuit against, by Tesla, 117
    Nobel Prize for, 120
    patent status for invention of the radio, 109, 160
    radio transmission research, 65, 67, 68, 72, 90
    weapons research, 145–46
    wireless communication research, 97, 104
Maxwell, James Clerk, 35, 65
mechanical eye, 133–34
medical applications, 48, 76, 104
Merington, Marguerite, 50
Mestrović, Ivan, 162
Mische, Will, 92
missiles, guided ballistic, 130, 131, 164
Morgan, Anne, 50, 100
Morgan, J. Pierpont, 47
    death of, 118
    investment in Edison's DC system, 16, 27–28

investment in radio transmission, 68
investment in Wardenclyffe Tower, 98–99, 103, 104, 105–6
role in the Niagara Project, 58, 63
Morgan, J. Pierpont, Jr., 118, 144
motors, see also turbine engines
    alternating current, invention of, 11, 21
    cosmic ray, 142
    Edison jumbo dynamo, 20
    first electric, 10
    gramme dynamo, 9
    "no-wire," 40
    two-phase induction, see polyphase motors
Muzar, Charlotte, 153, 157
"My Inventions," 51–52
mysticism, 138. See also extrasensory perception

NASA, 134, 171
National Advisory Committee for Aeronautics, 114
National Air Intelligence Center, 163
National Electric Light Association, 42
National Rural Cooperative Electric Association, 120
navigational devices, 99
neon tube, 33, 37, 38
Nesbit, Evelyn, 118
"New Art of Projecting Concentrated Non-Dispersive Energy Through Natural Media," 147
Niagara Falls Power Project, 53, 54–63, 100
Nikola Tesla Company, 103, 118, 122
Nobel Prize, 120–21, 125
nuclear energy, 114, 138

Office of Alien Property, 158
oil industry, 78, 115, 171–72
oscillators, 43, 48
    isochronous mechanical, 77–79
    in radio transmission, 67, 68, 70, 95
    Wardenclyffe Tower, 100–8, 129
oscilloscope, 35
Oudin, P. M., 48

Papadopoulos, Dennis, 169, 170, 171
Paris Exposition of 1900, 103
patents
    application and claims process, 24, 71
    "Method and Apparatus for Altering a Region in the Earth's Atmosphere, Ionosphere, and/or Magnetosphere," 168–69
    on radio transmission, 67–68, 109

on X-rays, 75
patents by Tesla
  "Apparatus for Aerial
    Transporation," 139
  bladeless turbine engine, 111
  debate on invention of the radio,
    67–68, 70, 109, 160
  "Fluid Propulsion," 112
  "Improvements in Methods of and
    Apparatus for the Production of
    High Vacua," 136
  "Method of and Apparatus for
    Controlling Mechanism of
    Moving Vessels or Vehicles," 79,
    80
  "Method of Signaling," 131
  polyphase AC motors, 21, 23, 24,
    109
  power transmission through the
    earth, 89, 106
  radio transmission, 67, 68
  secure communications, control sys-
    tems, and robotics, 82
  sold to Westinghouse, 23–24
  step-up transformer, 37
  "System of Transmission of
    Electrical Energy," 67, 68, 70, 85
  "Turbine," 112
Paul, Frank, 130
Pelton wheel, 57, 111
phosphorescent light, 37, 38, 41,
  42–43, 75
photography, transmission of, 99
Pittsburgh Reduction Company, 61
Players Club, 47, 103
polyphase systems, 21, 23–24, 26, 33,
  47, 58, 59, 162
Pond, Otis, 53, 68, 130
power transmission, see distribution of
  electricity; radio transmission;
  wireless transmission of energy
power wires, see electrical wires
printed matter, transmission of, 99
"Problem of Increasing Human Energy,
  The," 97–98
psychological aspects of Tesla
  compulsive gambling, 10
  obsessive-compulsive disorder, 3, 19,
    50, 51–52
  visualization of research, 6, 21, 61,
    62
  well-developed memory, 3–4
pump, bladeless turbine engine, 112, 115
Pupin, Michael, 49, 68, 75, 97, 104

quantum physics, 137
Quinby, E. J., 68

radar, 127, 129, 146, 169–70
radio, definition of, 71
radiography, see X-rays
radio transmission, 64–73
  from Colorado Springs to Pikes
    Peak, 85–92
  debate over invention of, 67–68, 70,
    109, 160
  first announcement of, 42
  with other planets, 94–95, 151
  patents by Tesla, 67, 68, 70, 85
  principles of, 70
  role in World War I, 127
  Tesla coil and, 37, 43
  through the earth and ocean, 88–89,
    105, 169
Rankine, Edward Dean, 58, 59
Rayleigh, Lord, 40
remote-control
  ballistic missiles, 130, 131, 164
  robots, see robots
  vessels, 79–82, 107, 130
resonance, 43, 66, 70, 87
Rice, Warren W., 115, 123
robots
  "individualization" of, 81, 131
  patents by Tesla, 79, 80
  remote-controlled, 79–82, 107,
    130, 162
Rockefeller, John D., 47, 98
Roentgen, Wilhelm, 75
Roentgen rays, see X-rays
Roentgen tubes, 92
Roosevelt, Franklin Delano and Eleanor,
  154, 157, 159
Rothschild, Lord, 58
Royal Institution, 68
Ruch, Charles, 149, 151
Ryan, Thomas Fortune, 47

satellites, 134, 171–72
Sawyer-Man lamps, 28
Scherff, George, 52–53, 86, 104, 106,
  137, 155
Scott, Charles F., 62
secure communications and control sys-
  tems research, 81, 82, 127, 131
"Seesaw" project, 163
shadowgraph pictures, 75. See also X-rays
Skerritt, Dorothy, 117, 118, 133, 137
Smithsonian Institution, 71–72,
  160–61
Sniffen, E. H., 149, 151
Société Française de Physique, 50, 68
Société Internationale des Électricins, 68
solar power, 98, 114
Soviet Union, weapons development,
  161, 163–64

SS Oregon, 17, 19, 20
standing waves, 37, 106
Stanley, William, 13
Star Wars program, 164, 165
Stone, John Stone, 160
"stopper" lamps, 28
Story of Youth Told by Age, A, 4
submarine detection by radar, 129
Suffold Land Company, 100
Swezey, Kenneth, 141, 154
Szigety, Anital, 11

telegeodynamics, 77–79, 151
telegraph communication, 65, 99, 127
telepathy, 67
telephone technology, 11, 29, 99, 134
television, 99, 134
Tesla, Angelina (sister), 3
Tesla, Dane (brother), 3, 117
Tesla, Josif (uncle), 5, 9
Tesla, Marica (sister), 3
Tesla, Milka (sister), 3
Tesla, Milutin (father), 3, 10, 143
Tesla, Nikola
  appearance, 13, 50–51, 133
  awards and citations, 120, 121,
    122–23, 133, 161
  credit for invention of the radio,
    109, 160
  decline and death of, 147, 149,
    153–55, 157–59, 162
  early years, 3–7, 9, 10–11, 27, 143
  Edison and, 17–21, 63, 112
  education, 5, 9
  family, 3, 5, 9, 10, 117, 121, 134,
    143
  fate of research papers after death
    of, 157–58, 159–60, 161,
    163–65
  health problems, 9, 11, 47, 117,
    119, 133, 155. See also psycho-
    logical aspects of Tesla
  laboratories, see laboratories of
    Tesla
  lawsuit against Marconi, 117
  lectures, 38, 40, 42, 68, 75
  marriage, speculation on, 50, 135
  patents, see patents by Tesla
  as poet and visionary, 132–39, 172
  research, see specific projects and
    concepts
  work habits, 19, 52–53, 112
  work with Westinghouse
    Corporation, 24–26
Tesla coil, 107, 162
  in high-voltage research, 43–45
  principles of, 36–37
  in telegeodynamics, 78

used to manifest poltergeists, 138
  for wireless transmission to Pikes
    Peak, 87
Tesla Electric Light Company, 21
Tesla Institute, 147
Tesla Memorial Society, 120
Tesla Museum, 162, 170
Tesla Pad, 104
Tesla-Schumann cavity, 89
Tesla Turbine, 109–15
tesla unit, 172
Thaw, Harry K., 118
Thompson-Houston Company, 28, 56
transformers, 15, 23
  air core, 87
  frequency, 170
  step-down, 57
  step-up, patent by Tesla, 37
  for the Wardenclyffe Tower, 104
Trbojevich, Nikola (nephew), 10,
    134–35
Treatise on Electricity and Magnetism,
    35
Trump, John G., 160–61
turbine engines
  bladed, 110, 112
  bladeless rotary, 9, 109–15
  gasoline, 113–14, 139
  in the Niagara Falls Power Project,
    55, 57
  Parsons, 111
  steam-driven, 112, 113
  turbo-pumps, 112, 115
Twain, Mark, 47–48, 118, 149
two-phase induction motor, *see*
    polyphase systems

ultraviolet rays, 106, 146
United Nations General Assembly, 170
U.S. Air Force Intelligence, 163, 164
U.S. Army, 163
U.S. Department of Defense, 165, 170
U.S. Naval Radio Service, 127

U.S. Navy, 89, 115, 127, 160, 163,
    170
U.S. Patent Office, 24, 68, 85, 109
U.S. State Department, 145
U.S. Supreme Court, 68, 70, 160
U.S. War Department, 81
USS *Maine,* 79

vacuum tube, *see also* cathode tube
  electrodeless, 37, 42–43
  open-ended, *see* "death beam"
  triode, 70, 71
Vanderbilt, Mrs. Cornelius, 16, 17
Vanderbilt, W. K., 58
vertical short takeoff and landing plane,
    139
vessels
  bladeless tubines in, 112
  remote-controlled, 79–82, 107,
    130, 162
Viereck, George Sylvester, 137, 147
Vivekenanda, Swami, 50, 138
voltage, 15, 57, 59, 92
von Zeynek, R., 48
VOR, 89

war, Tesla on, 125, 126, 127, 129
Warden, James D., 100
Wardenclyffe Tower, 100–107, 129
War of the Currents, 19, 23–33, 56,
    63, 104
War of the Turbines, 110
Watson-Watt, Robert A., 129
weapons, 125–31. See also "death
    beam"
  ball lightning, 95
  based on Tesla's patents and ideas,
    161, 163–66, 168–69
  radar detection, 125, 129
  remote-controlled, 80–82
  Tesla's views on, 47–48, 80–81,
    126, 131
weather modification, 98, 168, 170

Westinghouse, 15
  acquisition of Tesla patents, 23–24,
    47
  contract for the Chicago World's
    Fair, 28–29
  funding for new laboratory, 65
  investment in turbine engines, 110,
    112–13
  investment in Wardenclyffe Tower,
    104
  role in the Niagara Project, 56, 58,
    63
  Tesla's consulting role with, 141,
    149
Westinghouse, George, 23, 41, 63,
    103–4, 118
"Westinghousing," 27
White, Stanford, 100, 117–18
Whitesall, John C., 114
wind power, Tesla on, 114
wireless transmission of energy, 171. *See
    also* radio transmission
  control of robots by, *see* remote-
    control
  patents by Tesla, 67, 68, 70
  post-research demonstrations, 53
  research, 37–40, 41–43
  Tesla's prophecies on, 49, 63
  through the ionosphere, 85–92,
    105, 106, 167
  "World System," 99, 104, 105
World War I, 77, 125–27, 143
World War II, 143, 145, 153, 160

X-rays, 75–76

Yugoslavia, 142–43, 153, 157

Zivić, Fritzie, 152

PHOTO CREDITS

Tesla Museum Archives: pages 2, 3, 4, 5, 6, 7 top, 11, 18, 23, 33 top, 34, 36, 37, 38, 39 top, 41, 42, 44, 45, 46, 49 right, 50, 51 left and right, 52, 58 right, 64, 69 top right, 74, 76, 77 left, 84, 86, 87, 89, 91 bottom, 93 bottom, 94 right, 95, 96, 99, 100, 102 top, 103, 104, 108, 109, 110, 111, 113, 115, 116, 121, 124, 133, 135, 140, 145, 147, 148, 149, 150, 154 left, 155, 159, 173 right.

Tesla Wardenclyffe Project Archives: pages 31 right, 35, 47, 71, 73, 77 right, 79, 81, 82, 93 top, 101, 102 bottom, 107, 123

right, 126, 130 right, 132, 142, 152, 156, 157, 160.

Westinghouse Archives: pages 14, 22, 25, 26, 28, 29, 30, 32, 39 bottom, 55, 56, 58 left, 62, 72, 118 left.

Leland Anderson Archive: pages 65, 105, 118 right, 125, 128, 130 left, 151, 168.

Rusty Kolb: pages 83, 90, 91 top, 92, 119, 164.

Charlotte Muzar: pages 154 right, 161, 163, 173 left.

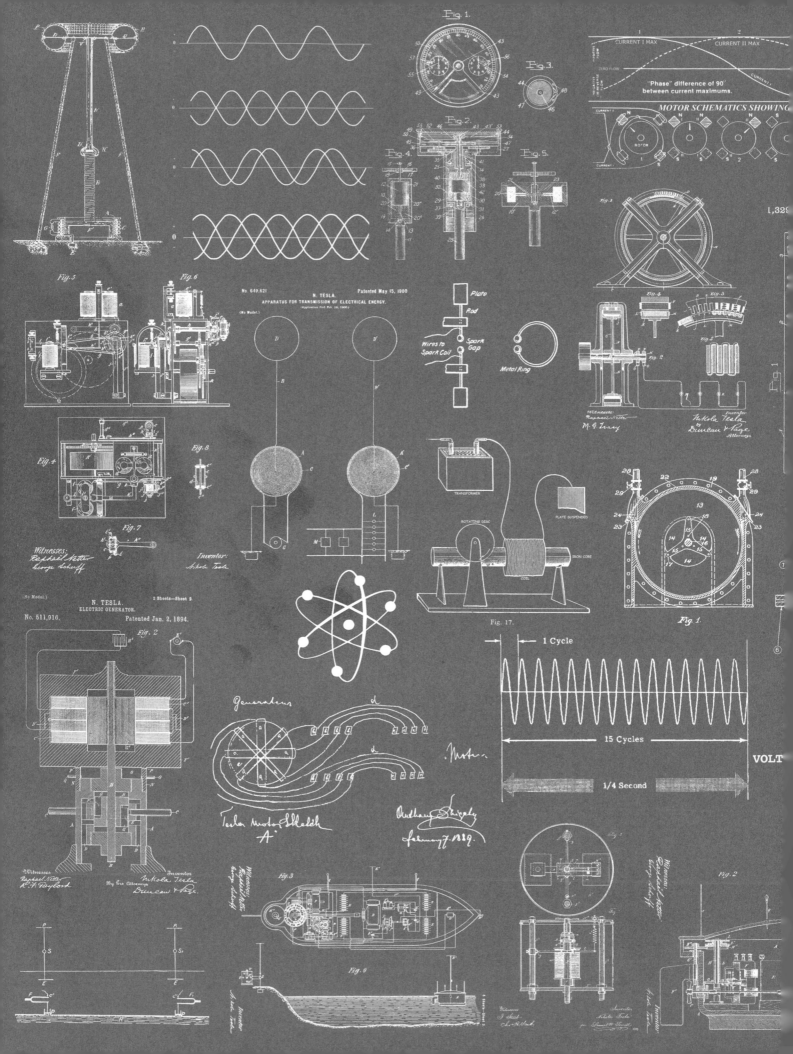